Building
A
People
Of Power

Building A People Of Power

IAN ANDREWS
AND
ROSEMARY ANDREWS
WITH
LUCY ELPHINSTONE

WORD PUBLISHING

WORD (UK) Ltd
Milton Keynes, England

WORD AUSTRALIA
Kilsyth, Victoria, Australia

WORD COMMUNICATIONS LTD
Vancouver, B.C., Canada

STRUIK CHRISTIAN BOOKS (PTY) LTD
Maitland, South Africa

ALBY COMMERCIAL ENTERPRISES PTE LTD
Balmoral Road, Singapore

CHRISTIAN MARKETING NEW ZEALAND LTD
Havelock North, New Zealand

JENSCO LTD
Hong Kong

SALVATION BOOK CENTRE
Malaysia

BUILDING A PEOPLE OF POWER

Copyright © 1988 Word (UK) Ltd

ISBN 0–85009–143–8 (Australia 1–86258–050–2)

Scripture quotations unless otherwise stated are from the New
International Version © 1978 New York International Bible Society.

Typesetting by Suripace Limited, Milton Keynes.
Reproduced, printed and bound in Great Britain for Word (UK) Ltd. by
Cox & Wyman Ltd, Reading.

91   92   93   /   10   9   8   7   6   5   4   3   2

ACKNOWLEDGEMENTS

* To my wife Rosemary, who has supported me when I've been down, prayed for me when I wanted to give up and has shared her life with me for over twenty five years - both privately and in the ministry, and now through the joint effort of this book.

* To my son Stephen, whom I love dearly and who means so much. He has sacrificed both knowingly and unknowingly as we have tried to help others. He will share in the rewards, both now and in eternity.

* To Lucy Elphinstone, who has laboured through blood, sweat and tears in the production of this book and to her patient husband Charles for being such a loving support all the way through.

* To Word Publishing for all their help and encouragement.

* And finally, a thanks to our Lord Jesus Christ who is the one and only star of this book.

CONTENTS

Introduction

There has not been a time in history when people's needs have been greater than they are today. We may think we have grown more sophisticated with our medical knowledge, scientific achievements and material affluence, but all this has resulted in an independence, and a self-sufficiency apart from God, which have led to broken relationships and wounded hearts, mental breakdowns and all manner of illnesses. The devil is not on the defensive but on the offensive in many people's lives, especially in the areas of sickness and disease, causing misery, pain and suffering to many people. For this reason, we as God's people need to be thoroughly equipped and informed so that we can work effectively with God in carrying out His will to heal the sick and set the captives free in the name of Jesus.

Up until the 60's and early 70's, there were a few of God's people who were praying for the sick and seeing results. This seemed to happen more in America than in England! Perhaps it is because by nature we are shy and reticent, so we were willing to stand back and let our American brothers and sisters step out of the boat into healing ministries. And so often in the past, they have given us an example of what God could and would do if we believed in Him.

I believe we are in a new day when God's Spirit is moving through all the earth in signs and wonders. He is raising up an army of men, women and children through whom He can move to display His love and power to a broken and needy society; people who are just waiting to be shown what God's love is all about, not only with words but by a demonstration of His mercy in healing power.

God is not looking for success, for brilliance or for head knowledge, but He is looking for volunteers, those of us who will say 'YES' to Him, 'Use me Lord'. We may feel weak and inadequate, but if we look at the way the Apostle Paul describes himself in the book of Acts, we shall see that it was like that for him many times. Through experience though, he learnt that when he let the Holy Spirit move through him, demonstrating the word of God, the results were mighty. There we see an amazing combination of the human and the divine: God putting His treasure, the Holy Spirit, into human beings. And that's the way He likes it, God and man working together. God uses our hands, our mouths, our bodies and our minds. He allows us the thrill and joy of this experience, and yet we know that it is His power flowing through us as He does the healing. We all know that **we** couldn't heal a fly with a headache. Jesus said, 'Apart from me you can do nothing,' and in another instance He said, 'The words I say to you are not just my own. Rather, it is the Father, living in me, who is doing his work.' We want to give credit where credit is due. All the credit for any healing goes to Jesus and all the glory to God the Father.

Jesus did, however, give us a great commission to 'go into all the world and preach the gospel to every person', 'to heal the sick, set the demon possessed free, to heal those who are broken in spirit and hurting, and tell them the good news that the Kingdom of God has come' (Mark 16, verses 15-18). He has not only told us what to do, but has given us the power in the Holy Spirit and the authority in His name to carry it out. As we proclaim and teach this message of liberty, that the price to redeem man from suffering has already been paid in full by Jesus Himself, God says that He will confirm His word with signs and wonders and miracles.

How is this all going to come about? The needs are so great, the sicknesses so many and the workers so few.

We can change the course of this world by being changed ourselves and then being people-changers. You may not be able to change the whole world, but you **can** change somebody's world! We can do it together.

Some of us will find ourselves called to a ministry instead of secular employment; some will be speaking to large crowds; some will function alongside others in the church, or take the church out onto the streets where the sick people are; some of us may be used with our next door neighbour or the person in our office at work. Everybody needs somebody, and that 'somebody' is you and me. Jesus says to His disciples, 'I chose you to go and bear fruit - fruit that will last'. I remember a translation of this into Pidgeon English: 'Big Boss wants me and He thinks me good enough to do His work.'

Don't wait, just volunteer. It's always nerve-racking to step out in faith for God. Look at Peter. He stepped out of the boat but then he panicked with fear when he looked down at the sea, and began sinking. But Jesus immediately saved him, and walked back with him to the boat. Peter had a lot to learn but he was willing, and instead of being a **reed** he became a **rock** in the church, and God did mighty things through him.

Our motive to see the sick healed is **love**. God so loved that He gave Jesus to die for sickness. We sometimes wonder if we've got it wrong when God heals those who (in our secret opinion) least qualify for healing! But God is a God of grace and love and has pity on those He has created, showing mercy to those who least deserve it.

We hope that you will be part of this vast army God is building to invade the territory of sickness, disease and sin in Jesus' name. As you study and put into practice what you learn, then your faith will grow and things will begin to happen. God moves when we move. So let us go on, not having attained, but still learning - still pressing on to take hold of that prize which Christ Jesus won for us.

It was a few years ago, during a time of fellowship with friends, that God spoke as we were praying about His will for the future in the ministry of healing. Someone saw a picture of a mountain, but instead of its usual rocky face, there were men and women packed tightly together, filling every space. The interpretation of the vision was that God wanted us to build a mountain of men and women who would be equipped to minister healing as a normal part of the message of God's grace whenever the opportunities occurred. Since then Ian and I have been holding training seminars where teaching and practice are the main emphases. The response from those attending has been very positive and folk have come away with new vision, new confidence and a definite biblical and spiritual authority for healing. They have left determined to put into practice what they have learnt, in their homes, in the church and in evangelism. In fact, some have seen wonderful healings take place through them (much to their surprise!) and have begun to get a reputation for praying for the sick.

One important factor in this new move of God's Spirit is that He obviously intends both men **and** women to be involved in the healing ministry. Wherever a man is called to this work, it is of great benefit if his wife recognises the invaluable contribution her own gifts and perspective give to the ministry. And, of course, if much travelling and living by faith is involved, then it helps if there is a mutual commitment to this calling. Another great advantage of establishing teamwork in the healing ministry is that we have seen, with much sadness, the pitfalls of one-man ministries. The pressures this situation puts on the individual are enormous, the dangers and temptations often unbearable: put on a pedestal by those who mistake the source of the ability and power demonstrated, they find themselves striving to live up to a reputation which at first may have seemed gratifying, or overwhelmed by the constant pressure to 'perform' and deal with every problem of sickness they encounter. Often alone, isolated from family and fellowship while travelling, these men are subject to undue emotional and even moral problems through loneliness and opportunity, and frequently their own family life suffers; and we who view these men as super-spiritual beings endowed with a special power have only ourselves to blame when we experience shock and disillusionment at their downfall. So wherever possible we seek to encourage people to enter into this ministry in couples and teams, making sure our aim is to point people to God as the source of their health and teaching them to remain in and minister this life to others.

We have received a great encouragement in this vision recently. For a long time now, it has been on our hearts to bring this gift of God's healing to a far wider audience through the media. Previously, the door into television seemed to be firmly shut, although we felt somehow sure that this would eventually change, so we were very excited when last November Ian received a letter from BBC Scotland asking him to take part in one of a series of programmes called *High Spirits* that they were doing on aspects of supernatural or miraculous movements within the church. The timing was ideal and fitted into our schedule perfectly. Our prompt reply was 'Yes', provided the subject was to be treated in a sympathetic manner and allowed the viewing audience to make up its own mind as to the genuineness of God's power. Three other church leaders were invited for their opinions in order to give the necessary balance and credibility on the programme.

The original uncut film took about six hours in front of a studio audience. It was pretty nerve-racking with technicians, cameramen and bright lights creating a very artificial setting. Would it work in such a clinical atmosphere? Suppose no-one got healed?! In spite of all our fears, God proved that this had indeed been His idea and He was about to show what He could do.

The first few words of knowledge were surprisingly alarming: they referred to someone who had been abused, perhaps, and had been afraid to tell anyone about it. (What a way to start!) Amazingly, the girl responded and was wonderfully released. Faith began to rise as many others came forward to receive their healing following more words of knowledge, and it had a great effect on the television crew filming the scene. One cameraman remarked that this was the best religious programme he had ever done. I suppose it **was** a little unusual!

Not surprisingly, we have had many enquiries following the programme, some from people wondering if there would be any more healing 'shows', a number from sick and depressed people asking for help, and our fair share of weird-and-wonderful letters. Many letters also came from Christians whose faith had been really encouraged and who felt the programme had helped them in talking to others about healing. Plainly there is an openness and thirst for the subject which was not present some years ago.

We are positive that there will be more opportunities in the future to bring the message of God's healing into people's homes through television so that people can turn to God rather than to other sources of help. Already we know of other Christians who have been approached to make programmes on various aspects of God's healing and the occult, so things are on the move to demonstrate to this nation the infinite ability of God over the works of Satan. As we hold our city meetings throughout the country, the ignorance and misconceptions concerning God's miraculous power are being broken down. God wants to use us all to bring in the light of His healing and His kingdom. Some of us will have a more specialised ministry and use certain gifts more than others, but the key word is involvement - being prepared to be used in any way in God's healing work - and to be involved you need understanding.

The understanding, or knowledge, that we need is revelation knowledge from God's Spirit to our spirits. He has promised to lead us into all truth (John 14, verse 26) and to teach us all things concerning

Himself. This kind of knowledge imparts life: it switches on the light inside, and causes us to change in our thinking and actions - if we allow it. There is nothing so exciting as when Jesus shares Himself with us through His Word, just as He did with the disciples as they walked together on the Emmaus road. Didn't they say that their hearts burned within them as they talked along the way and Jesus shared about Himself from the Scriptures? They were kept from recognising Him but now God has given us His Holy Spirit so that we can know Him and the power of His resurrection (Philippians 3, verse 10) so that we can be filled with all the fullness of God.

I remember some years ago that Jean Darnell had a vision of lights beginning to burn brightly all over Britain from the North to the South as God's people began to rise like a mighty army just as Ezekiel saw in his vision of the dry bones, as God's Spirit was breathed into them. This is already beginning to happen now. Up and down the land there is a stirring and awakening in God's people as we begin to 'redeem the time because the days are evil'. Each one of us has our part to play. Both individually and corporately we are making way for perhaps the last big wave of the Holy Spirit before Jesus returns. God works with us and we help it to happen.

Healing is God's love for His people, and He has made it available to all who can believe and receive. It is very difficult to serve God effectively while carrying a burden of sickness, whether emotional, psychological or physical, so He wants to restore and heal in the church, as well as outside. Can we, in turn, extend that love to those who as yet do not know that Christ is alive today?

Nothing is so effective as experiencing God for ourselves. We need to be aware that we are all working for the same side, no matter what denomination or background we have come from. It is not by being Baptists, Anglicans, Methodists, Reformed or House Church or members of any other church that we will make it to heaven, but by being **born again**. And those who love God must also love one another (John 4, verse 21).

Every big city can have regular outreach meetings. Ian and I would like to go on a regular basis to many cities and see how God will demonstrate His healing and saving power there, so dethroning principalities and powers that have reigned in those areas of our land. I believe we all really desire to put action to our words, demonstrating that greater is He that is in us than he (the devil) that is in the world. We have a message worth declaring, that 'Jesus Christ is the same yesterday and today and forever'. He is always full of mercy and compassion and wants to lift the misery out of people's lives. His promises are sure: He died that we might live, He was whipped and tortured so that we could be made whole. This is the gospel of power unto salvation for healing and for deliverance, and we must proclaim it, expecting God to confirm it with signs following so that we set this whole land talking about God's power.

All of us are aware that time is running out and men's hearts are failing them for fear - fear of violence, fear of unemployment, fears about the future and fears of nuclear war. Many die prematurely of heart attacks and other stress-related diseases. It is very like the days of Noah when men lived for sensual pleasure, and were completely uninterested in God. He was not even in their thinking, and as for being saved in an ark, they thought Noah must be mad. 'It's never rained before,' they said, 'it probably won't ever happen.' So all perished except Noah and his immediate family. What a tragedy. Yet this is the thinking that is polluting our society today, and I think that we have had enough.

As Christians, we care about our fellow beings, but until recently we have been so preoccupied with ourselves and our own fears that we have retreated. I believe God's Spirit is taking hold of us so that love and concern drive out our fears. This is still a day of God's mercy before the final flood; it is the day of the Lord for evangelism, for communication, for concern, for signs and wonders and all kinds of functions and ministries in the body of Christ. This is a day prior to the ushering in of the fullness of all things. There will be a fullness of evil, but **there will also be a fullness of God's power.** The word of God that was first spoken by the prophets is coming to pass and we can take heart and encourage ourselves in the Lord. For where sin abounds, grace abounds much more. As God says to Habakkuk: 'But the Lord is in his holy temple, let all the earth be silent before him' (Habbakuk Chapter 2, verse 20). He is on His throne and working His purposes out. There are those of us who have a tendency to view the problems as too big to solve and so retreat, or become completely taken up with the negative spirit of the current crisis to the exclusion of all else. Let us not be guilty of either but, fixing our eyes on Jesus, use our spiritual weapons and the power of the gospel to snatch men from the fire and bring light into the darkness. Consider the prophetic song of Isaiah in Chapter 42, verse 13:

> The Lord will march out like a mighty man
> Like a warrior he will stir up his zeal,
> With a shout he will raise the battle cry
> And will triumph over his enemies.

He is amongst us as we proclaim our God is alive, our enemies defeated. He has come to set the captives free, and is good news to the poor, the sick and the hopeless; He is life to all who will receive Him. So let us spur one another on and put on the whole armour of God, thinking of others more than ourselves, so that together we can make an impact on those around us, so that the world may know and believe that Jesus lives.

It is a well known fact that anybody who has made a mark in any field of work, be it social or creative, has derived their inspiration from somebody else's achievements or personal life. They have been motivated enough for their dreams to become a reality. The Bible says that our young men shall see visions and our old men dream dreams. Take these away from a man or woman and he or she becomes a depressed and unfulfilled person.

Everyone needs a vision from God, for their own life, family life and ministry. God had a wonderful dream which became a reality. He saw the church, a glorious church, with you and me as vital functioning parts. He saw us as His sons and daughters in His image, in a love relationship with Him where He is a Father caring and providing and nurturing us into maturity. God's dreams became and are still becoming a reality, as the Holy Spirit urges us forward into the glorious vision and possibilities that God has in His mind. He is not only a wonderful creator but He is so convinced of His plans that He has spoken them out and has faith that they will come to fruition through us. He watches over His word to perform it as He entrusted those first disciples with a commission, a blessing and an anointing to bring His plans to pass. Many more sought the vision and were inspired and empowered by the Holy Spirit to do the works that Jesus did. 'The works that I do shall you do also' (John 14, verse 12).

Ian and I have been greatly influenced by many people in the body of Christ, by their lives and by their gifts and ministries. Many dear people have also encouraged us with love, prayers and correction, for which we are extremely grateful. It's good to give credit where it's due and so I will mention the names of a few special people who have had particular influence on our lives and ministry.

Firstly, Sid Purse, who was the Pastor at South Chard fellowship when we arrived in need of help in 1968. He introduced us to Jesus and always encouraged us to go on when the chips were down, offering us a shoulder to cry on more than once. He inspired us with his love for the Lord and his hatred for the devil. He believed in the Holy Spirit's power to deliver and heal and was always seeking to bring out God's life and gifts through us. He was never too tired or too busy to spend time on us no matter what time of day or night we might need him, and that seemed quite often! He lovingly forgot himself and his own needs, moved by his vision that every member of the body of Christ would be functioning in the power of the Holy Spirit, and that we should be witnesses to the fact that Jesus was alive in us. God's love and desires were his one passion, and for that he paid a price. We would never have got off the ground without the support of Sid and his wife, along with many other friends at Chard.

Having received the Holy Ghost and being keen to get going, we devoured every tape we could about signs, wonders and the power of the Holy Spirit. Doing the housework in the bedroom, the bathroom or the kitchen, everywhere we could plug in the tape recorder, we would listen. I think that tapes must have been stronger in those days to withstand the wear and tear they had through constant listening! We were fascinated and never tired of the Holy Spirit's ministry, believing that somehow the truth and the anointed word would get into us if we soaked it in long enough.

We heard the American evangelist T.L. Osborne pray for the crippled and deformed whilst holding crusades in Trinidad and Tobago. His messages were so simple and were all taken from the gospel stories of Jesus healing the blind and the lame. You could feel faith rising in the crowds as he spoke, and his voice wasn't a great macho voice but rather the reverse. He utterly believed in the simplicity of the gospel of Jesus Christ, that it is the power of God to salvation to them that believe, and the word did the work. Thousands were saved, the demonically oppressed were loosed and the sick healed. God was doing the healing and T.L. preached the gospel message. The delivery was simple, but he seemed to be utterly one with the words he spoke. We also studied his book *The Healing Christ* which simply opened up the Word of God to us and revealed that it was God's will that we should be free of all sickness and pain because Jesus had borne them for us.

We also came in contact with Morris Cerullo, an American evangelist who revealed another dimension of God's work, showing us how to release the power of the Holy Spirit in praying for others. Sometimes during his meetings in London he had to be carried onto the platform, so great was the anointing of God upon him at that time! As you can imagine, a great reverence for God would come upon the people and many lives were changed and miracles happened. He brought the convicting power of the Holy Spirit in his meetings and the call to men and women to serve God and put their lives in order. The Holy Spirit moved on us many times to go forward and respond to God's will in our lives, receiving a fresh anointing of the Holy Spirit. One of his favourite messages was taken from John's Gospel: 'What shall we do, that we might work the works of God? ... Believe on him whom he hath sent' (John 6, verses 28 - 29). We listened to that message many times, eager to squeeze every drop of revelation from it and not wanting to miss anything which would fill us with faith and help us to see more clearly. His messages were never very long and were in fact quite repetitious, but brought with them a sense of reverence for God and were always followed by deliverances and healing.

During the 50's there were a number of men moving mightily in healing and deliverance, and one man in particular influenced our lives through his tapes. Jack Coe, a very loud Pentecostal, was considered to be a rather uneducated and even crude preacher, but he had a profound effect on us when we listened to tapes of his ministry in a tent meeting in Washington D.C, U.S.A. For the first time we heard miracles take place. He called out a lady who had her voice box eaten away through cancer, and as he commanded the demon to leave she began to speak, first in a whisper and then more clearly: 'Praise the Lord, I love you Jesus'. It was beautiful - God had performed a miracle and, as you can imagine, there was not a dry eye in the place, nor at home where we were listening to the tape! Jesus was really alive and proving it by performing so many miracles. It created a deep desire in us for the **reality** of this new life, and so we listened to the tapes over and over again until the messages were coming out of our ears! We knew them almost word-perfect and we became motivated to seek God to do the same things.

Another man called William Branham was moving in the gift of the word of knowledge with great power and authority. He used to see the angel of the Lord's presence moving on people in the congregation and as he did so would call them out to the front, sometimes sharing their problems and sometimes even giving their name and address. He spoke with such accuracy, knowing that God had revealed their need and he didn't even have to pray for them. God's knowledge flowing through to people under the anointing of the Holy Spirit is truly wonderful and can bring release to the sick, oppressed and crushed believer and unbeliever alike.

As you will see later on in this book, Kathryn Kuhlman also left her mark on our lives. We had read a few of her books of healing testimonies but were privileged to attend several of her meetings in the United States, and experience for ourselves the grace and love of God in healing. I say 'grace' because when you are in the presence of the Holy Spirit, you forget yourself and your problems and get caught up with the person of Jesus. That is what Kathryn Kuhlman conveyed to the sick, helpless and dying. She was just a channel for the Holy Spirit to use for His glory, and without that anointing of His presence she was helpless. We were filled with awe as she followed the Holy Spirit, calling out the various illnesses from which people were suffering. They would then rush out to the front and tell everyone what God had healed them from whilst they were sitting in their seats! Nobody had touched them, only Jesus. Many people had come from great distances to receive their healing, and such was the expectation that many were healed as they travelled, or stood outside in the crowd waiting for hours to get into the building. The worship was tremendous: one minute we were laughing, the next we were crying, as we watched Kathryn follow the Holy Spirit and repeat what He told her to say to the sick people. Her whole face and expression was one of wonder for Jesus, like a child coming down on Christmas morning to a tree filled with presents. We know from experience that she was just flesh and blood like each one of us. It was Jesus in her that we saw, in His compassion and mercy for the ill and suffering; she was just willing to be used by Him. She so frequently said in her meetings, 'Jesus, we want You to be seen not me, and we'll be careful to give You all the praise and all the glory for every healing taking place'.

There have been many more people who have influenced our lives and ministry, too numerous to mention, but our grateful thanks go to God for all of them, for the inspiration and sacrifices they have made to help others.

In a sense these were men and women who pioneered a vision of the healing message of Christ, often bearing the burden alone. Today is a new day in God's purposes, and He deserves that we all understand that His will is to heal the sick and oppressed as we make ourselves available to Him, to bring release and joy into people's lives. He wants us to push back the kingdom of darkness and bring in the Kingdom of God's dear Son. We pray and believe that as we support one another, and move forward in faith, love and courage, the Holy Spirit will be poured out, mighty signs and wonders will take place throughout all the world, and many will come into the Kingdom of God acknowledging Jesus Christ as Lord.

This book has a cutting edge. But at the same time, we have tried to be as honest as possible about our own experiences - the failures as well as the successes - and to share something of our spiritual journey. The book has a blend of personalities - it is the fruit not only of our own lives, but of some of the lives we have shared in over the years. Should you recognise yourself in any of the illustrations, we trust that none of you will be offended; rather, we hope that you will rejoice to know that your story can be the means to help someone else.

We believe more and more that God wants to move in a powerful way through **every** member of His church and He draws us together as a team to fulfill His call to 'Go ye'. Let us take up the challenge and fix our eyes on Jesus, the perfecter of our faith, sharing freely with all men and women the good news that Jesus not only saves from sin but also heals our bodies. Surely He carried the load of our sickness in His own body and with the wounds He bore, we were healed (Isaiah 53). Jesus was the substitute for our pains and sickness, and I can't resist shouting, 'Hallelujah, what a Saviour!'

None of us have arrived, and most of us haven't perceived half there is to know on the subject of healing. As we progress in our Christian lives, we find that our perspectives are being changed. That means that what we have written here is in no sense a final statement; even now we are seeing new insights, and we trust that will always be the case. We are learning all the time, but we share with you that which we have seen and heard, so that you can be more fully equipped for this day of God's power.

Rosemary Andrews   August 1988

Chapter One

What is Divine Healing?

It seems to me there have always been two basic systems of healing: one is man's way and the other is God's. Man's system aims at **treating** the problem; God's way **heals** it. When the Lord Jesus came to this earth, He must have done Luke out of a job. Not once did He send anyone to Luke for a pill or a potion. In fact, Jesus might have suggested, 'You'd better take up writing, Luke, because your doctoring days are over!'

Now let me say straightaway that I have nothing against doctors. (I believe they are marvellous evangelists to get the unsaved into the kingdom of God!) In thousands of ways, medical science can give relief from pain and sickness for those who do not believe they can receive it from God. It is God's grace, anyway, which provides the medical knowledge and the miracle of the healing process. (A doctor can set a bone but the actual knitting of the bone is something over which he has no control). In most cases, though, as I have suggested, there is **treatment** but not **healing, recovery** but not full **restoration.** If you have cancer of the stomach, the doctor can remove half your insides, which may get rid of the problem, but it's not **wholeness.** If you go to Jesus and He heals you, you still have your stomach and you are completely restored too. If you go to the optician, he can prescribe various lenses for you and cause you to see clearly but there is no healing there. If you have a bad tooth, the dentist gets the probe and says, 'Now this isn't going to hurt very much,' (which is usually the first lie you hear) then he drills out three-quarters of your tooth and fills it up. The toothache has gone, but you are not healed; you've merely had your problem treated.

God is merciful in giving us this safety net, BUT HE HAS AN

EVEN BETTER WAY. **Jesus paid the price to be our doctor.** Through His Son, God has committed Himself to making us whole. When we realise the responsibility is with **God** to restore and sustain us, when we see the completeness and the certainty of His provision for our health, we stop being full of fear and doubt, and start **expecting** to get well. We 'enter into rest', as the Bible puts it, and that is the place where we are able to receive God's blessings. As long as we are striving, it is difficult for God to get through to us with His gift of healing, for He rewards faith, not fear.

In our ministry, our whole concept of divine healing is based on this response of faith and love to God's love and faithfulness. This book isn't simply about how to get rid of your sicknesses. It is about how to have **abundant life through a relationship with God.** Healing is so often looked upon as a sort of magic trick: if we can only find the secret word or the magic formula, then in a puff of smoke, all our problems will disappear - until the next time. Over the years, various theories about spiritual life have come and gone on waves of popularity, with people shouting, '**This** is the way to do it'. But often they just leave a sad trail of confusion in their wake. There is no doubt many have brought encouragement - the teaching on positive confession, on words as a creative force and on signs and wonders, for example, to name just a few, have been wonderful in bringing a new realisation of the believer's authority, the power of the spoken word of faith, and the need for a transformation of our thinking in order to allow God's healing to be received. But we have to remember we can't **make** healing happen simply by getting right all the factors in the equation. The very nature of God, infinite, immortal spirit, means we can't reduce the way He works to a set of formulae. If we could produce healing like a rabbit out of a hat, we would be bringing God down to the level of a mere puppet who can be manipulated.

Having said all this, I do believe **God wants to heal everyone** (just as He desires everyone to be saved) and He wants us to learn about His provision, His laws and His unchanging character which He demonstrates in all His dealings with man, so that at least we can put ourselves in a position where we can receive. But much more than knowledge alone, **God wants us to discover the joy of living in a father-child relationship with Him.** Children don't (usually!) **demand** food, clothing, and shelter from their parents as a legal right, though they have more reason than anyone to expect such care from them. A child's confidence in his mother and father isn't based on his legal standing; he doesn't have to keep threatening his parents with his birth certificate or a phone call to the Social Services. His confidence flows from the security of knowing that he is loved and his parents **want** to look after him - and are committed to doing so. God wants us, in turn, to commit **every area** of our life to Him - our minds and spirits, as well as our bodies - accepting His lordship over them all. For His part, He promises to look after us to the smallest degree, changing us from glory into glory, just as everything in His kingdom is ultimately made whole and perfect. God wants to heal our bodies - His heart is full of compassion when He sees suffering in any form - but His ultimate desire is that we receive His **life in all its fullness and spend eternity with Him.** And a living faith in Jesus is the only cure for the terminal sickness of sin.

This, then is what we see as the wonderful uniqueness of God's healing - His grace and our faith mingle in a reciprocal relationship of love to bring **wholeness in every part of our being** and to **sustain us in health.** We don't have to keep getting sick and getting healed; God empowers us to share His freedom from pain and disease. It is not a matter of self-effort or knowledge of some theory or philosophy. There are plenty of alternative therapies which may claim to be holistic - bringing a harmony to body, soul and spirit - and, without going into their dangers and deceptions, it often appears they achieve some success. They acknowledge that a physical complaint may have its roots in the mental, emotional or spiritual realms. But their chief failing is that they cannot minister forgiveness and break the curse which holds all mankind in bondage. Only divine healing touches **every** aspect of human life that is under the influence of Satan, bringing:

> *Forgiveness of sin
> * Restoration from sickness
> *Freedom from the hold of poverty and adverse social
>   circumstances
> *Deliverance from demonic power and influence
> *Raising to life for the dead

More specifically, on a personal level, God is able to restore His image in every area of our life which has been distorted by sin, including our psychological, emotional, intellectual, sexual, social and spiritual functions. Other forms of healing may claim to offer, for example, peace, enlightenment, self-realisation, harmonization of energies, reincarnation even deification. But **only God** is able not merely to repair or extend our existing potential, but to fashion a **New Creation** (2 Corinthians 2, verse 17) within which He Himself dwells by His Holy Spirit.

Some of you may feel it is taking things too far to link healing so closely with salvation. Do we need to talk about repentance and sin when we are discussing healing? Is it necessary to receive forgiveness for something before we get rid of our sicknesses? And what has pain and illness to do with Satan? But this, I feel, is the starting point of getting healed: to realise that pain and sickness are an essential part of the curse which separated man from the state of perfection and wholeness God gave him in the Garden of Eden; and health is at the very heart of the eternal life Jesus won for us when He redeemed mankind on the Cross. This wholeness is what God planned from the moment Adam and Eve stood before Him in guilt and shame, and was promised throughout all the ages until the wonderful fulfilment at Calvary:

> Surely he took up our infirmities and carried our sorrows, yet we considered him stricken by God, smitten by him, and afflicted. But he was pierced for our transgressions, he was crushed for our iniquities; the punishment that brought us peace was upon him and by his wounds we are healed.
>
> (Isaiah 53, verses 4-5)

To realise that pain and suffering were never part of God's original plan, and that it was always His intention, after the Fall, to offer those who acknowledged the saving work of His Son the same power over them which Jesus enjoyed, changes our whole attitude to sickness and disease. Instead of passively accepting them as inevitable, or blaming God for His apparent lack of compassion and power, we begin to see we are allowing Satan to rob us of our inheritance and denying Jesus the ability to give us the full measure of blessing He won for us on the Cross.

Just look at the central place given to physical suffering in the sentences pronounced on the three offenders in the Garden of Eden. To the serpent, God said,

> Cursed are you above all the livestock
> And all the wild animals!
> You will crawl on your belly
> and you will eat dust
> all the days of your life.
> And I will put enmity
> between you and the woman,
> and between your offspring and hers;
> he will crush your head,
> and you will strike his heel.
>
> (Genesis 3, verses 14-15)

Satan was sentenced to the lowest place on the earth for his destructive work of inspiring perpetual conflict between God's people and his own evil offspring. And we see both in Scripture and in the ministry today, how physical afflictions are often demonically-inspired. But we also catch a glimpse of hope: 'He will crush your head.'

> When the time had fully come, God sent his Son, born of a woman, born under law, to redeem those under law, that we might receive the full rights of sons.
>
> (Galatians 4, verses 4-5)

God Himself in the flesh would provide the sacrifice that would satisfy the claims of justice, and pay the penalty of sin by death. The One who is the very source of existence would throw off the principalities and powers who had wrought such havoc in God's world, nailing all our sins and disobedience to a cross. Jesus would be 'bruised' as Satan struck back at the real King taking His rightful position over him, but the triumphant words, 'He (Jesus) will crush your head' would mean a deadly blow of utter defeat upon the Evil

One. Once the head is crushed, there is no more life, and so would be destroyed forever the serpent's poisonous lies and destructive power.

Then came the act which must have broken God's heart, for He had to curse the man and woman He had so lovingly made to enjoy fellowship with Him. For the woman, what should have been a great joy would become painful. For the rest of time, child-bearing, child-rearing and the relationship between husband and wife would be full of suffering and stormy conflicts:

> I will greatly increase your pains in child-bearing;
> With pain you will give birth to children.
> Your desire will be for your husband,
> and he will rule over you.
>
> (Genesis 3, verse 16)

To the man, God as judge makes it very clear what is the real source of Adam's fear and guilt at facing his Creator. It is not nakedness but disobedience which causes Adam to hide and lie. Though Adam protests that the disaster is all God's fault for giving him a woman who led him astray, God brings the responsibility firmly back to Adam since he had abused God's highest gift of free-will in choosing to ignore the command not to eat the forbidden fruit. The curse on Adam resulted in all creation becoming his enemy. Instead of enjoying the fruits of his labours in a world without disease, or decay, flood or drought, he would now have to strive continually to scrape an existence from the hostile land.

> Cursed is the ground because of you;
> through painful toil you will eat of it
> all the days of your life.
> It will produce thorns and thistles for you,
> and you will eat the plants of the field.
> By the sweat of your brow you will eat your food
> until you return to the ground,
> since from it you were taken;
> for dust you are and to dust you will return.
>
> (Genesis 3, verses 17-19)

Here is man's greatest tragedy. For the sake of a fruit, he defied God and exchanged immortality for death - and before death, a life of struggle, toil and disappointment. In the world today, we see this curse so graphically demonstrated: while one half of the world dies from stress and anxiety, from immorality and self-abuse, the other half starves through the greed and selfishness of its richer brothers and sisters. Man has lost his way and his only certainty (yet also his greatest dread) is death. Even though our bodies merely return to the dust from which we were made, death still holds a reign of terror over many people, possessing, perhaps, as they do, an inner knowledge that the real sting of death is the eternal separation of the spirit from the source of Life which was the true result of Adam's disobedience, 'for the wages of sin is death' (Romans 6, verse 25).

What a hopeless situation it all seems - until we read the rest of the verse from Romans: **'but the gift of God is eternal life in Christ Jesus our Lord'**.

Even as God was declaring the inevitable judgement on Adam and Eve which sin demanded in God's perfect world, He was forming His awesome plan for redeeming them. To Adam and Eve, God's act of providing them with garments of skin might have seemed no more than an expression of the love and thoughtfulness He had always shown them. But to us who stand beyond Calvary, we see the mighty significance in God killing an animal to provide for their helplessness. Until this point, there had been no blood shed in Eden. But God now provided the first animal sacrifice to show that He Himself would send the blood offering, the covenant sacrifice, which would cover men's sin forever. Adam and Eve's attempts to hide their shame by sewing fig leaves together remind us that our own efforts and religiosity can't put us right with God; only He can provide the robes of righteousness which symbolise our new life in Christ.

> For if, by the trespass of the one man (Adam), death reigned through that one man, how much more will those who receive God's abundant provision of grace and of the gift of righteousness **reign in life** through the one man, Jesus Christ.
>
> (Romans 5, verse 17)

What a promise! Through the sacrifice of Jesus on the Cross, the curse on Adam is overthrown, and man is restored to his original royal place of rule and authority. No longer sentenced to being a slave, he can be a son! If anyone acknowledges his need and turns to Christ, he will become a child of God and co-heir with Christ of everything in the Father's kingdom:

> If the Spirit of him who raised Jesus from the dead is living in you, he who raised Christ from the dead will also **give life to your mortal bodies** through his Spirit who lives in you.
>
> (Romans 8, verse 11)

It has always been God's plan, then, to restore to us the blessings of His kingdom. Healing is at the very centre of God's purposes. It is an essential part of salvation. A person healed by God finds, like Job, that he receives twice as much as he had before. Not only does the pain or sickness leave, but he finds he has renewed strength and joy:

> He forgives all my sins and heals all my diseases. He redeems my life from the pit and crowns me with love and compassion. He satisfies my desires with good things so that my youth is renewed like the eagle's.
>
> (Psalm 103, verses 3-5)

But even more than this, compassion and the desire to heal form the very essence of His character. It is an enormous aid to our faith to see how, throughout the whole of His dealings with mankind, God displays this overflowing faithfulness and love. In fact He is a God of such integrity and perfection, that it would be impossible for Him to withhold blessing and healing from those who earnestly seek Him. Let us just look at the nature and names of God, and see how deeply we can trust Him.

Chapter Two

God the Healer

What's in a name? The difficulties parents-to-be have in choosing names for their children reflect the importance we place on a name. Each one has a different connotation, and bears a particular meaning. Many of us feel that the name we choose will have an everlasting effect on our child - and it's true that our name can provoke a reaction wherever we go (there must be disadvantages in being called Ann Teake for example, and I once knew a lady called Victoria Station). Writers often use pen-names because they are aware their own names don't carry the correct romantic associations. Whenever we want to assert ourselves or promote a sense of authority, we often use our surnames and title or status. In the past, surnames often signified the craft or profession of the bearer - like Carpenter, Butcher, Cutler, Mason, Hedger and so on. And in the last century names like Patience, Faith, Mercy and Constance were very popular, as if parents hoped that by naming their children after these virtues they would blossom automatically into these temperaments. Names have power. And one way or another they are meant to tell us something about a person.

What grounds do we have for trusting God? What character is implied by His name and what actions would His name lead us to expect? (We can have a good idea what sort of King Ethelred the Unready was, for example!) There are two reasons for asking questions like this. First, as I minister throughout the world I frequently find a certain problem even among seemingly mature Christians: many people know a great deal **about** God, but few really know **Him.** They have accumulated **facts** about Him but often have never entered into real fellowship with God. Many Christians grow in head knowledge of Scripture but flounder around unable to overcome habits and receive answers to prayer because they haven't understood the heart of God and the provision He has made to draw us into a unique relationship with Him. This is Paul's urgent prayer for the Ephesians. They already had faith in the Lord Jesus; they had committed their lives to Him and served Him as their Lord, but they still needed to know the Father. This, Paul implies, is not a matter of intellectual study but a spiritual process mediated through our trust in God's grace:

> For this reason, ever since I heard about your faith in the Lord Jesus and your love of all the saints, I have not stopped giving thanks for you, remembering you in my prayers. I keep asking that the God of our Lord Jesus Christ, the glorious Father, may give you the spirit of wisdom and revelation so that you may know him better. I pray also that the eyes of your heart may be enlightened in order that you may know the hope to which he has called you, the riches of his glorious inheritance in the saints, and his incomparably great power for us who believe.
>
> (Ephesians 1, verses 15-19)

Paul repeats this theme in his letter to the Colossians:

> For this reason since the day we heard about you we have not stopped praying for you and asking God to fill you with the knowledge of his will through all spiritual wisdom and understanding. And we pray this in order that you may live a life worthy of the Lord and may please him in every way, bearing fruit in every good work, growing in the knowledge of God, being strengthened with all power according to his glorious might...
>
> (Colossians 1, verses 9-11)

It seemed to be of vital importance that people with a new-found faith in Christ grew in spiritual knowledge of God Himself. This seemed to be the foundation which would support a life of power and righteousness. We will explore this deeper relationship with God more fully in a later chapter.

The second reason for exploring the meaning of God's name and so deepening our understanding of His character is because God says, 'For my thoughts are not your thoughts, neither are my ways your ways' (Isaiah 55, verse 8).

Now usually we assess a person's character by the way he acts and the things he says. 'He's a mean old toad,' we complain of someone whose uncharitable actions have branded him the local scrooge. Sweet Aunt Alice, on the other hand, who always remembers the children's birthdays and sends us socks every Christmas, is a 'dear old thing who wouldn't hurt a fly'. We judge people by the things they do. Few of us can sum up a person's character at a glance.

What's more, we expect people to conform to our own standards of behaviour, and we are surprised or shocked by the actions of those who have a different set of values from our own, however legitimate those values are to them. This is particularly true in areas such as morality and business. Or we may think it rude if a person from another culture disregards all our table etiquette along with his knife and fork and dives into his food with both hands. Similarly we would be surprised to find, in a Moslem country, that we had given great offence by showing the soles of our feet!

But if we approach God in the same way, judging His actions by our own standards and basing our assessment of His character on our human ideas of justice or rationality, we can become bewildered and discouraged. He often works in ways beyond our natural understanding, for higher purposes than we can perceive, asking us simply to trust Him that, 'In all things God works for the good of those who love him' (Romans 8, verse 28).

It is far better then, if we approach God in a different way and interpret all His actions towards us in the light of what we already know about His unfailing love, compassion and grace.

The Bible is wonderfully geared towards this understanding of God. Names in Scripture always have a special significance. Many characters receive new names to illustrate God's intervention or divine purpose in their lives - Abraham, Sarah, Peter and Paul, for example. And God Himself is referred to by a number of titles, each one revealing another aspect of His character and the role He promises to fulfil towards His people. In fact, the two are inseparable. Just look at some of the names we find for God in the Old Testament:

Jehovah Sabaoth	The Lord of Hosts
Jehovah Jireh	The Lord will provide
Jehovah Rapha	The Lord that heals
Jehovah Nisi	The Lord my banner
Jehovah M'Qaddishkhan	The Lord that sanctifies
Jehovah Shalom	The Lord sends peace
Jehovah Rohi	The Lord my shepherd
Jehovah Tsidkenu	The Lord our righteousness
Jehovah Shammah	The Lord is there

What a God of integrity! Everything He does is an expression of what He is. Blessing overflows from Him like a spring of water. We who are used to being let down by people and who often fail to keep our word ourselves, find it hard to imagine a God so trustworthy. For in these titles alone, God promises to:

*be our King
*remove our sicknesses
*fight for us
*make us holy
*give us peace
*lead and protect us
*restore our relationship with Him
*be with us always

Then, when we take in the other names that are applied to God, we have an overwhelming picture of love, protection and provision: He is a God of Salvation, Faithfulness, Mercy, Justice, Comfort, Hope, Light, Love, Life and Refuge; the Lord is our Rock, our Fortress, our Shield, our Sun, our High Tower, our Deliverer, our Shepherd, our Helper, our Lamp, our Light, our Portion, our Inheritance, our Reward, our Shade, our Redeemer, our Strength and Song, our Resurrection and our Counsellor. All the power within God is directed towards our blessing. When we see divine healing within this overall context of restoration and provision, sickness begins to lose its hold of fear over us for we see it is part of God's unchangeable nature to make us whole.

In the New Testament, El Shaddai, the God Almighty, reveals Himself as the tender Abba - Father (or more exactly, Daddy) - of His children. This **Fatherhood** of God is the aspect of His nature stressed most strongly by Jesus and He taught His disciples to approach God with the trust and simplicity of a child, encouraging them to address God as Father and to trust in His commitment to care for them:

> Therefore I tell you, do not worry about your life, what you will eat or drink, or about your body, what you will wear. Is not life more important than clothes? Look at the birds of the air, they do not sow or reap or store away into barns, and yet your Heavenly Father feeds them. Are you not much more valuable they they?... So do not worry saying, 'What shall we eat?' or 'What shall we drink?' or 'What shall we wear?' For the pagans run after all these things, and your Heavenly Father knows that you need them. But seek first his kingdom and his righteousness and all these things will be given to you as well.
>
> (Matthew 6, verses 25-26, 31-33)

> Which of you, if his son asks for bread, will give him a stone? Or if he asks for a fish will give him a snake? If you then, who are evil, know how to give good gifts to your children, how much more will your Father in Heaven give good things to those who ask him!
>
> (Matthew 7, verses 9-11)

Not only does Jesus teach us repeatedly about God's loving character, but He demonstrates it in His own life, in all His words and actions. His very name, Jesus, means 'God saves'. He is Emmanuel, living proof that 'God is with us'. As the Son of God, the Word of God in the form of man, Jesus perfectly expressed the nature of God:

> In the beginning was the Word and the Word was with God and the Word was God. He was with God

in the beginning... The Word became flesh and lived
for a while among us.. We have seen his glory, the
glory of the one and only Son who came from the
Father, full of grace and truth.

(John 1, verses 1-2, 14)

Jesus said:
'Anyone who has seen me has seen the Father.'

(John 14, verse 9)

and:
'I and the Father are one.'

(John 10, verse 30)

As the Messiah, the Christ, the Anointed One, He came to do the
Father's will and He did only those things He saw His Father doing. He
never suffered any illness or disease. He healed people of sickness
wherever He encountered it. He fulfilled the prophecy of Isaiah 61 and
set the captives free. His word, His touch, brought freedom and
wholeness to everyone who sought His help:

Great crowds came to him, bringing the lame, the
blind, the crippled, the dumb, and many others, and
laid them at his feet, and he healed them. The people
were amazed when they saw the dumb speaking, the
crippled made well, the lame walking and the blind
seeing. And they praised the God of Israel.

(Matthew 15, verses 30-31)

Jesus discerned the root of the physical ailment and often declared
forgiveness of their sin or commanded them to sin no more. Again and
again the Bible records His compassion and love expressed in healing.
As John Wimber comments:

The gospels record forty-one instances of physical
and mental healing by Jesus... Of the 3,774 verses in
the four gospels, 484 relate specifically to the
healing of physical and mental illness and the

resurrection of the dead. More impressive, of the
1,257 narrative verses in the gospels, 484 verses -
38.5 per cent! - are devoted to describing Jesus'
healing miracles... He also equipped the disciples to
heal, that they might effectively advance the
Kingdom of God. He trained and sent the Twelve
and the Seventy Two (Luke 9: 1-9; 10: 1-24);
included healing in the great commission (Mark 16:
14-20); and throughout the book of Acts the disciples
healed the sick.

(*Power Healing* p 58-59 Hodder & Stoughton 1986)

The wonderful fact that Jesus spent most of His ministry healing the
sick and bringing light, hope and release to those in any form of
bondage, shows that this is God's main concern. The very heart of God
which Jesus reveals is **COMPASSION.** This is the personal dimension
of the loving kindness which was the essence of the Old Covenant.
Jesus often healed in response to faith (in fact He **always** rewarded
faith with healing) but He frequently went beyond this to heal before
petition because His heart was touched with the feeling of our
infirmities. Look at how Jesus responds to the sick when He Himself is
full of grief and weariness after hearing of the murder of John the
Baptist:

When Jesus heard what had happened, he withdrew
by boat privately to a solitary place. Hearing of this,
the crowds followed him on foot from the towns.
When Jesus landed and saw a large crowd he had
compassion on them and healed their sick.

(Matthew 14, verses 13-14)

What grace! Overcome with sadness He did His utmost to escape all
the noise and demands of the crowds for a while. How would we have
reacted if we had landed at our retreat, worn out with the pain of loss,
only to find the deserted beach packed with five thousand crying,
desperate, needy people all clamouring for attention? Yet in Jesus there
is no trace of anger, resentment or self-pity. With a heart overflowing
with love, there is no room for those feelings. Looking away from His

own needs, He is moved by the helplessness of the people and heals all their sick. After that, He could legitimately have packed them off home, but His compassion extends to the smallest need and He proceeds miraculously to provide food for everyone. Not just a scrap to keep the wolf from the door but a **feast,** more than they can eat so that there were twelve baskets left over! How can we doubt that God sees our every need and wants to provide for us? We don't have to try and persuade Him to heal us. He hasn't forgotten or overlooked our problems and our sicknesses. All these people did was to be in the right place at the right time and then to ask. They were where Jesus was.

God has always been the same. His nature will never change. Throughout the Scriptures, from Genesis, where we read:

> And God saw all that he had made and it was very good.
>
> (Genesis 1, verse 31)

to Revelation, where John says:

> Then I saw a new heaven and a new earth... Now the dwelling place of God is with men and he will live with them and be their God. He will wipe away every tear from their eyes. There will be no more death, or mourning, or crying or pain, for the old order of things has passed away.
>
> (Revelation 21, verses 1, 3-4)

God shows there is no deviousness in His character:

> Every good and perfect gift is from above, coming down from the Father of heavenly light who does not change like shifting shadows.
>
> (James 1, verse 17)

Creativity, order, beauty, productivity, harmony and restoration are reflected in all His dealings with mankind, transforming sorrow into joy, suffering into victory, death into life. Knowing His character we can be confident that these are the fruits that He wants to bring out of every situation, however dark and hopeless it might appear. He **cannot** fail us, for He cannot act contrary to His nature. We can trust God to keep what we have committed to Him and so be free from the burden of fear and anxiety, having the confidence of David to trust that God desires wholeness in body, soul and spirit:

> Lord, you have assigned to me my portion and my cup; you have made my lot secure. The boundary lines have fallen for me in pleasant places, surely I have a delightful inheritance. I will praise the Lord who counsels me, even at night my heart instructs me. I have set the Lord always before me. Because he is at my right hand, I shall not be shaken. Therefore my heart is glad and my tongue rejoices; my body also will rest secure because you will not abandon me to the grave. Nor will you let your Holy One see decay. You have made known to me the path of life; you will fill me with joy in your presence, with eternal pleasures at your right hand.
>
> (Psalm 16, verses 5-11)

Remember that when David wrote that, he was hiding in the wilderness in fear of his life from Saul. What amazing trust! Was David just a man of great faith or was there a further reason for his confidence? I think the secret lies in the fact that (i) He knew the character of God, (ii) He knew God personally - he had a relationship with Him, (iii) He knew that God was a covenant-keeping God - the God of Abraham and Isaac and Jacob - and David was a beneficiary of the promise made to his forefathers. What **was** this covenant, this promise, this contract?

Chapter Three

Covenant Terms

I have just read that some cars, particularly the Swedish makes, are now sold with an unlimited guarantee against rust. The promise that the bodywork on your vehicle won't wear out, or if it does, will be mended free of charge, is very tempting and it would be wonderful if we could take out the same guarantee on our own bodywork!

Maybe there is a sense in which we can. We have already seen that God's whole nature and purpose is to restore, make whole and bless. He has done everything necessary for us to live in health and joy and peace. But what is the problem? We often seem unable to appropriate His blessings into our lives. The blockage lies partly in our understanding of the concept of covenant. In our 'civilised' society we have lost the knowledge of the contract and relationship which was interwoven through the whole fabric of the Ancient World and still forms the basis of social interaction in some communities, such as in parts of Africa, today. When Jesus spoke about making a new covenant, His disciples would have grasped immediately the awe-inspiring implications of what He was doing.

For the most basic sense of covenant is **everlasting commitment.** It means that all I am and all that I have is yours - forever - and in our sophisticated Western society, the idea of such absolute loyalty and devotion is an alien one: the more civilised we become, the more disloyal we get. The Arabs have a saying, 'Blood is thicker than milk'. In other words, blood covenant brothers are closer than in a natural family relationship. Our culture reverses that principle.

In the Ancient World, a covenant was generally an agreement forged between two tribes. Each of them picked a representative who would sum up the feeling of the whole tribe, containing in his own person the qualities, abilities and characteristics of everyone else. Each representative would take off his coat and give it to the other. This symbolised 'all that I am I give to you'. They would then exchange belts, on which hung their sword, dagger and their bow and purse, representing their commitment of their strength to fight on behalf of the other tribe in time of danger, as well as a dedication of all their material wealth. After this a covenant animal, usually a bull, would be killed and then split down the backbone. The two representatives would then take the walk of covenant through the two walls of blood in a figure of eight which signified infinity, an everlasting bond, which they called upon whatever gods they worshipped to witness. Finally, they cut their wrists and held them together so that their blood mingled, and they swore to keep the covenant between them. The scar they would carry to the grave represented the seal of the covenant, the sign to the world that they had made an eternal, irreversible commitment to one another. They had become Friends. How shallow our modern interpretation of that term is compared to its profound implications in the Ancient World. Not just anyone could be called a friend, for a covenant brother was in fact the friend who 'sticks closer than a brother'. That is the true significance of that verse in Proverbs 18, verse 24: Jesus is a covenant friend, with all that signifies of a deeper bond than natural brotherhood.

After these solemn proceedings, the representatives would share a covenant meal, usually of bread and wine. Sometimes their blood was dripped into the wine as if to say, 'I am giving you my very life and I am drinking your life'.

The last effect of a covenant in those days was a name change. Tribe A became Tribe AB and Tribe B became Tribe BA. Henceforth they would be inseparably identified with one another, with mutual sharing, love and protection.

There is a particular covenant word which describes this unique relationship and which cannot be adequately conveyed in any single English word. The Hebrew word is **hesed** and once you understand the full implications of the covenant bond, you will see that only this original word sums up all its qualities. The Authorised Version of the Bible translates it as **mercy.** The New American Standard calls it **loving kindness.** Other words are love, compassion, loyal love, covenant or bonded love. But only **hesed** itself conveys the idea that 'all that I am I give to you, all my strength, my possessions, my abilities, my intellect are at your disposal; anyone who raises a hand against you, will have me to reckon with; when you are in any sort of need, I will always come to your aid; I will never fail you or leave you.'

There are other outstanding features of **hesed**:

1. **Hesed** is a **choice** word; it is not based on feelings but on an act of the will, a promise of unfailing loyalty.

2. It is a submissive love which is willing to yield in order to serve. It is a love which constantly looks for opportunities to bless.

3. **Hesed** is like a parent-love or womb-love; it is ferociously protective and willing to sacrifice everything to defend the loved one.

4. It is a responsible love. You are your brother's keeper, an activity which is one of joy and not drudgery to you.

> Be strong and of good courage. Do not fear or be in dread of them: for it is the Lord your God who goes with you; he will not fail you or forsake you. It is the Lord who goes before you. He will be with you, he will not fail you or forsake you. Do not fear or be dismayed.
>
> (Deuteronomy 31, verses 6 and 8)

Plainly, **hesed** does not come from our human nature. Its selfless devotion and commitment are found perfectly only in the character of God Himself, an expression of the **agape** love which is the essence of the Godhead.

With this deeper understanding of the meaning of covenant, then, the examples of covenant in Scripture give an exciting new dimension to our relationship with God. Suddenly we realise the potential for joy and power and fulfilment which is at our disposal. Now when we re-read the famous story of David and Jonathan's covenant, we perceive the full wonder and grace of what God has done for us:

Jonathan became one in spirit with David and he loved him as himself... and Jonathan made a covenant with David because he loved him as himself. Jonathan took off the robe he was wearing and gave it to David, along with his tunic and even his sword, his bow and his belt.

(1 Samuel 18, verses 1-3)

David and Jonathan were covenant representatives of their families; all their unborn children in every succeeding generation were to come under the blessing of the vows they took. For Jonathan said to David:

'May the Lord be with you as he has been with my father. But show me unfailing kindness like that of the Lord as long as I live, so that I may not be killed, and do not ever cut off your kindness from my family - not even when the Lord has cut off everyone of David's enemies from the face of the earth...' 'Go in peace for we have sworn friendship with each other in the name of the Lord, saying, "The Lord is witness between you and me, and between your descendants and my descendants for ever".'

(1 Samuel 20, verses 13-15, 42)

We have to remember that these words come from the son of a man who hated David and was already seeking to kill him. Saul was insanely jealous of David and must have been sowing seeds of suspicion and fear amongst his family towards David for years. Despite this, Jonathan bore a love for David far beyond all natural or reasonable ties. When David was hiding in the desert for fear of his life from Saul's marauding search parties, we read:

Jonathan went to David at Horesh and helped him to find strength in God. 'Don't be afraid,' he said, 'my father, Saul, will not lay a hand on you. You shall be king over Israel and I will be second to you. Even my father Saul knows this.' The two of them made a covenant before the Lord.

(1 Samuel 23, verse 17)

The story is well known - how David escapes from Saul, and after the death of Saul and Jonathan by the Philistines and the murder of Saul's son Ishbosheth, he eventually sits as God's anointed king on the throne of Israel. Time passes and peace returns to Israel. But every day, when David is getting washed in the morning, his eye is caught by the scar on his wrist. Each time he remembers the covenant he made with his beloved friend Jonathan. The word 'remember' is a covenant word. It means 'to hold you always in the forefront of my mind'. So one day, as he remembers again his friend, a surge of love and grief makes him cry out:

> Is there anyone still left of the house of Saul to whom I
> can show kindness for Jonathan's sake?
>
> (2 Samuel 9, verse 1)

There is the covenant word again. **Hesed!** From the scars of David flows the **hesed** of the covenant. If there is a living descendant of Jonathan, he will be entitled freely and undeservedly to all the riches and blessings of David's family. And hiding in a place called Lo Debar (which means 'load of nothing'), miserable, terrified, in despair, is Mephibosheth the son of Jonathan. He has been a cripple since the age of five when he was dropped by his nurse, who panicked and tried to flee when she heard that his father had been killed. Brought up in an atmosphere of suspicion and hatred, he has been indoctrinated by his grandfather with the idea that David is his worst enemy, and if he ever falls into David's hands he will surely be killed. When David becomes king, Mephibosheth's life is dominated by the thought that one day David will hunt him out and murder him. No wonder he calls himself a 'dead dog' (2 Samuel 9, verse 8).

So when a party of David's soldiers ride up one morning to the house where he is in hiding, his heart sinks to his boots. Unable even to walk, he knows he cannot attempt to escape; giving himself up for lost, he allows himself to be taken to the palace without even asking any questions. But instead of being thrown into a dungeon, he is led into a beautiful room, given a luxurious bath, and dressed in fine new clothes. Bewildered and scared he imagines this must be some subtle form of sadism for his execution must come soon - and sure enough, here comes the command to come before the king. This is it, he thinks dully, and when he is led into David's presence, he doesn't even see the smile and the outstretched hand, but throws himself face down on the floor. Then, amazingly, instead of blows, gentle and unbelievable words fall on his ears:

> 'Don't be afraid,' David said to him, 'for I will surely show you kindness for the sake of your father, Jonathan. I will restore to you all the land that belonged to your grandfather, Saul, and you will always eat at my table.'
>
> (2 Samuel 9, verse 7)

'I will show you kindness' **Hesed!** the mercy and grace of covenant love. Not because of anything he is or has done but simply on the basis of a covenant made between his father and David, Mephibosheth will now not only inherit all the worldly goods which had once belonged to his grandfather, but will also be part of the royal family and take a share in everything the king possesses. How hard it must have been for Mephibosheth to grasp this incredible truth, that instead of death he was receiving glorious life; no longer was he to be a dog of a servant but he was to reign like a prince. Impossible to understand - until at breakfast next morning as David is passing the marmalade, Mephibosheth catches sight of the deep scar on David's wrist and he realises that this is not some wonderful dream but the outworking of **hesed,** the profound, unfailing love of a covenant bond. So Mephibosheth doesn't need to worry whether this might just be a passing whim of David's and tomorrow he might decide he would like to chop off Mephibosheth's head. It doesn't matter that he deserves nothing and, in fact, all his efforts couldn't win any more. Freely he has received every blessing, and goodness and mercy will follow him all the days of his life:

> And Mephibosheth lived in Jerusalem because he always ate at the king's table.

Terrific! David could provide for him, give him a royal lifestyle, watch over him, fight for him, protect him. Yet despite all this the episode still ends on a slightly sad note for one thing remains unchanged. The verse goes on, 'and Mephibosheth was crippled in both feet'.

David could give him all these blessings, but he **couldn't heal him.** Mephibosheth had a wonderful life materially but he would always be a cripple because the covenant was made between two men. Covenant blessings extend only as far as the abilities and possessions of the covenant makers. So what happens when **God** makes a covenant with man?

In Genesis 12, we find Abram living in the sacred city of Ur, in the country which we today would call Iraq in the Persian Gulf. This was a city dedicated to the god and goddess of the moon, and every inhabitant was considered to be a sacred servant-priest of those deities. Yet somehow, amid this saturated atmosphere of magic and idolatry, Abram has retained his faith in God Almighty for the Lord says to him:

> 'Leave your country, your people and your father's household and go to the land I will show you. I will make you into a great nation and I will bless you; I will make your name great and you will be a blessing. I will bless those who bless you and whoever curses you I will curse: and all peoples on earth will be blessed through you.'

What a promise! Adam walked out of Eden responsible for 'all people on earth' being cursed; here is God revealing His great plan for reversing that curse through Abram. God's promise is three-fold:

1. Abram will be given a land.
2. Abram will become a great nation.
3. Through Abram all the families of earth will be blessed.

I can't imagine Abram really being able to comprehend what God meant at all. First, lone men don't normally get given a whole land to possess, particularly when they are foreign exiles. And second, he is seventy five years old, his wife isn't much younger, and they have no children and no prospect of being able to have any. So, although Abram has made a tremendous act of obedience and open repentance by leaving Ur and showing that he is serving the invisible God, I'm not sure that he really has much faith yet that God will fulfil His word.

In fact, just to 'help' God, he takes along with him Lot. By adopting his orphan nephew into his family, he is providing himself with a son and heir. He must have got rather hot under the collar when his herdsmen and Lot's herdsmen started to quarrel, as it looked as if there might be outright fighting between them. Abram manages to prevent violence, but there is a split between him and Lot which means that Abram is really in trouble: he's lost his heir. In despair, he must have questioned how on earth God was going to bring a great nation out of him, so once more, he gives God a hand by making his servant, Eliezer, his heir. God has to intervene. A promise alone is not going to convince Abram. Only a covenant will persuade him that God is eternally committed to him and will perform all the miraculous things He has said. So now God initiates the first step of covenant with the **exchange.** But instead of coat, shield, sword and belt, He gives Abram **Himself.** 'Don't be afraid, Abram. **I am your shield** and your very great reward.' I AM, God Himself, will be your strength and protection. What grace to offer mere man all that He is and has! Small wonder that Abram is still unable to comprehend the magnitude of what God is doing. So with great patience, God explains that it will be Abram's own son who will be his heir. Then He takes him outside and says,

> 'Look up at the heavens and count the stars - if
> indeed you can count them ...... so shall your
> offspring be.'

(Genesis 15, verse 5)

For the first time we read that Abram actually **believes** the Lord. He takes his eyes off the impossibility of Sarai's conceiving and looks to the power of God Almighty. But a moment later, his faith begins to waver again as he tries to come to terms with the next promise - that he will take possession of the land of Canaan. Or perhaps he thinks that if God will give him a sign that he really will possess the land, then he can believe the Lord for the greater miracle that he will have as many descendants as the stars in the sky. Anyway, he dares to ask God for some proof. And God proceeds with the one mighty, awesome act which will put a seal of unfailing certainty on all He has promised:

> So the Lord said to him, 'Bring me a heifer, a goat,
> and a ram, each three years old, along with a dove
> and a young pigeon'.
>
> (Genesis 15, verse 9)

God didn't exactly spell it out, but Abram must have been realising by now with growing excitement that he is being told to prepare a **blood covenant sacrifice:**

> And Abram brought all these to him, cut them in
> two, and arranged the halves opposite each other; the
> birds, however, he did not cut in half.

Just as everything is ready, the precious sacrifice is almost stolen, for birds of prey come down on the carcasses and Abram has to drive them away. I believe many things can try and rob us of God's provision - doubt, fear, the devil; we need to exercise our own faith and strength of will to cast out these works of darkness.

Then we read that:

> As the sun was setting, Abram fell into a deep sleep,
> and a thick and dreadful darkness came over him.

One of the joys of the blood covenant relationship with God is that we can enter into **rest.** We can cease from our own works when we realise that God makes available to us His ability and power. He put Abram to sleep because there was absolutely nothing that Abram could contribute in a covenant with the Lord God Almighty. What **could** Abram give God? All that he had came from God - his health, his wealth, his strength. So God made him fall asleep and then,

> When the sun had set and darkness had fallen, a
> scorching fire pot with a blazing torch appeared and
> passed between the pieces.

We have already learnt that in a blood covenant, the two representatives walked in a figure of eight through the pieces of the sacrifice, between a wall of blood. So here we witness the amazing miracle of Jesus making a covenant with His Father on Abram's behalf, the Light of the World walking through the pieces. And,

> On that day the Lord made a covenant with Abram
> and said, 'To your descendants I give this land'.
>
> (Genesis 15, verse 18)

But, as yet, God still doesn't finish the covenant. They have not yet shared the covenant meal together. For God can see that Abram has still not come to the point of covenant **faith** which means total commitment to God. He still cannot just receive what God has promised. He still tries to offer God something. So despite this wonderful sign, Abram still cannot leave the problem of having a child up to God.

I shouldn't think Sarai was much encouragement. She hadn't been in on any of these talks with the Lord and she probably thought Abram's ramble about having a baby was senile decay or the product of too much sun. After ten years of nothing happening, Abram began to wonder if she wasn't right, so when she suggested he tried to have a child by her servant Hagar, he gave in and slept with her. Thus Ishmael was born, and Abram was thrilled. At last, at last, he had an heir. Now God's promise could be fulfilled. But how sad. Abram thought he could help God, but he was way off the mark, and he was only delaying God's blessing. How can you fault a person who is trying to fulfil God's purpose, though? Satan is so subtle. The whole idea of covenant with God is supernatural, however, and there is nothing man can do to bring it to pass.

For thirteen years, Ishmael was brought up as Abram's son and heir, shown every honour, and showered with love. Then just as he was at the point of entering manhood, God yet again appeared to his father, and repeated His original promise. But this time He revealed more of His plan and character to Abram, and by the way He spoke, made it clearer that there was a New Covenant relationship between them:

> 'I am God Almighty; walk before me and be
> blameless. I will confirm my covenant between me
> and you, and will greatly increase your numbers...
> ... You will be the father of many nations. No longer

> will you be called Abram; your name will be
> Abraham for I have made you a father of many
> nations.'
>
> (Genesis 17, verses 1-5)

Here is another mark of covenant - an **exchange of names.** The very essence of God's name, the sound in the centre of Yahweh, which no-one knew exactly how to pronounce but which was almost like a breath, was incorporated in Abram's name. And henceforth God deigned to be called the God of Abraham. This incredible blessing is conveyed on Abraham's wife too:

> 'As for Sarai your wife, you are no longer to call her
> Sarai; her name will be Sarah. I will bless her and
> will surely give you a son by her. I will bless her so
> that she will be the mother of nations; kings of
> peoples will come from her.'
>
> (Genesis 17, verses 15-16)

And Abraham falls on the floor, laughing. Even after all that has happened he still can't see beyond the human limitations. He thinks that through Ishmael, the promises of God can come true without having to resort to the supernatural (or the ridiculous!) God can't be serious. He must mean Ishmael:

> 'If only Ishmael might live under your blessing!'

'Yes,' says God, 'but I have an even higher plan':

> 'Your wife Sarah will bear you a son and you will
> call him Isaac' (which means 'he laughs', or more
> exactly in Hebrew, 'hahaha'!)

It is almost as if God is laughing with Abraham, for in the womb of human helplessness, God has formed His answer for mankind. This is the hilarity of true faith, when we come into the joy of abandonment to God, beyond struggle, beyond reason, beyond hope - **into faith.** And now the covenant is almost finalised for Abraham is **circumcised,** taking upon himself and on every member of his family the sign of his remarkable agreement with God. The tragic point is when he has to go and tell Ishmael that he is no longer the son of promise. There are many people we hurt, like Ishmael, through our unbelief.

So now Abraham, at the age of ninety nine, is expecting a son within the year. But there remains one problem. Sarah still thinks he is a silly old fool. She is, after all, **barren**. Always has been. And she is an old woman. God hasn't given **her** any of these wonderful promises. She only has Abraham's word to go on, and, quite honestly, she doesn't believe men have much of a clue about babies. There's only one thing for it: she has to hear the Lord Himself saying these things. A few days later, Abraham is resting at the entrance of his tent in the middle of the day when he sees three men approaching. Hospitality is the hinge-pin of his culture and Abraham begs the men to stay while he hastily orders a delicious meal. While they eat, Abraham stands a little way off, watching them discreetly from the shade of a tree. They look like ordinary men, but with the eyes of his growing faith, Abraham begins to realise that one of them is the Lord. For as he sees one of them break the bread and hold some out to him, the glorious fact dawns on him that this is his covenant Lord sharing the **covenant meal**, the meal which signifies, **It is done.** Sure enough, when his ears hear the wonderful promise repeated once more, Abraham is convinced that this is indeed El Shaddai, the Lord God Almighty:

> 'I will surely return to you about this time next year and Sarah your wife will have a son.'
>
> (Genesis 18, verse 10)

Suddenly from behind the curtain of the tent there is a great explosion of laughter. Sarah has been eavesdropping on the conversation, and the thought of her having a baby at her age with a husband who is nearly a hundred years old has her doubled up with mirth and her apron over her head. The Lord can read her thoughts perfectly, but instead of being angry at her unbelief, He makes allowances for the limitations of human understanding and reassures them:

> 'Is anything too hard for the Lord? I will return to you

at the appointed time next year and Sarah will have a
son.'

(Genesis 18, verse 14)

And now, at last, Abraham has entered into covenant faith. All the
terms of the covenant have been fulfilled by God Himself, and
Abraham recognises that he is now a covenant beneficiary. He has
come to the end of all his own ideas and ability. It is now completely
up to God and Abraham has confidence that God will perform what He
has promised. As far as his eyes can see, and his mind can understand,
the situation is still hopeless but now it doesn't bother him. Even when
Sarah is taken accidentally by Abimelech as a wife (remarkable when
you consider she is almost ninety!), Abraham still believes that God
can fulfil His promise. So we read in Hebrews 11, verse 11:

> By faith Abraham, even though he was past age - and
> Sarah herself was barren - was enabled to become a
> father because he considered him faithful who had
> made the promise.

The Hebrew is ambiguous here, and this verse could refer to Sarah.
Anyway, both of them were now completely committed to God's way
of doing things, and this faith gave them the physical ability to
conceive a child. This was not virgin birth. Isaac was the natural, yet
supernatural, child of their own bodies:

> Against all hope, Abraham in hope believed and so
> became the father of many nations, just as it had been
> said to him, 'So shall your offspring be'. Without
> weakening in his faith, he faced the fact that his body
> was as good as dead - since he was about a hundred
> years old - and that Sarah's womb was also dead. Yet he
> did not waver through unbelief regarding the promise of
> God, but was strengthened in his faith and gave glory to
> God, being fully persuaded that God had power to do
> what he had promised. This is why 'it was credited to
> him as righteousness'.

(Romans 4, verses 18-22)

After all his doubts, it was the **covenant** which gave Abraham the strength to believe God. He now had not only a promise but an oath:

> Because God wanted to make the unchanging nature
> of his purpose very clear to the heirs of what was
> promised... God did this so that, by two
> unchangeable things in which it is impossible for
> God to lie, we who have fled to take hold of the hope
> offered to us may be greatly encouraged.
>
> (Hebrews 6, verses 17-18)

Having entered into covenant with God, Abraham was able to face everything in his situation which should have made him give up, and actually **praise God.** As he gave glory to God, his faith grew even stronger. He was as pregnant with faith as Sarah was with child, and at the appointed time the vindication of his faith was revealed to the world:

> Now the Lord was gracious to Sarah as he had said,
> and the Lord did for Sarah what he had promised.
> Sarah became pregnant and bore a son to Abraham in
> his old age, at the very time God had promised him.
>
> (Genesis 21 , verses 1-2)

It is Sarah who sums up the real reward of this long trial of faith.

> God has brought me laughter, and everyone who
> hears about this will laugh with me.
>
> (Genesis 21, verse 6)

Joy is always the outcome of faith. It is the fruit of clinging to the Lord's promises, of trusting in the faithfulness of our covenant God who promises to give us all that He is and has.

Before we leave the story of Abraham, we should note that it reveals one important feature of covenant faith. It is trust in the covenant **maker** not in the covenant **provision.** God had become everything to Abraham. All possibilities for life and peace lay in El Shaddai. God had revealed to Abraham His very nature, and Abraham had come to put his trust in that faithfulness and love, and not in the miracle he hoped for. How else could Abraham have gone through with the incredible test of being told to sacrifice Isaac, his miraculous son of promise? After years of waiting, the impossible had happened and Abraham might have thought he had reached his goal of faith. But God asked him to go one more mile. And if you are mature in your faith, God might well ask you to do the same. After going through years of refining and discipleship, God leads you into a wonderful ministry of preaching, or teaching or healing - only to tell you to give it up, to lay it on the altar as a burnt offering. Without covenant faith, you may fight for your ministry. But if you have trust in the perfect love of your covenant God you will know that whatever He asks will be for your good, and you will be prepared to lay down the thing you most treasure in order to receive God's best for you. He may well give it back to you at the last minute, as He did with Abraham, but the important thing is being prepared to lose, to die, in order to gain Christ.

In this part of the story, Abraham was entering a new dimension in his covenant relationship with God. Hitherto he had been told to believe a promise which could only bring him joy; now he was being asked to destroy the very fulfilment of that promise with no explanation or reassurance. Abraham's amazing prompt, unquestioning obedience reflects the fact that his long years of waiting have so refined his faith that now he really does know his God. Before God even reveals another of his covenant names, 'The Lord Your Provider', Abraham has confidence that the Lord will again perform some miracle to bring joy out of disaster. This is why he calls this terrible act of killing Isaac **worship.**

> 'Stay here with the donkey,' he said to his servants,
> 'while I and the boy go over there. We will worship,
> and then we will come back to you.'

Abraham is so convinced of the **loving kindness** of the Lord that he is sure that somehow he will return with his beloved son. Even if he has to go through with the sacrifice, Abraham believes that God can raise him from the dead because God has promised that through this son all the nations of the world will be blessed. And God cannot lie. So when Isaac asks,

> 'The fire and wood are here, but where is the lamb for the burnt offering?'

Abraham replies,

> 'God himself will provide the lamb for the burnt offering, my son.'

Yet he still has to get to the point of lifting his knife to slay Isaac, before the angel of the Lord stops him:

> 'Do not lay a hand on the boy. Do not do anything to him. Now I know that you fear God, because you have not withheld from me your son, your only son.'
> And Abraham looked up and there in a thicket he saw a ram caught by its horns. He went over and took the ram and sacrificed it as a burnt offering instead of his son. So Abraham called that place, 'The Lord will provide'.
>
> (Genesis 22, verses 12-14)

So it is not until we reach that point of total abandonment to God, of utter commitment to HIM over and above all other hopes and desires, that we receive His provision. For it is only in that realm of true worship when we lay down our life on the altar that God is able to provide for our needs. Let us look in more detail at how, in our helplessness, God is our strength, and how, ultimately, God provided an even better covenant of life and blessing based not on law, but on grace.

Chapter Four

Covenant Provision and a New Covenant

> The Israelites groaned in their slavery and cried out,
> and their cry for help because of their slavery went
> up to God. **God heard their groaning - and he
> remembered his covenant with Abraham,** with
> Isaac and with Jacob. So God looked on the Israelites
> and was concerned about them.
>
> (Exodus 2, verses 23-24)

Here we find the seed of the miracle which took place on the night of the Passover. **God remembered His covenant with Abraham.** All that He planned to bless Abraham's descendants with was brought forcibly to His mind, and He prepared the remarkable plan which would set them free. The first thing He did was to call Moses from the burning bush and appoint him as His covenant representative. And Moses was convinced He'd got the wrong man. To be fair, anyone else would have thought that too. He might have been brave enough, in the heat of the moment, to kill the Egyptian beating a fellow Hebrew, but as far as being a leader and a spokesman was concerned, he was just a joke. Not only was he meek and timid, but there is every possibility he actually had a speech defect:

> 'O Lord,' Moses said, 'I have never been eloquent
> neither in the past nor since you have spoken to your
> servant. I am slow of speech and tongue.'
>
> (Exodus 4, verse 10)

But all these inadequacies are irrelevant when God has given him

His covenant promise that He will bring the Israelites out of Egypt into a land flowing with milk and honey. Not only that but God's oath is sealed by His own name, by which God assures Moses that all that I AM will be given to His people, for He is committed to them forever:

> God said to Moses, 'I am who I am. This is what you are to say to the Israelites: "I AM has sent me to you." ' God also said to Moses, 'Say to the Israelites, "The Lord, the God of your fathers - the God of Abraham, the God of Isaac and the God of Jacob - has sent me to you." This is my name for ever, the name by which I am to be remembered from generation to generation.'
>
> (Exodus 3, verses 14-15)

The Hebrew for 'Lord' sounds like and may be derived from the Hebrew for 'I AM'. Up till now, God has been known as El Shaddai, God Almighty; with the forging of the covenant, God has made possible a more personal relationship with His people, and by revealing this name I AM WHO I AM, or THE LORD, He promises to carry out all He has said He will do, because He is a God of integrity and faithfulness. In other words, He is showing them that He **loves** them. By revealing to them this name, God is trying to quicken the Israelites' faith and revive their memory of the covenant He has made with them. Humanly, their situation is hopeless, but if they can recall the covenant, they can lift up their heads and look towards the promised land. He even repeats this new name by which He will be known to them and gives them through Moses a further promise of deliverance:

> '**I am the Lord.** I appeared to Abraham, to Isaac and to Jacob as God Almighty, but by my name the Lord, I did not make myself known to them. I also established my covenant with them to give them the land of Canaan, where they lived as aliens. Moreover, I have heard the groaning of the Israelites whom the Egyptians are enslaving, and I have remembered my covenant.

Therefore, say to the Israelites: "**I am the Lord,** and I will bring you out from under the yoke of the Egyptians. I will free you from being slaves to them and will redeem you with an outstretched arm and with mighty acts of judgement. I will be your God. Then you will know that **I am the Lord your God,** who brought you out from under the yoke of the Egyptians. And I will bring you to the land I swore with uplifted hand to give to Abraham, to Isaac and to Jacob. I will give it to you as a possession. **I am the Lord.**" '

(Exodus 6, verses 2-8)

Four times God promises the Israelites that He will be true to His perfect character of righteousness and love. Four times He reassures them that He will not fail them, that He will deliver them and bless them - and not because of a passing whim but on the basis of two unshakable, unchangeable things: His **character** and His **covenant.**

How sad that the Israelites are too discouraged and oppressed by their bondage to believe these promises (Exodus 6, verse 9). And this is sometimes the case with healing, that even though we come to a sick person with a word of knowledge or the message of God's covenant love and provision, they are too depressed by their pain to believe there is any hope. It is pointless praying for their healing until the root of discouragement and dismay has been dealt with, and they have received God's love and the Lordship of Jesus. Because the Israelites couldn't see any other lords except the Egyptians, God kept saying, 'I am your Lord', but every moment of their tortuous day, they were reminded that Pharaoh ruled over them. And sometimes our illness can become our lord. It dictates all our thoughts and actions. Everything we do is with reference to our physical condition. But if we reject that domination, or are delivered from that bondage and receive the yoke of Jesus instead, we are able to step outside our problem and share God's perspective which means health and deliverance.

It takes **nine** plagues, nine incredible demonstrations of God's power, before the Israelites begin to see a genuine glimmer of hope. Only when they are told of the last terrible plague to come upon the Egyptians, the death of all the first-born, and of God's protection over the Israelites, do they realise that, true to His word, God **is** going to deliver them. Nothing about their circumstances has changed yet, but their hearts have changed. Look at the difference in their response to Moses' command to prepare the Passover meal:

> Then the Israelites bowed down and worshipped.
>
> (Exodus 12, verse 27)

This, then, is the attitude in which they take a lamb and sacrifice it for this remarkable meal. WORSHIP. And when we let go, and fall at the Lord's feet in worship, He is then able to deliver us from bondage. That day two million slaves prepared a feast for themselves as if they were kings. It must have really rattled the Egyptians. 'What on earth are those crazy Israelites doing now?' The air is filled with the smell of 250,000 lambs roasting on spits! And the Israelites are praying and praising their God. Have they gone mad? If we rejoice in the Lord in the face of our enemies, in the midst of sickness and Satan's bondage, we too will confuse and overthrow the opposition.

When the lambs were slaughtered, the Israelites had been told to dip a bunch of hyssop, a bitter herb symbolising their bondage, into the blood, and paint the posts and lintels of their doors. Then all the family were to walk through the door and eat every scrap of the meat which had been cooked. Did they do so with a growing, amazed realisation that they were partaking in a covenant meal? Perhaps, but Moses certainly knew that all that was happening was the outworking of God's covenant promise, so he may not have been as astounded as the rest of them when they ate the lamb and found themselves healed of every affliction. For they had walked through **the walls of blood,** just as one would do in a covenant sacrifice. And now they were eating a meal and breaking unleavened bread together, the bread of repentance, and a statement, therefore, that they were leaving behind sin, as if to finalise that covenant. Anyway, what they did was an amazing act of faith, standing eating this meal in their travelling clothes when everything about their situation said that they would be back under the whips of the Egyptians in the morning. But not far away, there were wails of grief and despair as family after Egyptian family discovered the eldest son dead in his bed. God was faithful. That very night Pharaoh ordered the Israelites to go and a few hours later, laden with the gold and silver of the Egyptians, they were on the road to freedom. And not alone:

> By day the Lord went ahead of them in a pillar of cloud to guide them on their way, and by night in a pillar of fire to give them light, so that they could travel by day or night. Neither the pillar of cloud by day, nor the pillar of fire by night, left its place in front of the people.
>
> (Exodus 13, verses 21-22)

Deliverance had come, and the encouraging thing from our point of view is that they hadn't shown mountains of faith in the past nor deep spiritual understanding. All they did was OBEY GOD: they fed on the right food which was, in a spiritual sense, the Lamb of God, the Lord Jesus Christ, even though they had no idea that this act prefigured the New Passover, the deliverance that would come to all mankind through the sacrifice of the Lamb. What is more, we read in Psalm 107, verse 37:

> He brought out Israel, laden with silver and gold, and from among their tribes **no-one faltered.**

After years of poverty and ill-treatment not a single one of the two million Israelites stumbled or fainted on the way. Weak and undernourished as they must have been before that Passover Meal, now they were supernaturally restored and empowered with the strength for this epic escape in the face of huge dangers and obstacles. What a remarkable thing! And what an encouragement to us to see the life and restoration available in the blood of Jesus, the New Passover Lamb.

Very soon, however, the Israelites encountered their first trial of faith. They were overjoyed they had been delivered **from** the Egyptians, but what had they been delivered **into?** We read that they wandered round the land in confusion, hemmed in by the desert (Exodus 14, verse 3) and then, suddenly, they looked up and saw the entire Egyptian army with horses, troops and chariots marching after them. And they couldn't escape for in front of them was the impenetrable barrier of the Red Sea. After the wonderful proof they had had of God's power and love, what did they do? Panic.

> They were terrified and cried out to the Lord. They said to Moses, 'Was it because there were no graves in Egypt that you have brought us to the desert to die? What have you done to us by bringing us out of Egypt? Didn't we say to you in Egypt, "Leave us alone; let us serve the Egyptians"? It would have been better for us to serve the Egyptians than to die in the desert.'
>
> (Exodus 14, verses 10-12)

We may have this experience in healing - that after the first deliverance or touch, the problem comes back with a vengeance. This may be due to one or two factors which we will discuss in the section on 'How to pray for the sick', but it is worthwhile just noting here what Moses' reply was in this situation:

> 'Do not be afraid - Stand firm and you will see the deliverance the Lord will bring you today. The Egyptians you see today you will never see again. The Lord will fight for you; you need only be still.'
>
> (Exodus 14, verses 13-14)

Whatever the cause of the return of the problem, it is no good fretting and striving. We need to **stand firm** in our faith, **be still,** and see the Lord accomplish the deliverance. Fear will stop us seeing beyond our problem. But if we look to the Lord, the Red Sea of our difficulties or sickness will open up before us and we will cross over safely.

At last everything was going well for the Israelites. The Egyptian army was all drowned and they had a marvellous time of rejoicing on the shore of the Red Sea, singing, dancing and praising God for their wonderful deliverance. It didn't look as if they could ever doubt God again. But only three days later they found themselves in the wilderness, wandering around in the heat and dust without water. And when they eventually did find water at Marah, it was undrinkable.

This is another trial of faith. Now trials of faith are sent to develop our faith, not destroy it, to deepen our trust in God, not to undermine it. But this doesn't happen automatically. Only if we **look to the Lord** will our faith grow stronger. And that requires a conscious and sustained effort of the will. It means denying your senses, your feelings and your reason. But if we look at our problem, it gets bigger and bigger until it finally overwhelms us. We can't see anything except how hopeless everything is. So we have to be ruthless with ourselves and give not only our problem, but our very selves, over to the Lord for **His** answer.

God was testing the Israelites. Now testing implies trying out the quality and strength of something and God was wanting to discover what was in the hearts of the people. At least, **He** knew very well what was in their thoughts, but **they** didn't know themselves. Very often, difficulties draw out what is hidden inside us, the bad as well as the good, just as refining of gold and silver requires it to be heated until all the impurities rise to the surface and can be scooped off. With the Israelites, after years of slavery, when they had little freedom of choice, no rights, and were totally dependent on the Egyptians, they had to learn that they must look somewhere else for all their needs to be met. (There is, after all, a certain security in bondage. This is why some people ultimately prefer their sicknesses to the responsibility of health). God wanted to teach them to rely wholly on Him. Now that they were no longer forced to serve a ruler and work for hard taskmasters, He longed for them to choose to obey Him out of love. Even at this stage, God was seeking an intimate relationship with His people rather than a rule of law. Already He was demonstrating that He wanted to be a **father** to them. This purpose is seen clearly in Deuteronomy 8 as they finally near the promised land:

> Remember how the Lord your God led you all the way in the desert these forty years, to humble you and to test you in order to know what was in your heart, whether or not you would keep his commands. He humbled you, causing you to know hunger and then feeding you with manna, which neither you nor your fathers had known, to teach you that man does

not live on bread alone but on every word that comes from the mouth of the Lord. Your clothes did not wear out and your feet did not swell these forty years. Know then in your heart that as a man disciplines his son, so the Lord your God disciplines you.

(Deuteronomy 8, verses 2-5)

God knew that they would be full of enthusiasm for serving Him so long as He was rolling back the waves of the Red Sea and drowning their enemies, but would they trust Him and love Him when things weren't going so well, when God's help seemed to be absent? Would they demonstrate covenant faith or human faithlessness? And would a 'proud and stiff-necked people' allow God both to reign over them and provide for them (for it can sometimes be as hard to be served as to submit)? Or would they want to go their own way now they were free from domination?

Unfortunately, the Israelites had short memories. Unlike God who constantly 'remembered' His covenant with that faculty of covenant faithfulness and commitment, they turned their back on Him at the first hurdle. They began to mutter and complain as moment by moment they felt their tongues swelling. Then as they looked around and saw nothing for miles but rock, sand and more sand, they really began to panic. You can just imagine it:

'We're all going to die in this God-forsaken wilderness. What was the point of escaping from Egypt just to rot here in this desert? We must have been mad to trust Moses. We always thought he was a bit stupid and now he's proved it...'

Poor old Moses. If the people of Israel thought they had a problem, his was about two million times the size. After all, he was responsible for the whole tribe. They had followed his leading, and in this time of crisis, he had to find the faith to hold on to God's promise, and bring His divine provision to the people. Moses had a choice. He could either stare at the undrinkable water and feel hope ebbing away like the tide, or he could look to the One who gives living water, the Lord God. Glancing at the people wailing around the pool, Moses knew that soon he was going to have a riot on his hands. So what did he do? He lifted up his head and **cried out to the Lord.** He didn't waste time trying to dig holes to find water. He just threw himself upon His covenant Lord and gave God the problem of saving them all from dying of thirst. For God's covenant promise was that when they were in trouble, He would deliver them. **How** He would do it was God's responsibility; Moses' trust was in Him and His faithfulness, not in the answer. And because he let go of his problem, God was able to release that answer to Moses, just as a drowning man can only be saved when he stops clutching and grabbing, and trusts in his rescuer.

> Then Moses cried out to the Lord. …And the Lord
> showed him a tree.
>
> (Exodus 15, verse 25)

What sort of an answer was that? A fork of lightning flashing into the pool would have been a bit more convincing, and certainly more impressive. But quite often the Lord's provision doesn't look like a very good idea at all from our point of view. Sometimes it seems far too simple; or else God asks us to do something which seems quite unrelated to our immediate problem - look at the story of the blind man Jesus told to go and wash in the Pool of Siloam. But God is sometimes testing us to see whether we will be obedient, and we will only obey if our heart is full of love and trust. Moses could have felt he was going to lose all remaining credibility in the eyes of the Israelites. And God wanted to see what mattered most to him - the praise of the people, their good opinion, or favour with God by doing His will. Where were his eyes - on the people or on the Lord? Fortunately for them all, Moses didn't waver. He had asked God for help and he believed that the tree was His provision so he threw it right into the heart of the problem. Picking up the piece of wood, he hurled it into the water:

And the water became sweet.

So often, we have to take the first step and God confirms. In the New Testament we read that God confirmed His word with signs and wonders, so the disciples evidently had to preach and act on their faith first and then God did the rest. There are many instances where people had to actually rise up and walk first before they knew they were healed, and then often would come the verbal confirmation that their faith had made them whole. So here, Moses acted in faith, received the miracle and then God confirmed it again with a promise. For there at the pool of Marah, God covenanted to be their Healer. He had proved to them He could to it, and now **He committed Himself to being their health.** He revealed to them the wonderful fact that His very nature generates the gift of healing and strength. For He tells them of yet another name by which He may now be known: Jehovah Rapha - the Lord your healer.

> There the Lord made a decree and a law for them, and there He tested them. He said, 'If you listen carefully to the voice of the Lord and do what is right in his eyes, if you pay attention to his commands and keep all his decrees, I will not bring on you any of the diseases I brought on the Egyptians for **I am the Lord who heals you.'**
>
> (Exodus 15, verses 25-26)

Notice, though, that the Lord's promise of healing here was conditional. He didn't say, 'I love you so much that whenever you get sick, I will heal you immediately'. Of course, this was God's provision under the law, before the grace of the New Covenant had come, but, still, it shows God's desire for **wholeness**, for spiritual and moral health, rather than physical well-being alone. In fact, some people do discover that being well in itself is of little good if they are without peace, without joy and without hope in the world. But, sadly, others are so disillusioned with life that they don't really expect peace, joy and hope anyway, so they are quite happy to settle for physical health alone on the basis that it is better to be miserable and **healthy** than miserable and **sick**!

We see then that the basic principle God lays down here is that their healing is conditional upon their obedience to His laws and His ways, that health is the reward of righteousness, and throughout the Old Testament we see God blesses those who keep His commands. It does not always follow, though, that those who sin automatically get sick, and it is a question often raised in the Old Testament - why do the righteous sometimes suffer while the wicked prosper? Psalm 73 puts this into God's eternal perspective, and concludes that, ultimately, the wicked do perish, and even in this life their comfort is often short-lived. But still, our own experience tells us that on many occasions we find God healing non-Christians who may or may not subsequently turn to Him, or sometimes even healing people who are living blatantly immoral or disobedient lives, who even while reaching out to God on a strand of faith, do not necessarily have any intention of changing their ways, and who, even in the light of God's manifest power and love, may subsequently refuse to turn and thank Him. Such is God's mercy. As we have seen, the very **essence** of God's character is to heal and restore, and these gifts **overflow** from Him. With the redeeming sacrifice of Jesus and the establishment of the New Covenant, such a river of divine love and grace flooded over mankind that some people get healed simply by 'being in the way', with their tiny portion of faith. And repeatedly through the history of the Israelites in the wilderness we find God having mercy on them and healing them despite their continued doubt and disobedience. Usually, though there **was** faith somewhere which God honoured on behalf of the rest of the nation, or there was a measure of repentance:

> *Further on in the desert, the people of Israel thought they would die of hunger and railed at God for abandoning them - He replied by sending manna and quails to sustain them.
>
> (Exodus 16)

> *Their rebellion against God grew so great that He sent a plague to destroy them - but the faith of Moses and Aaron stopped His anger and brought the plague to an end.
>
> (Numbers 16)

> *Miriam was smitten with leprosy for speaking against Moses - but God healed her when Moses pleaded on her behalf.
>
> (Numbers 12)

> *Despite the lessons of Marah, the Israelites thought they would once more die of thirst in the wilderness

of Zin (Numbers 20), and raised another cry of self-pity and reproach - and God provided for them when Moses struck the rock with his rod and released the water of Meribah.

*They complained again about how much better off they would have been in Egypt and so God sent a plague of fiery red serpents among them - but when they repented, God told Moses to set a bronze snake on a pole and anyone who looked at it would be healed.

(Numbers 21)

Never in the history of mankind has there been a record of such consistent faithlessness on one side and such overwhelming love on the other. In these examples, we see how the full grace of the New Covenant, reflected in the awesome sacrifice of God's only Son, is foreshadowed in the Old. Blessing and restoration, then, are promised to all who keep God's laws:

If you pay attention to these laws and are careful to follow them, then the Lord your God will keep his covenant of love with you and bless you and increase your numbers. He will bless the fruit of your womb, the crops of your land - your grain, new wine and oil - the calves of your herds and the lambs of your flocks in the land that he swore to your forefathers to give you. You will be blessed more than any other people, none of your men or women will be childless nor any of your livestock without young. **The Lord will keep you free from every disease. He will not inflict on you the horrible diseases you knew in Egypt**, but he will inflict them on all who hate you.

(Deuteronomy 7, verses 12-15)

Wonderful promises to the Israelites! So how much more can we expect who live under the New Covenant? God never contradicts Himself and His eternal purpose is always the same. But what has changed is that the New Covenant has made it possible for our **hearts** to be changed, for the righteousness of God, which is Jesus, to dwell inside us so that we live lives pleasing to God, for 'We have been made holy through the sacrifice of the body of Jesus Christ once for all' (Hebrews 10, verse 10).

This amazing new relationship with God, based not on law but on love, is prophesied by Jeremiah:

> 'The time is coming', declares the Lord, 'when I will make a new covenant with the house of Israel and with the house of Judah. It will not be like the covenant I made with their forefathers when I took them by the hand out of Egypt because they broke my covenant, though I was husband to them,' declares the Lord. 'This is the covenant that I will make with the house of Israel after that time,' declares the Lord. **'I will put my law in their minds and write it on their hearts. I will be their God and they will be my people.** No longer will a man teach his neighbour or a man his brother, saying, "Know the Lord," because they will all know me, from the least to the greatest,' declares the Lord. 'For I will forgive their wickedness and remember their sins no more.'
>
> (Jeremiah 31, verses 31-34)

These, then are the terms of the New Covenant:

1. God's laws will be in our hearts.
2. We will be a 'peculiar' people, a people set apart for God.
3. We will know God personally.
4. Our sins will be forgiven and forgotten.

In the light of what we now understand about covenant, let us look briefly at the way in which this New Covenant was made.

First, a covenant representative was required. As with Abraham, no ordinary man could make a covenant with God because he had nothing to offer an almighty, perfect God. What was needed was someone at once completely human yet also completely sinless.

And since no-one could be without sin except God Himself, the representative had to partake of the divine nature. As the Son of God, Jesus fulfilled all the requirements of the covenant. Sometimes we are so intent on proving Christ's deity that we forget He is also a man. We have only to see the importance laid on Christ's genealogy in the Gospels, to realise that the disciples saw Him as truly one of them, not a visitor from outer space. He was born of Mary and took on our humanity; He wasn't suddenly found under a gooseberry bush. Made of flesh and blood, He was tempted to sin just as we are because He didn't know He couldn't sin. He was One Person worth the entire human race.

Ever since the night of that dramatic escape from the Egyptians, the Passover was celebrated every year by the Israelites. It became the cornerstone of their faith, a solemn commemoration of God's covenant faithfulness, and a statement of their belief that one day the Great Deliverer Himself would come and crush the oppressor called the Serpent. Gradually lambs were bred specifically for the Passover, and at the feast itself, three bags of unleavened bread would be placed on the table to represent Abraham, Isaac and Jacob. The host would then take out the middle wafer, signifying Isaac, the son of promise, and break it before passing it around for everyone present at the meal to eat. Wine was added to the meal but one cup was never drunk. This was the cup for the Messiah, and symbolised their faith that in the fullness of time God would send the Anointed One.

And one year, on the tenth of the month, the very day the Passover lambs were brought into Jerusalem to be examined by the Levites in the courtyard of the temple, Christ entered Jerusalem and was soon being questioned by the Sadducees and Pharisees in the same courtyard. Then came the Passover meal, and the Lamb of God Himself officiated at the last Passover of the Old Covenant which became through His words, in His hands, the covenant meal of a wonderful new contract of grace. Jesus took out the middle wafer of bread and with growing wonder the disciples would have seen that here was indeed **the** Son of promise. When He broke it and said: 'This is my body,' what could He mean but that in some way His body would be broken on their behalf for their benefit? And then He took the cup, the Cup reserved for the Messiah, and for a moment their hearts filled with joy. But it turned to grief as they heard Him say,

> '**This is my blood of the new covenant** which is poured out for many for the forgiveness of sins. I tell you, I will not drink of this fruit of the vine from now on until that day when I drink it anew with you in my Father's kingdom.'

No-one had spoken those words since the time of Jeremiah. There was no mistaking it for these men whose whole culture revolved around the idea of blood covenant. Jesus was going to be not only the covenant representative but also the sacrifice on behalf of mankind in an incredible new covenant which would provide forgiveness of sins once and for all. By the shedding of His blood, which bore both the human and divine elements in His nature, the life of man and God would be joined together in an eternal covenant of love. For Jesus was both the covenant sacrifice and the burnt offering, the lamb sacrificed as an atonement for sin, and as the spotless Lamb of God He was to pay forever the debt of sin.

It may be that to talk in these spiritual terms draws a veil over the full horror and nightmare of what Jesus was doing. But if we look at Gethsemane, we begin to realise the extent of the price that was paid on our behalf. It is in Gethsemane that the real sacrifice took place, in Gethsemane that the redeeming blood began to be shed, for that was where Jesus really yielded Himself to God's will. And that caused Him such agony that it almost killed Him. As He faced the despair of alienation from God, blood burst from His forehead and God had to send an angel to sustain Him in case He never made it to Calvary. What can have caused Him such desperate agony? Was Jesus afraid to die? No, it wasn't simply the thought of crucifixion which made Him sweat great drops of blood. Jesus knew He was the Passover Lamb, and what He could see before Him was the dreadful fire of God's judgement which He was to suffer on behalf of sinful man. Lambs had to be roasted, after all. 'Could there by **any** other way?' He cried out in torment. But no, such was God's love for mankind that He was prepared to sacrifice His only Son so that the law of sin and death might be fulfilled and then abolished. So Jesus' cry on the Cross, 'It is finished,' was a cry of triumph not despair. He had fulfilled all the terms of the covenant. All that He was and all that He had He offered up to God on the cross, and, in return, God made available to us, who are heirs of this covenant, all the righteousness and peace and health of Christ Himself. As we partake of the Lamb through repentance and faith, we receive a new nature; we become a new person in Christ; when God looks at us He sees not our sin, but the righteousness of Jesus who dwells inside us. And when we participate in the Lord's supper, we celebrate the fact that our sins and iniquities are remembered no more, and we proclaim to devils, angels and man that we are now a **covenant people.** We have within us the treasure of God, Jesus Christ, and on the basis of His righteousness we are able to receive the riches of His life. Remember Jeremiah 31. It is God who makes the promises. We have nothing to give Him. All we can do is rest and say thank you, keeping His commands by the power of His Spirit of love within us.

Chapter Five

Origins of Sickness

We have begun to see some of the blessings available to us under the New Covenant. Included among them is not only forgiveness but physical health. Sickness was never part of God's plan, any more than sin, and neither of them have any place in His eternal Kingdom. Sin and sickness originate from the devil. The Bible describes him as a thief, and his whole aim is to rob us of our inheritance, to steal our health and peace and joy. He has usurped the throne of this world and seeks to spread his kingdom of darkness over the lives of men, filling their hearts with evil so that sin, sickness, war and want are generated and regenerated in a demonic cycle empowered from the pit of hell.

> But thanks be to God who gives us the victory through our Lord Jesus Christ!
>
> (1 Corinthians 15, verse 57)

Jesus' death and resurrection makes it possible for us to recover the order and wholeness which God established at the Creation. As we read in 1 John 3, verse 5,

> The reason the Son of God appeared was to destroy the devil's work.

And Jesus spent most of His time destroying sickness, infirmity, demonic-inspired problems and death.

According to Paul, death is the last enemy to be destroyed (1 Corinthians 15, verse 26) and it is good just to remember for a moment that death is an enemy, not a friend. Yes, death no longer has a sting because we go to be with the Lord, but God never intended us to die. He made us to live forever, dwelling in free fellowship with God, eating from the tree of life (Genesis 2, verses 9 and 17), but through man's disobedience, death entered the world, the enemy which could cut man off from God eternally. Nevertheless God still declares His will for man:

> With long life will I satisfy him, and show him my salvation.
>
> (Psalm 91, verse 16)

And He plainly makes it possible for us to enjoy many more years than we usually expect, giving us a foretaste of the time when death will be conquered forever. As Moses told the people of Israel:

> These are the commands, decrees and laws the Lord your God directed me to teach you to observe in the land that you are crossing the Jordan to possess, so that you, your children and their children after them may fear the Lord your God as long as you live by keeping all his decrees and commands that I give you, and so that you may enjoy long life.
>
> (Deuteronomy 6, verses 1-2)

Three score years and ten was a curse not a blessing if you read the context in Psalm 90, verse 10.

So long life is what we should be expecting. I do believe that death is something we can put off as long as we have knowledge to put it off. By that I mean that by keeping God's commands and living by faith in Him we can go on to be 'full of years' until we receive from God the message that it is time to come home. Then it should be a question of yielding up our spirit, just as Jesus did. He wasn't killed, He knew His work was accomplished and He voluntarily went to His Father. I would like to be like Moses:

> Moses was a hundred and twenty years old when he died, yet his eyes were not weak nor his strength gone.
>
> (Deuteronomy 34, verse 7)

I know several beautiful Christians who seek to love and serve God in the spirit with all their heart and soul. They pray, they study God's Word daily, and at ninety years old they don't wear glasses, they don't need a stick, they have hair on their heads and they are planning to go on like that until they fall asleep in their beds, yielding up their breath to go home to their Lord. That's what I'm aiming for anyway, but if I die next year prematurely, don't think I was deceived, because God's Word convinces me that this is what He desires for His people. Having said that, God doesn't generally get His will more than 25% of the time! If we look at the parable of the Sower we see that only one of the four types of soil allows God's Word to bring forth fruit. So let's look at a few of the blockages:

> Hear the Word of the Lord, you Israelites, because the Lord has a charge to bring against you who live in the land:
> 'There is no faithfulness, no love, no acknowledgement of God in the land. There is only cursing, lying and murder, stealing and adultery; they break all bounds and bloodshed follows bloodshed. Because of this the land mourns, and all who live in it waste away; the beasts of the field and the birds of the air and the fish of the sea are dying...my people are destroyed from lack of knowledge.'
>
> (Hosea 4, verses 1-3 and 6)

What a picture of disunity and despair. Social order has given way to anarchy and war, bonds of kinship and friendship have disintegrated, people are literally wasting away with sickness, and even the natural world is gripped by suffering and decay. What is the cause? 'There is no faithfulness, no love, no acknowledgement of God in the land... my people are destroyed from lack of knowledge.' What sort of knowledge is meant here? Surely not intellectual wisdom, a rational understanding of facts or ideas. It was a spiritual knowledge which the Israelites were lacking, an acknowledgement of God, of His laws and of His provisions. A lack of knowledge of these things could stem from one of two causes:

1. Sin
2. Ignorance and misunderstanding

With the Israelites it was plainly the former.

In the past God had made clear to them how they could enjoy peace, health and prosperity - the choice was theirs, of life or death, and they had chosen death.

> See, I set before you today life and prosperity, death and destruction. For I command you today to love the Lord your God, to walk in his ways and to keep his commandments, decrees and laws; then you will live and increase, and the Lord your God will bless you in the land you are entering to possess.
>
> But if your heart turns away and you are not obedient, and if you are drawn away to bow down to other gods and worship them, I declare to you this day that you will certainly be destroyed. You will not live long in this land you are crossing the Jordan to enter and possess.
>
> This day I call heaven and earth as witnesses against you that I have set before you life and death, blessings and curses. Now choose life so that you and your children may live, and so that you may love the Lord your God, listen to his voice and hold fast to him. For the Lord is your life, and he will give you many years in the land he swore to give to your fathers, Abraham, Isaac and Jacob.
>
> (Deuteronomy 30, verses 15-20)

Now the people of Israel obviously knew **about** God. With religious laws woven into the very fabric of their daily lives, almost every act, on one level, was an acknowledgement of God. But did they know God personally? Did they worship Him in their hearts? Plainly the Israelites in the time of Hosea had rejected all God's moral and spiritual commandments, and had given themselves up to selfishness and greed. By turning away from God, they had cut themselves off from the source of all hope and blessing, thereby choosing death instead of life. Without life and light, they quickly degenerated into darkness and despair.

The plight of the Israelites was an extreme one, brought about by wanton disobedience and pride. Their lack of knowledge of God and His laws was a matter of choice, a deliberate disregard of their conscience. In these circumstances, sin brought about its own reward, sickness being not so much the fire of God's wrath but the tool of His discipline. There is a sense in which mercy is shown in fact, for God doesn't utterly destroy them but seeks, through the decay which they have brought upon themselves, to turn their hearts back to Him. God was not the creator of their suffering but since through disobedience they surrendered themselves to the forces of evil, He allowed it and utilised it to bring about their repentance.

There are several instances in the Old Testament of sin reaping sickness in this way. David evidently knew this connection between sin and sickness. There was no doubt in his mind as to the source of his own pain and illness which he records in Psalm 38:

> Because of your wrath there is no health in my body; my bones have no soundness because of my sin. My guilt has overwhelmed me like a burden too heavy to bear.
>
> My wounds fester and are loathsome because of my sinful folly. I am bowed down and brought very low, all day long I go about mourning. My back is filled with searing pain; there is no health in my body. I am feeble and utterly crushed; I groan in anguish of heart.
>
> (verses 3-8)

Again in Psalm 41, he cries:

> Oh Lord have mercy upon me; heal me, for I have sinned against you.
>
> (verse 4)

We also read in Numbers Chapter 12:

> Miriam and Aaron began to speak against Moses

because of his Cushite wife, for he had married a
Cushite. 'Has the Lord spoken only through you
Moses?' they asked. 'Hasn't he also spoken through
us?' And the Lord heard this.

Straightaway God summoned the three of them out to the Tent of
Meeting where He appeared in a pillar of cloud. He charged Aaron and
Miriam with speaking against His anointed servant, Moses, and His
anger 'burned against them'. When the cloud of His presence lifted,
Miriam had been stricken with leprosy. No disease was so associated
with shame and dishonour, not to mention fear, for it meant not only
pain, disfigurement and ultimately death, but social ostracization as
well. This sounds harsh, but the severity of her affliction only matched
the seriousness of her offence, for she had criticised the Lord's own
servant, thereby rebelling against God's order and authority. Not only
that, but pride and greed had made Aaron and Miriam jealous of
Moses' leadership and they were seeking to assert themselves as
vessels for God's Word.

In total contrast to this self-regard, we read that 'Moses was a very
humble man, more humble than anyone else on the face of the earth'
(Numbers 12, verse 3). And it showed amazing humility and grace to
cry out to the Lord to heal someone who had criticised and slandered
him. No wonder that the Lord had mercy and restored Miriam after
Moses' prayer, though her sin alienated her from her friends and family
for a while (she was confined outside the camp for seven days, in
accordance with the laws for cleansing) and the scene had its
repercussions on the whole community, for the people were not able to
move on until she had been brought back. This, then, suggests a further
aspect of sin-related sickness: it can cause both individuals and those
connected with them - family, friends, church, community - to be
blocked in their walk with the Lord.

In fact, God had already stated that sin could have such far-reaching
effects. In His Ten Commandments, He had declared that they
shouldn't bow down to any other gods, for,

'I the Lord your God am a jealous God punishing the
sins of the fathers to the third and fourth generation
of those who hate me, but showing love to thousands

who love me and keep my commandments.'
(Deuteronomy 5, verse 9)

Not only could sin have an effect on the immediate community, then, but the repercussions could be felt years later in subsequent generations. We read in Lamentations 5, verse 7:

Our fathers sinned and are no more, and we bear
their iniquities.

Like ripples from a stone cast into a pool, so the effects of sin travel ever outwards. This seems to be true even when the sin is unintentional, illustrating again how the breaking of certain divine laws brings its own consequences which God allows to get the attention of the individual so that His perfect order might be re-established. Look at the story of Abimelech. Poor Abimelech. There was nothing wrong with him. He couldn't believe his eyes when Abraham arrived on the scene with a really attractive woman called Sarah, who he said was his sister. He had no idea that Abraham had told his wife to play up to this half-lie because he was terrified of getting killed by someone who wanted to make off with her. Yet despite his ignorance and, in fact, perfectly honourable behaviour, he and all his family and household became unable to conceive a child. Fortunately Abimelech was a God-fearing man and he remembered to ask God what the trouble was. When he realised the situation he made restitution by returning Sarah to Abraham and giving handsome gifts to them:

Then Abraham prayed to God and God healed
Abimelech, his wife and his slave girls so they could
have children again...

(Genesis 20, verse 17)

It is important to remember that it is not that God is vindictive or is angrily punishing wrong-doing as a judge might sentence an offender. As we have already been seeing, sin puts the individual outside the protection of God, exposing him to the threat of 'the fowler's snare and... the deadly pestilence... that stalks in the darkness and the plague that destroys at midday'. We find here the beginning of an awareness of the forces of darkness always threatening the covenant world. As yet not fully personalised, Satan's destructive influences were recognised as being ever present to afflict those who stepped outside God's will and protection.

This may seem a very simplistic, even harsh picture, but the situation described in these examples is borne out by medical and psychological fact. The Israelites did not have the scientific knowledge to understand the very real connection between sin and sickness. Doctors and psychiatrists have established the relation between emotions such as guilt, anger and grief and certain forms of illness; the whole subject of psychosomatic illness centres around the interplay between the emotional and physical realms; stress is well known to be a contributory factor in medical problems such as high blood pressure and heart disease; abuse of the body from over-eating, smoking, lack of exercise, and over-work, for example, can directly produce physical disorders; with babies being born with VD, addicted to heroin, and now with AIDS, there has never been more certainty that immoral lifestyles, particularly those which are sexually immoral, may well result in serious illness; and within the Church, there is a growing awareness of the possible physical effects of involvement in the undisputed works of darkness, such as witchcraft, spiritism and other forms of the occult. We are reaping what we have sown:

> Your wound is incurable, your injury beyond healing. There is no-one to plead your cause, no remedy for your sore, no healing for you... because your guilt is so great and your sins so many.
>
> (Jeremiah 30, verses 12-14)

Fortunately, there is hope - in the mercy of the Lord if not in anything else:

> 'But I will restore you to health and heal your wounds,' declares the Lord.
>
> (verse 17)

And God says:

> 'Repent! Turn away from all your offences; then sin
> will not be your downfall. Rid yourselves of all the
> offences you have committed, and get a new heart
> and a new spirit. Why will you die, O house of
> Israel? For I take no pleasure in the death of anyone,'
> declares the Sovereign Lord. 'Repent and live!'
>
> (Ezekiel 18, verses 30-32)

What is more, for those of us under the New Covenant:

> In those days people will no longer say 'The fathers
> have eaten sour grapes and the children's teeth are set
> on edge'. Instead everyone will die for his own sin.
>
> (Jeremiah 31, verses 29-30)

True repentance brings healing. But ignorance of this promise of restoration, and a misunderstanding of God's Word, can prevent us from coming back into a relationship with God and enjoying His blessings once more. We can repent and yet not realise we are forgiven and restored to God's full favour. This is a more subtle problem which can afflict us even when we are really trying to do God's will and it takes two forms.

The first is that we do not read His Word enough, so we are simply unaware of the marvellous provision God makes for our restoration and welfare. There is a wonderful scene in the book *The Last Battle* by C.S. Lewis in which a group of dwarfs have been so blinded by the monkey god they have been serving, that when released from their stable prison and set before a sumptuous banquet of food they think they are still locked up in the darkness and eating straw and dung. Similarly, even when we have not been consciously disobedient to God, we are conditioned to look at our circumstances through the eyes of the world and to expect only what is humanly and rationally possible. We are like birds still sitting in our cage when the door is left open, so accustomed to imprisonment that we no longer recognise freedom. The devil is hardly going to be the one to point out that we are no longer locked in. Still we live as slaves, still under the bondage of sin and the devil, instead of reigning victoriously as legal heirs to all Christ possessed.

Second, it may be that we have heard these truths with our ears but have not opened our hearts (and spirits) to receive them. We give mental assent to the words that we read in the Bible, but somehow don't really grasp the possibilities of making those promises a reality in our own lives. We have a theoretical faith, not an experiential one. The words of God have not become spirit and life to us, transforming our minds so that we see how we really can live in a realm that goes beyond the limitations of our human understanding.

Living in the world, according to the world's standards and expectations, means, of course, living under a curse - a double curse really, sentenced to toil and pain and mortality, cut off from God as Adam and Eve were when they were cast out of the Garden of Eden, and also doomed to failure in keeping every part of God's law:

> Cursed be every one who does not continue to do
> everything written in the Book of the Law.
>
> (Galatians 3, verse 10)

And the effect of breaking God's law was far-reaching and catastrophic:

> The Lord will send on you curses, confusion and
> rebuke in everything you put your hand to.
>
> (Deuteronomy 28, verse 20)

It is possible to be born again and filled with the Holy Spirit, yet still not experience joy and victory over trials and temptations. This will certainly be the case if we are ignorant of what God's Word says and means:

> Christ redeemed us from the curse of the law by
> becoming a curse for us...
>
> (Galatians 3, verse 13)

Many Christians interpret this verse only in its primary sense of forgiveness of sin through the substitute death of Christ on the cross. But in the light of the comprehensiveness of what we have seen is given in the New Covenant, new possibilities for victory and fulfilment open up at every turn. For Calvary releases to us all the promises given to Abraham:

> He redeemed us in order that the blessing given to Abraham might come to the Gentiles through Christ Jesus, so that by faith we might receive the promise of the Spirit.
>
> (Galatians 3, verse 14)

And what does the Spirit do? He puts within us the spirit of sonship that enables us to cry 'Abba, Father'. So redemption involves so much more than merely being saved from something. **It is what we are saved into which is the exciting thing.** The blessing given to Abraham was to be drawn into a covenant with Almighty God; it was a promise of health, prosperity, peace and protection - and a Saviour who would extend His covenant to the whole world. Not only do we inherit all these blessings, but the curses are now reversed and become promises for us. So now when we read the curses in Deuteronomy 28, we can start to praise the Lord that we are not subject to them any more. I heard a story about a man sentenced to jail for theft. As he was taken into the prison he saw some words inscribed over the gates,

THOU SHALT NOT STEAL.

He hung his head and felt those very words justly condemning him for his offence. During his time in prison he had a wonderful experience of God and repented of all his wrong-doing. When he eventually left prison, he looked back over his shoulder and saw those same words. But this time, instead of a condemnation, he read them as a promise:

THOU SHALT NOT STEAL.

The very curse he had received for breaking the law had now become a blessing, that he would never steal again. He was now a new creation, with a new heart, and he would no longer give in to the old desires and temptations.

This puts a whole new perspective on life. Instead of being dominated by fear and anxiety, we can now live in security and peace, trusting in the faithfulness of our Covenant God to keep and bless us:

> You will be blessed in the city.

I know so many people in the city who live in terror of a bomb exploding in front of them, of being burgled, or ruining their health through pollution or stress. But God can turn these circumstances into a place of joy and rest.

> You will be blessed in the country.

Rural life doesn't have to mean isolation, power cuts and snowdrifts.

> The fruit of your womb will be blessed, and the
> crops of your land and the young of your livestock -
> the calves of your herds and the lambs of your
> flocks.

Are children a blessing? I know many families where, sadly, the parents would call them a curse. But if we know that Christ has redeemed us from the curse, then we don't have to wait for our little baby angels to become 'terrible twos' and our teenagers to take to drink, drugs, sex and the Loony Left. We can expect our homes to be places of joy and love, and our work and business to flourish.

> Your basket and your kneading trough will be
> blessed.

When we first started to live by faith my wife would give away our last packet of tea and trust that God would replenish it. He usually did - with two packets! By giving, we really proved that He was our provider. I remember her telling me one day how she went strawberry picking with the words 'Your basket will be blessed' running through her mind. As she went down the rows, she came across a huge basket of strawberries upturned and left, its precious load spilling on the ground. A shame for the other person, but God's wonderful provision for Rosemary! Gone are the days of dreading the next bill, of wondering where we will find the money to buy the food and to clothe

the children, of constant financial anxiety and strain. Instead,

> The Lord will grant you abundant prosperity.

Suddenly we realise we are plugged into God's limitless resources. He will supply all our needs according to His glorious riches in Christ Jesus, and that's different from having a fat purse in our hand - it's having a hand in God's fat purse!

> You will be blessed when you come in and blessed
> when you go out.

If we are living under the curse, when we go to work, we expect to be dominated, crushed, humiliated, unfairly treated; at meetings we're looking for problems and spiritual attack; in business, we live in fear of failure; when we travel we are terrified of an accident; when we get home we wonder if we will have been burgled. Redeemed from the curse we can feel completely secure, for

> The Lord will keep you from harm - he will watch
> over your life; the Lord will watch over your coming
> and going both now and evermore.
>
> (Psalm 121, verses 7-8)

In verse 22 of Deuteronomy chapter 28, we read that another effect of the curse of breaking God's law is being afflicted with wasting disease, fever and inflammation. How many people suffer from stress-related diseases these days? But under God's blessing,

> The Lord will keep you free from every disease. He
> will not inflict on you the horrible diseases you knew
> in Egypt, but he will inflict them on all who hate
> you.
>
> (Deuteronomy 7, verse 15)

Disobedience and sin can mean that 'the heavens above your head shall be like brass' (verse 23). Have you ever had that experience - of your prayers just bouncing back off the ceiling? I've got a way round that now - I say, 'Devil, it's no good you lying to me and saying I can't get through and there's a block between me and God, because that's only true under the curse, and, frankly, I'm under the blessing.'

When Jesus went from earth to heaven, He carved a great hole right through the principalities and powers of darkness so that there is always a way through to God for me. After praying that truth for about five minutes, I can start to feel the presence of God once more, because the devil just can't deceive me any longer.

> You will know the truth and the truth will set you free.
>
> (John 8, verse 32)

Verse 25 says that you will be defeated before your enemies. Many Christians have got such a distorted view of what persecution and turning the other cheek means that they anticipate being abused, badly treated, badly served in even the most mundane areas of life. They allow themselves to be baffled by townhall bureaucracy and walked over in issues at work or in the community. It's the doormat mentality. But when we see that Christ, 'having disarmed the powers and authorities, made a public spectacle of them, triumphing over them by the Cross' (Colossians 2, verse 15) we realise that our true position is to be seated with Christ in heavenly places and our whole attitude changes. We can get up in the morning, look in the mirror and say:

'**You** are more than a conqueror.'

'Who me?'

'Yes, you.'

'A conqueror?'

'Well not exactly - **more** than a conqueror!'

And after five minutes of that sort of conversation, you've grown about two inches and are ready to take on anyone.

And so it goes on. If we have been living a righteous life and yet recognise our situation in many of those curses, we can rebuke Satan for deceiving us into thinking that we have to be dominated by these things, and then step into the blessings. Once we were part of the kingdom of darkness, blind and without hope, but now we are

GOD'S OWN PEOPLE

(1 Peter 2, verse 9)

For he has called us out of darkness into His wonderful light. We are part of the kingdom of His dear Son, in this world but not of it. So we don't have to get the 'flu just because everybody else has it. It's marvellous. A new way of living opens up.

We find another reason why people get sick in Paul's first letter to the Corinthians:

> The Lord Jesus Christ on the night he was betrayed took bread and when he had given thanks he broke it and said, 'This is my body which is for you, do this in remembrance of me.' In the same way after supper he took the cup saying, 'This cup is the New Covenant in my blood; do this whenever you drink it in remembrance of me. For whenever you eat this bread and drink this cup, you proclaim the Lord's death until he comes.'
>
> Therefore whoever eats the bread or drinks the cup of the Lord in an unworthy manner will be guilty of sinning against the body and blood of the Lord. A man ought to examine himself before he eats of the bread and drinks of the cup. **For anyone who eats and drinks without recognising the body of the Lord eats and drinks judgement on himself. That is why many among you are weak and sick, and a number of you have fallen asleep.** But if we judged ourselves, we would not come under judgement. When we are judged by the Lord, we are being disciplined so that we will not be condemned with the world.

> (1 Corinthians 11, verses 23-32)

How do we 'recognise the body of the Lord'? The context here reveals at least two meanings. The first involves our understanding of the New Covenant, which we have already discussed. God's life flowed out to mankind in Gethsemane and on the Cross; all that God was and has was given to us through the blood of Jesus, winning for us forever the right to physical health as well as free fellowship with the Father through the forgiveness of sins. If we eat the bread and drink the cup of the Lord's supper with this understanding, we proclaim the Lord's death - in other words we make a declaration of faith to ourselves, the world, to the angels, to the powers of darkness and to the Lord God Himself, that Jesus' death makes available to us all the fullness and glory of His resurrection life. We need to be aware that when Jesus said, 'Do this in remembrance of me,' He was using that covenant word, and urging us to hold always in the forefront of our minds the terms of the covenant which entitles us to every blessing of His kingdom. So communion should be much more than a memorial service; it should be a means of re-affirming and receiving afresh the fullness of life given to us through the New Covenant.

If we fail to discern the Lord's body in this way, it does not mean that we get sick and weak as a curse or punishment. Rather, we need to realise that there is a law of suffering and death at work in the world generated by the devil, and fuelled by our own sin or ignorance, to which we will be subject unless we positively draw on the life which is the blood. So, as we have seen, unless we have a revelation of our entitlement as heirs of Christ in the New Covenant, we will find ourselves subject through deception to the curses which fall on the world.

We discover the second meaning of discerning the Lord's body in Paul's earlier words about disunity and insensitivity among the believers:

> In the following directives I have no praise for you, for your meetings do more harm than good. In the first place, I hear that when you come together as a church, there are divisions among you and to some extent I believe it ... When you come together, it is not the Lord's supper which you eat, for as you eat, each one goes ahead without waiting for anybody else. One remains hungry, another gets drunk. Don't you have homes to eat and drink in? Or do you despise the church of God and humiliate those who have nothing?
>
> (1 Corinthians 11, verses 17-22)

It's a sad fact that even within the Body of Christ there is gossip, criticism and suspicion. The Church is fragmented into denominations which vie with one another for a monopoly of the truth. And I don't just mean between the traditional denominations. Even amongst churches who claim to be moving in a new awareness of the power of the Holy Spirit, there is disunity and in some instances rifts verging on outright war. The various strands of non-denominational churches and fellowships have been deeply divided in many places reflecting a terrible disregard for one of the wonderful benefits of Christ's death:

> But now in Christ Jesus, you who once were far away have been brought near through the blood of Christ. For he himself is our peace, who has made the two one and has destroyed the barrier, the dividing wall of hostility, by abolishing in his flesh the law with its commandments and regulations. His purpose was to create in himself one new man out of two, thus making peace, and in this one body to reconcile both of them to God through the cross, by which he put to death their hostility.
>
> (Ephesians 2, verses 13-16)

So there is an even more serious dimension to the sin of not discerning the Lord's body. Unless we recognise that the death and resurrection of the Lord Jesus abolished the barriers of race and custom, unless we love one another, we will be liable to physical sickness and infirmity because we are refusing to accept the wholeness and order which the Cross won for the Body of Christ. It is possible then for our physical health to reflect the degree of unity and faith within the Church, both local and universal.

Insensitivity, and a lack of love and concern, form a further aspect of taking the Lord's supper in an unworthy manner and so turning the cup of blessing into a cup of judgement. If I am not in right relationship with my brothers and sisters when I take communion, not only will I not get healed, but I might end up sick if I was healthy in the first place. Some years ago, I took a series of teaching and healing meetings in a traditional denominational church. It turned the place upside down. On the first evening, many people were baptised in the Spirit, on the second evening, the gifts of the Spirit broke out spontaneously, and on the third evening, people were healed of arthritis, back conditions and one person even got out of her wheelchair and walked.

Unfortunately, this didn't go down too well with the clergyman's wife who was staunchly traditional and was horrified to see the safe, sedate boat being rocked. I think she could see their sound reputation, along with the minister's pension, just flying out of the window, and she rallied the members of the congregation of like mind to resist the 'Charismatic' influence. It split the church. Now I don't believe it was the people who got filled with the Spirit who caused the rift (though in situations like this it's possible for those who have had a dramatic experience of God to be over-enthusiastic and impatient); it was the traditionalists who created the split by getting terribly upset, insisting that the experiences being claimed were unbiblical and that someone had to stand for truth in all this deception.

A short time later on another visit, a lady came up to me, glared furiously, and said, 'You have totally ruined this church'. What a welcome. I was so taken aback I just blinked and said, 'I am very sorry'. 'The only service I enjoy now,' she rushed on as if she hadn't heard, 'is communion. The only problem is, I can't stand the minister's preaching and I am sure he is not a man of God at all.'

On and on she went, criticising everything about this man and his church. When she stopped to draw breath for a moment, I said carefully, 'May I give you a word of warning?'

Needless to say, that went down like a brick. No, she didn't need to be warned and what was more … but I stopped her, and explained that I believed I did need to warn her because if she was taking communion and was completely out of fellowship with just about everybody else in the church, she was liable to bring sickness to her body. You can imagine that she was hardly blessed by that and she stormed off. Very soon afterwards she developed rheumatoid arthritis - but sadly she still wouldn't accept that the root of her illness might lie in her criticism and resentment.

There once was a brother who sponsored a meeting I was booked to speak at. He was certainly keen but unfortunately he was one of those super-spiritual types - the sort who have to pray which shirt to put on in the morning. The dear man stood up to introduce me and said something like this:

'God has brought our brother Ian Andrews here tonight - but I know we don't want to hear from him, we want to hear from God, don't we? Now our brother lives by faith so he's not asking for any sort of offering or support. If you feel led or compelled to put something in the bowl for him, then praise the Lord, but if you don't, you must not feel under any obligation whatsoever.'

Not surprisingly, after the service (and we had a congregation of three to four hundred people) eight glorious £1 notes appeared in the bowl at the back of the hall. Now normally I wouldn't have said anything but on this occasion I felt the brother was in danger. So afterwards I took him aside and said quite gently,

'If God has brought me to speak to you all, He's brought me to speak and He's not going to speak through somebody else. God's very economical. By receiving me, you receive the God who sent me. But if you encourage everyone to ignore me because I am just a fallible human being, but tell them to look out for God, you make it very difficult for God to work because He is using my voice and my hands as a channel. Secondly, I don't live by faith. I live by the Word of God and that says that if I preach the gospel to you in spirit and truth, it's the church's responsibility to support me, materially as well as prayerfully. Now I'm not grumbling because I am not looking to the meeting to keep me going, I'm looking to God, but perhaps you would be wise to discern the Lord's body and recognise that I am ministering His life.'

Sadly that brother wouldn't be corrected and he took great offence at what I had said. Maybe it was a bit hamfisted but I really had tried to convey it as kindly as I could. Still, some months later, he became terminally ill and he went to many others in the Body of Christ for prayer but he wouldn't come to me. Now I am not saying that God would have healed him through me because I have some kind of hot-line no-one else has, but the fact that he had a broken relationship with me and refused to put it right made it difficult for him to receive healing. Tragically he died, with that rift still unbreached. There is no doubt that failing to discern the Lord's body is a very serious situation.

Some people will quote John 9 as a reason why they are sick. Here Jesus and his disciples come upon a man who has been born blind and his disciples are keen to know whose sin has caused the affliction, the man's or his parents'. But Jesus replies,

'Neither this man nor his parents have sinned, but this happened so that the work of God might be displayed in his life.'

(John 9, verse 3)

This verse has sometimes been used to argue that the reason for some suffering is to glorify God, but from what Jesus goes on to say, it seems that He meant that the glory of God is revealed in the man's healing, not his affliction:

'As long as it is day, we must do the work of him who sent me. Night is coming when no-one can work. While I am in the world, I am the light of the world.'

(verse 4)

Having said this, He went on to heal the man, manifesting the power and love of God, and proving in a most dramatic and graphic way that He was indeed the light of the world. So we shouldn't just accept our sicknesses because we feel it is the work of God being manifested through us. No direct work of God could be anything but the vehicle of blessing, joy, peace, wholeness and beauty. God might well glorify Himself through suffering because He can turn every situation into good, but that is only an intermediate purpose. We should be looking for the restorative, perfecting touch of His hand, for that is undoubtedly the work He wants to be revealed in our life.

In our zeal to discover the spiritual roots of sickness, we can easily overlook quite simple, practical reasons why we get sick. If we abuse our bodies in any sort of way, we can hardly expect to remain healthy - unless we have been called to a situation where long, hard hours, lack of food, physical hardship and so on are unavoidable, as in a missionary situation, for example. In that case we can expect God to sustain us miraculously. But we cannot choose to work overtime continuously, go without adequate sleep, take no fresh air or exercise, eat a poor unbalanced diet, have no time for relaxation and still expect to stay in good shape. It's very difficult, I know, when your job, and therefore your career, demand late hours in the office, but you don't always have to accept the situation and see your health and family suffering. Sometimes your boss might by surprisingly open to the idea that for both reasons you feel you should get home earlier - and even be challenged by the spiritual basis for your priorities.

On the other hand, I know a young man whose firm wasn't too impressed by the idea of taking care of your body or your wife if it conflicted with promoting the interests of the firm, and so he used to 'speak' to the mountain of work on his desk each day and command it to disappear. Amazingly the pile seemed to melt away, not because less work came in, but because his working hours seemed to be stretched so that it could all get done. He used to rebuke any sort of demonic influence which might disrupt the day and waste time - things like continuous phone calls, vital information being lost in the filing, or his secretary being off sick. So we really don't have to bow to the inevitable.

It's possible to get sick through our very spirituality, or should I say superspirituality. We can sometimes get so caught up with the disciplines of prayer and fasting that we don't realise it has become a law to us rather than a work of the Spirit. Either we feel that going without food and praying all night have in themselves some sort of power which acts as a lever to make God do what we want (though we would never admit this, or perhaps even realise that this is a sort of blackmail); or we fast and pray out of anxiety, fearing that unless we mortify our flesh, God won't answer us. No wonder we get sick - and we are almost glad - it's proof for us that our prayers must be doing some good.

We must be on the lookout for another weak area if we are feeling very spiritual. The devil is at his most subtle just when we are rejoicing in the blessings. That's when he slips in, when our guard is down and we have been feeling rather pleased with ourselves. When we have had a few answers to prayers, seen someone healed, led a meeting which has gone well, it is easy to take the credit ourselves almost without realising it, and to move away from a dependance on God. As soon as we take the glory ourselves and imagine that by our own wisdom and ability we can achieve spiritual success, we are stepping outside God's protection, and particularly in entering 'battle areas' like deliverance we put ourselves at great physical risk.

So, to summarise, Satan is the originator of all sickness. This world is dominated by his rule of sin, suffering and death and although we have been delivered out of the kingdom of darkness into the kingdom of our God we live bodily in this world and are threatened constantly by these destructive influences. The enemy is certainly like a prowling lion seeking whom he may devour and unless we consciously appropriate the life God has provided for us and resist what Satan tries to throw at us, we will be subject to all the same physical problems the world groans under. Evidently there is a battle going on, usually in our mind and our emotions. In the next chapter we will study this battleground and discover how we can have the victory.

Chapter Six

The Battleground - Six States of Mind

What shall we say, then? Shall we go on sinning so that grace may increase? By no means! We died to sin; how can we live in it any longer? Or don't you know that all of us who were baptised into Christ Jesus were baptised into his death? We were therefore buried with him through baptism into death in order that, just as Christ was raised from the dead through the glory of the Father, **we too may live a new life.**

(Romans 6, verses 1-4)

Therefore, if anyone is in Christ, **he is a new creation;** the old has gone, **the new has come!**

(2 Corinthians 5, verse 17)

There's something wrong somewhere. Is the world aware that there is a completely different species of human being on the earth - called. Christians? Or are most of us acting out the fairy tale of the Emperor's New Clothes, feeling so proud of our wonderful spirituality while the world just laughs at us for being so blind? Clearly, despite all the blessings, all the fellowship, all the teaching, there is still a discrepancy between this radically new life the Bible talks of, and the mediocrity of our actual experience.

To a large extent, the problem lies with our minds. Unfortunately, many of us have got into the kingdom of God on the wrong ticket. We accepted Jesus as our Saviour and thought we'd made it. But in fact, nowhere does the Bible speak of accepting Jesus as Saviour **alone.** We need to accept Him as Lord too - and that means a total and continual submission of every aspect of our lives; it means coming under a new rule, a new set of laws, a new discipline; it involves will-power - the conscious and constant dedication of our will combined with the power of the Holy Spirit to bring about our transformation into a glorious new creation.

Some of us have given our heads to God, but we have the same thoughts, the same problems, the same attitudes as before; we are new Christians, but not fully new Creations. When we succumb to the old temptations and difficulties we start rebuking Satan, asking for ministry, claiming the victory and pleading the blood - but we forget a very powerful little word that God has given us, and that word is 'No'! The Bible is explicit that the old way of thinking, our sinful nature, the 'old man', is something **we** have to cast off. A person I know, after being born again, baptised, and filled with the Spirit, found that his life wasn't really much different; he was still dogged by the same problems and attitudes but now he was going to heaven with them! Then he had a vision of an Egyptian-type mummy with burial bandages trailing on the ground, walking around and talking with people as normal. This made him realise that although he was a new **spiritual** creation, he was still dragging around with him all the trappings of his old life, the same habits, thought patterns and feelings, and he needed to cast them off and leave them in the tomb where they belonged.

God calls us to bring our minds, emotions and bodies under His control. By the power of His Holy Spirit, He is then able to mould them so that we grow more and more like Jesus. The Lord doesn't want to erase all the human part of our nature and make us into spiritual robots - Jesus was a person of warmth, energy and intelligence - but He does want these areas to reflect the holiness and purity of His life. Dedicating our lives to God in this comprehensive and practical way is what true spiritual worship really is. In this position, we are able to receive what God wants for us:

> Therefore I urge you, brothers, in view of God's mercy, to offer your bodies as living sacrifices, holy and pleasing to God - which is your spiritual worship. **Do not conform** any longer to the pattern of this world, **but be transformed by the renewing**

> **of your mind.** Then you will be able to test and
> approve what God's will is - his good, pleasing and
> perfect will.
>
> (Romans 12, verses 1-2)

The way to holiness, then, is not firstly through our outward behaviour and actions, but through our innermost thoughts being transformed so that we reflect the perfect nature of God in all we say and do:

> You were taught with regard to your former way of
> life, to put off your old self, which is being corrupted
> by its deceitful desires; to be made new in the
> attitude of your minds, and to **put on the new self,**
> **created to be like God** in true righteousness and
> holiness.
>
> (Ephesians 4, verses 22-24)

We need to be honest and recognise that however moral and upright our life has been, we still require this renewal of our minds: selfishness, pride and a lack of love do not need to manifest themselves in dramatically immoral ways for us to be failing to show God's character and life to the world, or to present a blockage in our receiving His blessings, provision, guidance or healing. Interestingly, the Bible talks of various states of mind by which we are basically governed, and if we can identify our areas of weakness we can more easily offer them up to the Lord to be made new by His Holy Spirit. There appear to be degrees in these attitudes, the 'lowest', if you like, to be found in those totally rejecting God, and the 'highest' affecting even the Spirit-filled Christian, but all of them represent more steps towards the goal of receiving '**the mind of Christ**'. We will examine more fully what that means later, but first, let's find out where we are by looking at the six states of mind we might possess before we develop a spiritual mind.

1. The Deluded Mind

> The coming of the lawless one will be in accordance
> with the work of Satan displayed in all kinds of

counterfeit miracles, signs and wonders, and in every
sort of evil that deceives those who are perishing.
They perish because they refused to love the truth
and so be saved. For this reason God sends them a
powerful delusion so that they will believe the lie
and so that all will be condemned who have not
believed the truth but have delighted in wickedness.

(2 Thessalonians 2, verses 9-12)

A deluded mind is one of the most dangerous states of mind to be
in, worse because it believes itself to be enlightened, even one of the
chosen elite. A classic example is Jim Jones, the man who caused
almost nine hundred people to commit mass suicide in Guyana. Now
he wasn't an apparently evil man, in fact, he professed to be a born-
again Christian, a pastor of a church in Indianapolis of over four
thousand people. He **chose** not to be true to God, and eventually
entered into orgiastic ceremonies and all sorts of immorality. He
became so deluded that he believed he was God, and then he was
beyond help. The story goes that he murdered eight people in Los
Angeles but such was his 'charisma' that not a single District Attorney
believed he was guilty. He dominated and controlled the minds of his
followers to such an extent that he was able to make them kill
themselves. A normal mind doesn't have that sort of power. Jim Jones
had a power similar to Hitler - and he was undoubtedly anointed by the
devil. It is a sobering fact that we will see more and more people with
this sort of supernatural power, satanically deluding themselves, who
through signs, wonders and miraculous healings will completely
deceive thousands, and lead them into the Pit. It is the Dr. Faustus
syndrome. It is possible, perhaps, to reach a point where one is not
able to repent, even if one is filled with remorse.

2. The Depraved Mind

The tragedy of this state of mind is that often it is found in a person
who has had some knowledge of God to start with:

For although they knew God, they neither glorified
him as God nor gave thanks to him, but their
thinking became futile and their foolish hearts were

darkened. Although they claimed to be wise, they became fools and exchanged the glory of the immortal God for images made to look like mortal man and birds and animals and reptiles.

Therefore God gave them over in the sinful desires of their hearts to sexual impurity for the degrading of their bodies with one another. They exchanged the truth of God for a lie and worshipped and served created things rather than the Creator.

(Romans 1, verses 21-25)

The paradox between the intellectual and philosophical acumen of ancient Rome and its blatant immorality and sensuality is well established. Pride in their own understanding and achievements made the Romans self-centred and unable to accept the sacrifice involved in true worship of the Creator. So they lied to themselves and said that by celebrating the pleasures of the physical world - food, drink, sex, the arts, sport - they were worshipping God. In fact, they fell from worship, through religious practice, into mere superstition and eventually they became so deceived that they set themselves up as gods (look at the Caesars who reckoned themselves divine) which gave them licence to indulge their sensual passions. So their very wisdom was their downfall, turning them into fools then hypocrites, and finally into creatures less than animals in their perversion, forsaking all appearance of spirituality:

Because of this, God gave them over to shameful lusts. ... Furthermore, because they did not think it worthwhile to retain the knowledge of God, he gave them over to a depraved mind to do what ought not to be done. They have become filled with every kind of wickedness, evil, greed and depravity.

(Romans 1, verses 26, 28-29)

We need to beware, then, of intellectual and religious pride. Scientists, philosophers and theologians whose studies should cause them to worship God for the wonderful perfection of His creation and laws, can end up serving the objects of their studies or deifying themselves. And all of us are in danger of doing that in some form. Materialism, worldly ambition, sensual pleasure, form the very air we breathe and it is so easy to absorb these values, priding ourselves on our ability and achievement, yet, in reality, becoming ever more foolish. And in the church we can get caught up with certain religious theories or practices, like prosperity teaching, positive thinking, signs and wonders ministries, when in fact we are simply gratifying our own desires for power, pleasure or excitement. It is a frighteningly short step, then, from that position into depravity. And we can never plead ignorance. No matter how far we sink, we still know we are doing wrong, but we do it anyway. We are perfectly aware that we have broken a covenant but we choose to ignore that and its consequences for the sake of our immediate pleasure. We can try and call our sin a sickness to abdicate responsibility but deep down our conscience is still alive to the fact that we are deliberately disobeying God. Homosexuality is not a sickness, for example; it is a rejection of God's commandments, and it is sin, however much it might seem like a 'natural', and therefore legitimate, instinct. Many people are being set free from that problem once and for all - if they first repent - and the so-called broad-mindedness which advocates either uninhibited self-expression, or treats it as an emotional or physical sickness, is in fact, the least helpful attitude we can take as it leads people from a 'darkened' mind into a depraved one.

3. The Blinded Mind

We have renounced secret and shameful ways; we do not use deception, nor do we distort the word of God. On the contrary, by setting forth the truth plainly, we commend ourselves to every man's conscience in the sight of God. And even if our gospel is veiled, it is veiled to those who are perishing. **The god of this world has blinded the minds of unbelievers,** so that they cannot see the light of the gospel of the glory of Christ who is the image of God.

(2 Corinthians 4, verses 2-4)

Have you ever told someone about Christ and been so excited by the wonder and power of the message that you have been expecting them to fall to their knees in repentance any second - until you suddenly realise they are staring at you as if you have two heads? They really haven't understood a word you've said. All the glorious perfection of God's plan for mankind has been double dutch to them. The idea of His love, the sacrifice of His own Son, the need for repentance, God's desire to bless and heal, has sounded completely crazy, whilst the concepts of the Virgin Birth and the Resurrection have had less credibility than fairy stories.

The problem is that their minds have been blinded by the devil, and the arguments that might have moved a person with an open, searching mind will sound incomprehensible to the one whose persistent sin has dulled his ears to the voice of God (see 2 Corinthians 13, verse 14). With a person like this, it is pointless trying to use reason - until the scales of blindness are removed from his eyes. And just as God **commanded** the light to shine out of darkness at the creation of the world, and **made** His light shine in our hearts (2 Corinthians 4, verse 6), so we need to come against the Prince of Darkness, and command the blindness to be removed so that the person is free to choose light or darkness. If the cause of the blindness lies in some sort of involvement with the occult, this will certainly require the prayer of authority, and even a time of prayer and fasting. After that, we need to 'set forth the truth plainly', attacking the dullness and hardness which remain by systematically putting forward the miracle of what God has done, line upon line, precept upon precept, until the shrouds of blindness are stripped away. The gospel is 'the power of God for the salvation of everyone who believes' (Romans 1, verse 16). We don't need to be drawn into subtle arguments concerning theology, morality or philosophy. The good news of Jesus, plainly and clearly put forward, reveals in itself the wonder of the new life in Him, 'foolishness to those who are perishing, but to us who are being saved it is the power of God' (1 Corinthians 1, verse 18).

I heard of a church situated in a part of the country where occult practices, covens, and witchcraft were rife, struggling for months to get through to the young people of the town the simplest facts about their lost condition. Although many of these young people had severe problems - they were on drugs, homeless or in trouble with the police - they still couldn't see that they were in any spiritual need, and the idea of God's love didn't touch their hearts at all. Eventually a word of knowledge came to the church that the barrier was caused by the satanic practices which had spread a blanket of blindness over the minds of most of the people in the town so that they weren't able to respond to the gospel. When this was revealed, the church had a period of prayer and fasting commanding this blindness to be stripped away, at the end of which they witnessed the most dramatic change. Suddenly there was an openness amongst the people with whom they shared the gospel; the young people in the town seemed at last to recognise their desperate situation and responded with sincere repentance to the message of Christ; and those who had committed their lives to God were able to receive the truths about His laws and life in His kingdom, and to grow steadily into maturity. Clearly we need to come against this particular work of Satan, blinding minds, and say, as it was in the beginning, 'Let there be light'.

4. The Carnal Mind

This isn't as awful as it sounds! If you have a carnal mind, it doesn't necessarily mean that you are vicious and immoral, it simply means you have a natural mind, that all your points of reference are based on human ability and understanding, and all your motivation is selfish and directed towards material pleasure and profit. That's not so terrible, that's just human, isn't it? But God didn't create us to be 'just human'; He created us to live forever and enjoy free fellowship with Him, and since He is Spirit, we need to worship Him in spirit and in truth (John 4, verse 24).

The New International Version states the case a bit more plainly. Here the 'carnal mind' is translated 'sinful mind', and from the context it is clear Paul is saying that it is perfectly possible to be a Christian yet still possess the sinful nature - not only possess it, but be controlled by it.

> Those who live according to the sinful nature have their minds set on what that sinful nature desires, but those who live in accordance with the Spirit have their minds set on what the Spirit desires. **The mind of sinful man is death**, but the mind controlled by the Spirit is life and peace; **the sinful mind is hostile to God. It does not submit to God's law,** nor can it

> do so. Those controlled by the sinful nature **cannot**
> **please God.**
>
> (Romans 8, verses 5-8)

Perhaps it is more serious than we thought, then. Unless our sinful mind is renewed, we might end up missing the mark altogether. This is a subtle problem and we need to be aware of the forms it can take. 'The mind of sinful man is death.' That seems a bit extreme. But we are given the reason why in the next sentence: 'the sinful mind is hostile to God.' A carnally-minded person may appear to be thoroughly good and moral; some of the most philanthropic actions and causes have been fielded by humanists, for example, and all sorts of quasi religious organisations seem to be showing more constructive love and concern than the true Church. But all the benevolence and idealism can't alter the fact that their minds are thinking **independently** of God. They are drawing on their own strength and understanding and this limits their effectiveness. And although the universal goal might be laudable, on an individual, personal level there is often dissension, corruption and a lack of inner peace, for only the mind controlled by the Spirit finds true life and peace.

For others with a carnal mind, God's laws may be in direct and open opposition to their own desires. Such people admit that they prefer immediate physical pleasure or gain to the 'vague' promise of spiritual benefits. Again, initially their aims might seem quite laudable - work hard, provide for the family, improve your standard of living, enjoy life to the full - but gradually there is less and less time or motivation to think of other people, their hearts become hardened, and their minds set on the insatiable pursuit of personal pleasure, with the desires of the flesh for food, drink, sex or other excitement ultimately squashing the earlier apparent idealism and morality.

As Christians, unless our sinful mind has been renewed, we will have the outward trappings of spirituality - we will pray, read the Bible, go to church - but we will still be governed by the same thoughts and desires as the rest of the world. And sometimes we don't even realise how much we are fooling ourselves because we have so much head knowledge **about** God that we think we are actually living it. Chorus-tapes are always on in our homes, we are booking up for all the good conferences, and we are talking to people about healing and

God's provision, but when illness or difficulties strike we react like everyone else. Why pray when you can worry?! Go to the doctor straightaway with your lump or rash or pain and find out all about it. Why ask God to heal you when it will only take a few days or weeks and a course or two of pills to make you better - or at least take away the symptoms? Why ask God to meet your financial needs when it's so much easier to arrange a loan or an overdraft, or just to panic? After all, there's no point in troubling God about it; it's too small (or too large), and anyway, He's not really interested in **practical** problems, just in getting people saved.

We're being reasonable, rational, sensible. And that's the problem. God is none of them, or at least not by human standards. He works by different laws and to follow Him we need to learn this new way of thinking. God made this plain right from the beginning.

> Now the Lord God had planted a garden in the east, in Eden, and there he put the man he had formed. And the Lord God made all kinds of trees grow out of the ground - trees that were pleasing to the eye and good for food. In the middle of the garden were the tree of life and the tree of the knowledge of good and evil...
>
> The Lord God took man and put him in the Garden of Eden to work it and take care of it. And the Lord God commanded the man, 'You are free to eat from any tree in the garden; but you must not eat from the tree of the knowledge of good and evil for when you eat of it you will surely die.'
>
> (Genesis 2, verses 8-9, 15-16)

Next God created woman, and the two of them lived in perfect security, perfect happiness and complete fulfilment, enjoying a wonderful face-to-face relationship with God. Then along came trouble (it always does when we think we're really walking close to God).

> Now the serpent was more crafty than any of the wild animals the Lord God had made. He said to the woman, 'Did God really say, "You must not eat from

any tree in the garden"?'

(Genesis 3, verse 1)

This is really subtle. He didn't ask, 'Did God really say you mustn't eat from the tree of the knowledge of good and evil?' He was playing on the woman's doubts and confusion. What **was** it God had said exactly? The tree of life and the tree of the knowledge of good and evil were **both** in the middle of the garden. Were they really only allowed to eat from one of them? And if so, which one? Satan always tries to confuse and deceive us by calling black white, and here he capitalises on the woman's obvious uncertainty by implying that the tree of the knowledge of good and evil is really the one that gives life:

> 'You will surely not die,' the serpent said to the
> woman. 'For God knows that when you eat of it your
> eyes will be opened and you will be like God,
> knowing good and evil.'

(Genesis 3, verses 4-5)

Again this is a clever lie. First, there is only one supreme God; no-one can be 'like' Him in the sense the serpent was implying - almighty, omniscient - as He is unique, the Creator who reigns over everything that He has made. Second, by eating of the tree of the knowledge of good and evil, they would not even acquire the power of Satan: only if they went on to eat from the tree of life after that would they become immortal. In fact, what happened to them was an unmitigated disaster. Their eyes were opened, but to what? The first thing they saw was that they were naked, and in came shame and therefore probably lust. Next they had to find something to clothe themselves with - and so they lost their dependence on God and trust that He would provide all their needs. And finally, when they heard God walking in the garden, they were afraid and hid themselves; fear, guilt and deception were to dominate man's attitude to God from that moment.

When we see just these immediate effects, we begin to realise why the knowledge of good and evil **in the power of man** is such a deadly thing. The trouble is that it presents us with a constant choice: is this good, is this evil? And with our limited wisdom and understanding, and our basically selfish nature, we are tossed about by fears and doubts as we try to make the right decision. It's like trying to measure the length of London Bridge with a pocket ruler: we don't have the right tools for the job. If we continue to feed off the tree of the knowledge of good and evil as Christians, then we run into a further problem - double-mindedness.

5. The Double Mind

> If any of you lacks wisdom, he should ask God, who gives generously to all without finding fault, and it will be given to him. But when he asks, he must believe and not doubt, because he who doubts is like a wave of the sea, blown and tossed by the wind. That man should not think he will receive anything from the Lord; he is a double-minded man, unstable in all he does.
>
> (James 1, verses 5-8)

Double-mindedness is not a state of back-sliding, it is a state of growth. Until we start feeding into our minds the Word of God, we don't have this problem because our thoughts are governed by the one human perspective. But when we start to claim the promises of God and live our life according to His laws, the trouble really starts. Because we **know** we have 'flu - our head aches, our nose is streaming, we have a hacking cough - and it's going to take a few days, and lots of aspirin, to get over it. But our spiritual thought says, 'By His stripes I am healed'. So what do we do? Do we give in to our human experience and rational understanding, or do we speak out the real truth which lies in God's Word and receive His healing? Bills, bills and more bills keep piling in, but God's Word promises prosperity and provision. Do we worry and strive or do we rebuke the devil as a thief and a liar, and release God's blessing into our experience? Unfortunately, when we have double-mindedness in a bad way we try to do both!

Look at Peter walking on the water. There's no doubting his enthusiasm and desire to serve the Lord. He really wants to grow in faith.

'Lord, if it's You,' (still got a bit of doubt, though), 'tell me to come to You on the water.'

'Come,' He said.

Then Peter got down out of the boat and walked on the water to Jesus. But when he saw the wind he was afraid and, beginning to sink, cried out, 'Lord, save me!'

Immediately Jesus reached out His hand and caught him. 'You of little faith,' He said. 'Why did you doubt?'

You can just imagine the humble way Peter had got out of the boat. 'Stand aside, James, the Lord's called me. Excuse me, John. It's all right for you to lean on the Lord's chest, but I want some action.' And he walked on the water. That was fine - so long as he kept his eyes on Jesus. But when he glanced sideways, he saw the waves getting bigger and a storm brewing. Panic gripped him, and with one bite of the tree of knowledge, he was up to his ears in water. If he hadn't been double-minded, he would have taken a big step in faith that day; as it was he scrambled back to the boat like a wet puppy with his tail between his legs.

By trying to keep one foot in the world and one in the kingdom of God, we end up getting the worst of both. We lose credibility in the eyes of our friends and colleagues, and we don't receive the blessings that unreserved faith in God would bring. So we end up sicker, poorer and more anxious than people in the world! What a testimony. We are like little children. Have you noticed how a three year old will find it very difficult to come to a decision and almost impossible to stick to it? 'Orange juice or Ribena?' Quick glance round the room to see what everyone else is having. He's not so concerned with what he would actually like as with what seems the best deal. He sees one friend with orange juice. 'Orange juice, please.' Five minutes later, most of the other children have chosen Ribena, and the little boy is throwing his orange juice on the floor and screaming for Ribena. In the same way, when presented with a decision or problem, we may start trying to trust God and claim His promises of guidance or provision, but then after a while (usually about a day!) when nothing seems to be changing and other people in the same position seem to be getting things sorted out without God's help, we decide to implement a back-up policy of incorporating the world's answer as well. But double-mindedness gives us double problems - we don't have confidence in either strategy, and we sway backwards and forwards between the two, 'unstable' in all we do.

The characteristic of this state of mind is **doubt**. The trouble is that we believe our doubts instead of **doubting** them. We wake up on Monday morning feeling awful and we're tempted to think that the joy we felt in the meeting the night before was all an illusion. God seems a million miles away, and all we can see ahead of us is a day of stress and hassle at work. With faith like this for a bad day, we'll certainly get one! But doubts always come from the enemy, so if we reverse these doubts we will get the truth. The devil feeds us the thought, 'You haven't got any joy, have you?'

Instead of plunging into guilt and condemnation, we should respond,

'But the joy of the Lord is my strength. Thank you for reminding me. I don't feel it right now, but I know I've got it. In His presence there is fullness of joy. Well, I am in Christ so I don't just have joy, I have **abundant** joy. And joy comes in the mornings! I'm going to feel that joy coming through any minute.'

And by this time, doubt has had to slink out of the door and we have built up so much faith that we are able to receive a day of real victory and praise.

Jesus said,

> 'Man does not live by bread alone, but on every
> word that comes from the mouth of God.'
>
> (Matthew 4, verse 4)

But how **do** we change our spiritual diet in this way? The clue lies in Ephesians Chapter 6, and the power of God's answer is seen more clearly if we look at it in the King James Version:

> Wherefore take unto you the whole armour of God,
> that ye may be able to withstand in the evil day, and
> having done all, to stand. Stand therefore, **having
> your loins girt about with truth**...
>
> (Ephesians 6, verses 13-14)

Now if we look over at 1 Peter 1, verse 13, we read:

> Wherefore **gird up the loins of your mind**, be sober,
> and hope to the end for the grace that is to be brought
> unto you at the revelation of Jesus Christ.

The analogy, in both cases, is drawn from the uniform of a Roman soldier. The article was a long shirt made up of eight or nine strips which was worn over the loin cloth tied round his waist. This wasn't the most practical of garments when there was any action around, so when he was about to go into battle, the soldier would gather up these strips and tuck them into his loin cloth. Then he could run and fight and have freedom to move without tripping over his clothes. So God is saying to us here that when we are being attacked by the enemy, we need to gather up our 'loopy' thoughts and tuck them into our belts of truth; in other words, strengthen our mind by bringing it into subjection to the Word of God. What we see and feel and understand is not the truth; only God's Word gives us the correct perspective on our situation. Take a woman with a husband and three children to rouse, dress, feed and send off to work and school. As the door bangs after them at 8.30 a.m. she turns round to face the scene of devastation and is immediately overwhelmed by the thought that there are twenty nine things to be accomplished that day, and the man is coming to mend the washing machine, mother-in-law is calling in for coffee and the baby has just been sick on the floor. Now she can either panic, or she can get hold of that 'loopy' thought and tuck it into her belt by saying, 'Devil, the Bible says, "He who believes will not make haste," so I'm going to have another cup of coffee…!'

Now if she doesn't do that, her mind will get into such a state of worry and confusion that she won't do anything properly because she can't think straight. She can try fighting the thoughts of panic and helplessness, but usually when we do that it just creates more tension because we are striving to control our situation by our own strength. That's the curse. (I lived like that for years: bills, letters, requests, telephone calls. 'I must get everything done,' I thought and I would get exhausted just looking at my desk.) But if that woman sits down with a cup of coffee and spends five minutes listening to a chorus-tape and rejoicing in the Lord, she will find that she enjoys her day instead of battling through it; she will get done far more than if she had leapt into action with a duster in her hand and panic in her head, and the things which don't get done she will accept quite happily because she realises they weren't so desperately important after all.

Nothing angers the devil so much. It's **him** who has the nervous breakdown: 'I've been trying **everything** to get this woman to crack up and all she's doing is praising the Lord.' Let him be the one to get high blood pressure. If we bring our natural thoughts into subjection to God's truth, we will find **life** instead of mere knowledge.

'The words that I speak are spirit and life' (John 6, verse 63).

And peace: 'You will keep him in perfect peace whose mind is steadfast because he trusts in you' (Isaiah 26, verse 3).

The other way to become spiritually minded is to be found in 2 Corinthians 10, verses 3-5:

> For though we live in the world, we do not wage war
> as the world does. The weapons we fight with are not
> the weapons of the world. On the contrary, they have
> divine power to demolish strongholds. We demolish
> arguments and every pretension that sets itself up
> against the knowledge of God, and we take captive
> every thought to make it obedient to Christ.

Paul may have been using an analogy here which would have had particular effectiveness with the Corinthian church. At the time Paul was writing, the Middle East was the granary of the world. Ships laden with wheat and maize would sail along the coast of Corinth bound for the store-houses which supplied the Roman Empire. Hidden in the narrow harbours along the coast were pirate ships which frequently seized these precious cargoes. It was known that these pirates came from the villages which clustered at the top of the steep cliffs above the sea, and eventually a task force of soldiers sailed from Rome to deal with the problem. At night, they maneuvered close to the cliffs and threw up grappling-irons. Some tiny houses perched right on the edge were actually pulled down into the sea, while elsewhere soldiers swarmed up ropes and took the villagers captive before they had time to flee.

So when we get a thought which 'sets itself up against the knowledge of God', which challenges God's Word or what our spirit feels He is saying to us, we need to send up a grappling-iron and pull it down, taking that lie captive and making our minds obedient to the law of Christ. There are a frightening number of road accidents in America and when I am driving along there and see a car in front swerve, it's easy to think, 'It could be me next'. What do I do when I get that thought? If I say, 'Satan, I rebuke you,' it usually becomes even more insistent! But what God wants me to do is throw a spiritual grappling-iron up, get hold of that 'imagination' as the King James Version calls it, and pull it down. 'No, devil, I'm kept by the power of God. He will bear me up if I even dash my foot on a stone.' I don't **fight** the thought; I just pull it down. Another time, the thought will come, 'This meeting will be a disaster,' or 'They won't receive you,' or 'There will be no miracles this weekend'. What do I do? Fight it, saying 'They **will** receive me, they **will** receive me'? Positive confession is no good on its own. It's the word of faith - the promise of God applied to the situation - which is effective.

If these two methods don't work, then another way to remove doubt is to fast. When Jesus said, 'This kind can come out only by prayer and fasting,' He meant not so much the deaf and dumb spirit as the **unbelief** in the disciples. 'Everything is possible for him who believes.' 'I do believe,' replied the father of the boy with the evil spirit, 'help me overcome my unbelief.' So he didn't need more belief, just less doubt. By fasting we starve our doubts and feed our faith. Starve our unbelief long enough and it will die; allow it to take root, and it will grow like weeds and strangle our faith. As single-minded people we must renew our thinking and be spiritually minded. In order for this to happen, we need to feed on God's Word and eat of the tree of life.

Another spiritual aid we often neglect is speaking in tongues. We need to be reminded of this wonderful gift and weapon against enemy strongholds. Paul said he spoke in tongues more than everyone and urged us to pray in the Spirit, and with understanding too. The way to deal with spiritual opposition is by spiritual means, which are effective when used in faith. The Holy Spirit prays through our spirit into a situation that needs changing. Often, as we mature as Christians, this gift is neglected or used only occasionally. We need to stir up this gift and use it much more. We often lose our inspiration because we grow bored with the same words or language and forget to put any faith behind the words that we speak. Rosemary and I find that we can speak with new languages deliberately as well as inspirationally. We can form new sounds, use new vowels and as we have said to people, start anywhere from A-Z, but don't keep repeating the same words forever. It has been exciting to hear God speak through people in a refreshing way as they experience new languages, even singing out a message in a tongue with an interpretation. We need to use these gifts and never let them grow stale. They are for the refreshing and encouragement of those in the church, and the testimony of Jesus to the outsider, and as we speak in tongues in our daily lives more and more it helps our minds to be still and hear God's thoughts. We become strengthened in our inward man. Our mind no longer dominates our spirit but becomes subject to it. Instead of analysing everything and taking it through our computer brain, we are more able to believe and receive from God, and His Word becomes easier to read and understand. As we speak in tongues His Spirit illuminates our way. We begin to get direction in our lives and discernment in many situations whether in counselling, ministry or for our own personal lives. If people have had a mental breakdown or are feeble-minded, it is especially helpful, if they are Spirit-filled Christians, for them to speak in tongues every day. In that way they will become stronger in their minds and healing will come more quickly.

When Paul said he spoke in tongues more than most he needed to do so because of all the circumstances he found himself in, but also because he knew in his ministry that the power to heal and deliver men and women from demons and sickness lay in the Holy Ghost and he needed to be constantly re-filled with the Holy Spirit.

6. The Feeble Mind

Comfort the feeble-minded.

(1 Thessalonians 5, verse 14 (KJV))

If we have got to the point of bringing our negative thoughts and doubts under control, all we need, to overcome the final hurdle and receive the Lord's provision, is courage and perseverance. **All** we need! Unfortunately, the idea of endurance is not a very popular one nowadays, when our society is so geared towards comfort and immediate results. Yet the Bible is full of exhortations to persevere and endure, to hold fast and not to give up:

Let us hold unswervingly to the hope we profess, for he who promised is faithful.

So do not throw away your confidence; it will be

> richly rewarded. You need to persevere so that when
> you have done the will of God, you will receive what
> he has promised. For in just a very little while, 'He
> who is coming will come and will not delay. But my
> righteous one will live by faith. And if he shrinks
> back, I will not be pleased with him.' But we are not
> of those who shrink back and are destroyed, but of
> those who believe and are saved.
>
> (Hebrews 10, verses 23, 35-39)

We may have to endure suffering from many quarters - from the
world in the form of mockery or persecution, and from Satan through
sickness, difficulties, temptations, spiritual attack - but God uses it to
bring us to a place of greater blessing by making us more mature in our
faith.

> We rejoice in the hope of the glory of God. Not only
> so, but we also rejoice in our sufferings, because we
> know that suffering produces perseverance,
> perseverance character, and character, hope. And
> hope does not disappoint us because God has poured
> out his love into our hearts by the Holy Spirit whom
> he has given us.
>
> (Romans 5, verses 2-5)

To many of us, this might sound like the headmaster of a boarding
school as he orders cross-country runs and cold showers before
breakfast. But while the goal for the headmaster is simply 'character',
for the Christian it is **hope**, hope which is the sure belief that God will
do what He has promised. If we see God's purpose, then, in all that
happens, and understand that He is merely disciplining us out of love
as a father disciplines his son, then we can resist the temptation to give
up, to be anxious, to question, to despair, all the feelings of weakness
which stem from a feeble mind,

> For God did not give us a spirit of timidity, but a
> spirit of power, of love, and of self discipline.
>
> (2 Timothy 1, verse 7)

A feeble-minded person looks at himself, at his own failings and limitations. Often he has been dominated by an overbearing parent as a child, and finds it very difficult to come to any decision on his own. He is easily led, and is vulnerable to being dominated by someone else's will. He is full of self-doubt and anxiety. At the first test of faith, he cries, 'There, I knew it wouldn't work,' and throws in the towel. He is usually first in line for ministry when a new speaker comes to the church, and needs regular counselling sessions with an elder, usually covering the same fears and problems. The feeble-minded person needs to be encouraged (not merely comforted and sympathised with) to '**consider him who endured**'. If God has promised. our own abilities or worthiness don't come into it. As Paul urges,

> Let us throw off everything that hinders and the sin that so easily entangles, and let us run with perseverance the race marked for us. Let us fix our eyes on Jesus, the author and finisher of our faith, who for the joy set before him endured the cross, scorning its shame, and sat down at the right hand of the throne of God. Consider him who endured such opposition from sinful men, so that you will not grow weary and lose heart. ...
>
> Therefore, strengthen your feeble arms and weak knees! Make level paths for your feet, so that the lame may not be disabled, but rather healed.
>
> (Hebrews 12, verses 1-3, 12-13)

Rosemary recalls a picture that flashed into her mind as she was cleaning. (That's when the Lord usually speaks to her and it certainly takes the drudge out of housework!)

> I saw myself when I was at Junior School on the playing field. We used to have a special sports day once a year. My favourite race was the egg and spoon because I seemed to come second or third quite often, but I used to fall apart when it came to anything else. I felt I'd lost before I began - there were so many good runners and I was nearly always

one of the last. That didn't do much for my inferiority complex, but this particular day was different. The eager parents were sitting around, all eyes on their children, full of encouragement, and all the girls were there with the teachers, enjoying the sunshine and a day off from classes. Two teachers were at the end of the 100 yard run holding the white tape. We all got lined up. 'On your marks, get set, GO' - and we were off! I was doing my best, but instead of giving up as usual when I thought that everyone else was doing better, I kept going. I didn't give up on the inside and think, 'Well, I may as well be the best loser'. The crowds were cheering, 'Go on Rosie!' I got to the tape and looked **back** - for the first time ever I had actually won! My name was being announced as the winner and I could hear a teacher saying in front of everyone, 'Rosemary, you have won the race. Well done! You have won the prize!' Now this may sound silly but it was just as if it was Jesus speaking to me. **He** made the announcement. **He** said I had won! I really laughed. He has already seen me at the finishing post and I am going to receive a prize from Him. How tremendous if we could all see ourselves winning the race God has marked out for us. Then when the devil came along and said, 'Give up now, it's too hard,' or 'You can't make it,' we would know that he is a liar.

For the joy that was set before Him Jesus endured the cross and the shame. We have to encourage ourselves in the Lord, and spur one another on. There is a Final Day coming; He has put His overcoming Spirit in us, and on the day when we meet Jesus face to face, we want to hear those wonderful words, 'Well done, you made it. You kept going against all difficulties; enter into My joy.'

It is as we strengthen our feeble spirits and minds, then, that we receive physical healing in our bodies. This is the will of God, holding on to our confidence in what He has said. **After we have done this** (Hebrews 10, verse 36), we will receive **in our experience** what He has promised.

This process of becoming spiritually minded has to be practised daily and is not something which happens overnight. It takes months, even years, of walking with the Lord before the fruits of love, joy, peace, patience, kindness, goodness, faithfulness, gentleness and self-control are manifested consistently in our lives. I have heard some people say, 'I have the mind of Christ now'. But that is not possible. Individually, we cannot have the mind of Christ, for as the Body of Christ is made up of many parts, so is the mind. **Collectively,** we possess the mind of Christ. In talking about spiritual wisdom in 1 Corinthians 2, Paul makes it clear that it is together that we come to an understanding of spiritual truths:

> We have not received the spirit of the world, but the Spirit who is from God, that we may understand what God has freely given us. This is what we speak, not in words taught us by human wisdom but in words taught by the Spirit, expressing spiritual truths in spiritual words. The man without the Spirit does not accept the things that come from the Spirit of God for they are foolishness to him, and he cannot understand them because they are spiritually discerned. The spiritual man makes judgments about all things, but he himself is not subject to any man's judgment: 'For who has known the mind of the Lord that he may instruct him?' **But we have the mind of Christ.**

> (1 Corinthians 2, verses 12-16)

A fellowship of spiritually minded people will, together, discern the Lord's will. Otherwise an individual, trusting in his own spiritual understanding, might say to you, 'I don't think you should do that brother, it's not wise. It just doesn't make good financial sense.' But who is talking about good, sound, financial common-sense? Jesus didn't very often. When money was needed to pay the temple tax, Jesus didn't open up His purse; He told Peter to go fishing:

'Go to the lake and throw out your line. Take the first

> fish you catch; open its mouth and you will find a
> four-drachma coin. Take it and give it to them for my
> tax and yours.'
>
> (Matthew 17, verse 27)

Peter was a fisherman. This must have sounded like a fairy story rather than sound financial sense. He must have felt very stupid going out in his boat that morning.

'What are you doing, Peter?'

'Trying to catch a fish with a coin in its mouth to pay the temple tax.'

But Jesus knew that Peter would have had pride in his ability and knowledge as a fisherman, and unless he was prepared to sacrifice that and to do what appeared foolish to his mind, he wouldn't find the Lord's provision - which cost him nothing, after all, except a little pride.

When God told me to go into the ministry of healing and live by faith, incidentally, I'm afraid that I told Him He was stupid:

'As an accountant, I can earn more than most people in the fellowship. I can tithe and keep a missionary on the mission field all the time. It's pointless sending me out in faith. You've picked the wrong man. Send brother so and so. He's out of a job.'

To which God's reply, not unpredictably, was,

'I don't need your money, but I do need you. And I didn't ask you if it was a good idea. I said it was a God-idea. So do it.'

Alone, we can find it difficult to discern the Lord's mind. But when several people seek the Lord together, He can make His will more clear through a variety of spiritual gifts. As individuals, we tend to see things only from our own particular viewpoint, and our vision is often narrow. I may only have a part of God's mind, a partial understanding of His purposes; you may have another part. As we lay down our prejudices and learn to trust one another, we will become much more effective, and our love and appreciation for one another will deepen. Quite often, the deepest truth God wants us to discover is how to live together in love, harmony and humility. Corporately, then, we discover the mind of Christ, even though we may hold different opinions. And this **is** the mind of Christ: life and peace.

Chapter Seven

The Renewed Mind - Looking to Jesus

We say of two people who have just fallen in love, 'They have eyes only for each other'. Oblivious to everything else around them, their love for one another makes every glance, movement and word of their beloved totally captivating. Their vision and thoughts are completely filled by the object of their desire, and this inspires them to noble acts and a disregard of themselves, making even the most mundane of tasks enjoyable.

Similarly, the centre of a baby's world is his mother. His eyes will follow her around the room, dismay crossing his face when she goes out for a moment, delight greeting her when she returns. Most of what he learns comes from her, both good and bad, and in trouble or pain it is always to her that he looks first.

To learn a difficult skill, the apprentice must do more than read the theory in text-books; he must spend hours, months, even years, watching the master craftsman until he has learnt every intricate movement to reproduce a work of equal quality.

What fills our vision, shapes our minds and dictates our actions? As Christians, what are our eyes fixed upon and what is influencing our thoughts and lifestyle? There is no doubt where we should be looking:

> Let us fix our eyes on Jesus, the author and perfector
> of our faith, who for the joy set before him endured
> the cross, scorning its shame and sat down at the
> throne of God.
>
> (Hebrews 12, verse 2)

In the context of healing, I find most people are absorbed by their illnesses. They spend most of their time looking at their symptoms, analysing their sickness, wondering if it's getting worse, and very little time looking away from their problem to Jesus. What's more, with a lot of ministries emphasising faith, I find many people putting their faith in their faith, so that when they come forward for prayer, they tell me they really do have faith - and sometimes I say, 'If you have that much faith, don't ask me to pray for you. Get healed.' I would much rather they said, 'I don't know if I have much faith but I'm looking at Jesus', because then Jesus would become faith to them.

Throughout Scripture we see people being presented with a constant choice - either look at the problem or look to the Lord. If you look to the Lord, you will find He will do something about your problem. It is so simple that most people reject it because they feel healing can't be that straightforward - mainly because they've already been prayed for by a lot of people and they are just as sick as ever. That was my experience for years. Most people with a healing ministry had a go at praying for me, and coping with the feeling of condemnation and anger afterwards when I didn't get healed was very difficult. I began to think that I didn't have enough faith, or maybe God didn't want to heal me. This is when I realised I was doing one fundamental thing wrong. I was looking for my healing. My mind was focussed on my problem - my stammer - rather than on the God who heals. The Bible says we walk by faith, not by sight, but that doesn't mean I close my eyes and refuse to look anywhere. It means I **fix** my eyes on the person who starts my faith, sustains my faith and brings it to perfection - the Lord Jesus Christ. Now when I do this, my sickness stops being mine, **my** problem by which I almost identify myself, and becomes a problem quite detached from me. Until then, I'm so wrapped up in my sickness that God can't reach past it to heal me.

The Greek verb which is translated 'let us fix our eyes on Jesus', carries the sense of looking **away from** one thing **towards** another. So we need to pull our attention **away from** our problem and look **towards** Jesus; turn away from our pain and look towards Jesus; turn away from doctors' reports and look towards Jesus. We must deliberately turn our eyes away from everything which causes us fear and dismay, and fix them on the One who **has** the faith to heal us.

Remember Moses at the Waters of Marah. We saw how he had to look away from the complaints of the people and the impossibility of the situation; he had to **keep on** looking to the Lord even in the face of what seemed a ridiculous answer to the problem. But by doggedly **fixing** his eyes on the Almighty God, he seemed to create a channel for the Lord's provision, and brought about the wonderful revelation of the Lord's healing purpose towards His people.

The same principle is illustrated a little further on in the Israelites' wanderings. Surprise, surprise, they were moaning again:

> 'Why have you brought us up out of Egypt to die in the desert? There is no bread! There is no water! And we detest this miserable food!' Then the Lord sent venomous snakes among them; they bit the people and many Israelites died. The people came to Moses and said, 'We sinned when we spoke against the Lord and against you. Pray that the Lord will take the snakes away from us.' So Moses prayed for the people. The Lord said to Moses, 'Make a snake and put it on a pole; **anyone who is bitten can look at it and live.**'
>
> (Numbers 21, verses 5-8)

Fortunately, Moses didn't blink an eyelid at this. He had learnt the lesson more than once that when God tells you something you do it, however daft it sounds. But can you imagine the reaction of the Israelites when Moses hoisted a bronze serpent up on a pole and promised they would be healed if they looked at it? Time was running out. That's the trouble with snake bites. You can tell exactly how long you've got before you die by how far your body has swelled up with the venom. So if you have a leg the size of a tree trunk, there's no time to play games. But since the nearest hospital was forty years away and you had to be a good swimmer to cross the Red Sea, most of the Israelites decided they had nothing to lose. (And I think that is why a lot of people with incurable illnesses get healed while people with colds still struggle; when you are desperate it's much easier to be whole-heartedly committed to God's way.)

Again, neither Moses nor the Israelites knew that the snake on the pole prefigured Jesus crucified on a Cross, fulfilling His prophecy that 'I, when I am lifted up from the earth, will draw all men to myself'

(John 12, verse 32).

They didn't know that by the stripes of Jesus we are healed. They would never see Jesus spread out His arms on the Cross and cry, 'It is accomplished'. They were simply being obedient, looking to Jesus, rather than relying on their own abilities or human understanding. And God's promise brought life:

> Then, when anyone was bitten by a snake and looked at the bronze snake, he lived.
>
> (Numbers 21, verse 9)

From this verse, perhaps not **everyone** could believe they could be healed by looking at a bronze snake on a pole. We suffer from the same temptations today. Rosemary narrates the following incident:

> I remember having an argument once (once?!) with Ian after which, during the evening, I had a terrible stomach ache, more like cramp really, a deep-seated pain which wouldn't go away. I tried to busy myself until bedtime, avoiding talking to Ian with whom I was still angry, but the pain was still there. Talk about 'The tongue has the power of life and death, and those who love it will eat its fruit' (Proverbs 18, verse 21)! This wasn't a verse I cared to dwell on just then. Law of Life No. 1 was being broken as all hope of communication seemed to have flown, and we went to bed to enjoy back-to-back fellowship! Laws No. 2 and 3 promptly went out of the window as we refused to draw together and went to bed with the matter unresolved. ('Don't let the sun go down on your wrath.' In other words, keep short accounts.)
>
> But I couldn't get away from God's mercy to me, so after tossing and turning for a bit, I did what I could to draw close to Him, saying, 'Oh, Lord, I know you still love me and you still died to heal me. Forgive me for my angry words and resentment and help me. I ask for your healing now in Jesus' name.'
>
> Then I tried to get as comfortable as possible, and

laid hands on myself, speaking healing to my body and praying in tongues. After a while, I fell asleep, but when I woke up, I felt as though I had been punched in the stomach. There were other guests in the house, but I was first up and went downstairs to make a cup of tea, with Ian still fast asleep. But suddenly the room started spinning round and I had to sit down. I could hear sounds of our friends beginning to stir and I called to them in some distress, but suddenly I panicked as the pain sharpened and I just cried out to the Lord, 'Jesus, heal me - quick!' And before anybody else could get there, all the pain and faintness had gone, and I was fine. I saw again how full of mercy Jesus is, rushing to rescue us when we cry out, and the first thing I wanted to do was be reconciled with Ian.

It was a stern reminder to me that when we break God's laws we are liable to judgement, and Satan certainly makes sure we feel guilty and wretched with his accusations. But we have an intercessor to plead constantly on our behalf and He can cleanse our conscience from sin. Still, we can't use that as an excuse to keep on falling into the same traps and being lazy about our attitudes and dealings with people. God has given us the ability to walk in His ways and be controlled by the power of His love if we want to be.

The trouble is, when you get sick, your body tells you you are sick, your mind tells you you are sick, and it is very difficult to **deny** yourself - to look away from all your feelings, the physical evidence, the negative remarks ('You really do look awful...') - and look to the Lord. Not so long ago, I lost my voice (again). It's preacher's throat or something! I was staying in a home in Norfolk that was centrally heated and double glazed, yet I have never felt so cold in my life. I shivered and shook, and thought, 'Oh, Lord, for the palm trees of Chard.' There were more meetings ahead, but when I woke up the next morning, my head was spinning, my throat felt like a cheese grater, my nose was blocked, and the last thing in the world I felt like doing was getting up and preaching. But I knew I had to do what I preached - look to Jesus. So, with a great effort (and not much enthusiasm), I said, 'Lord, I refuse to think about my nose or listen to my voice. I just look to You.'

And the Lord replied, 'You're resentful'.

'What do you mean, Lord, I'm resentful?'

'You resent staying in this house, don't you?'

That made me feel really stupid so I ummed and aahed and He said, 'Yes you do.'

So I had to admit it and repent.

'Lord I'm sorry. I do repent of being resentful. Thank You that I'm staying in this house. Thank You that I feel so cold. I praise and thank You, Jesus.'

In five minutes, I was healed.

I have a Catholic friend living in America who had been crippled for thirteen years. She had never been taught to read her Bible and so she didn't have much confidence in the idea that God could heal her, but eventually some friends persuaded her to go along to a renewal service. There all the Christians gathered round her and started to say, 'Sister, you can be healed. You can get out of that wheelchair and walk.' Well, she was terrified. She had some bones in her feet which wouldn't stop growing and her feet were incredibly painful and extremely deformed. She knew there was no way she could get up and walk. So she told them she wanted to be alone and talk to God. Pushing her wheelchair down to the front of the sanctuary, she found a huge crucifix on the wall, and her eyes were riveted by the feet of Jesus nailed to the Cross.

'Oh Lord,' she cried, 'Your feet are just like mine and yet You never once complained. I've spent thirteen years complaining. Please forgive me, Lord. I'm sorry, I didn't realise how You suffered and that I could have the privilege of suffering like You.'

She had never known God in a personal way, but her heart was right, and suddenly she found she just couldn't take her eyes off the feet of Jesus. The next thing she knew, a wonderful heat came over her head, down through her spine, through her legs and bathed her feet in tremendous warmth. As it did so, all the pain left and she cried out, 'Oh Lord, you've given me such grace to suffer. I can't even feel the pain!'

That gave God another problem because she was healed and didn't know it! She left the church that night still in her wheelchair, and three weeks later she was still thanking God she was able to suffer her disability without pain. Then one day her three little children got into a fight together and the two little boys came in with bleeding noses where the girl had bopped them both. Without thinking, the mother jumped out of her wheelchair to comfort them and they all shrieked, 'Mummy! Look at your feet!'

There she stood on two perfectly normal, healthy feet - and since that happened in the early 70's, she has never been back in a wheelchair.

Some years later, at an annual check-up, her doctor told her the devastating news that she had a malignant tumour in her womb.

'I'm very sorry but we'll need to remove the womb as soon as possible. You'll have to come in for surgery tomorrow.'

Despite her protests, he was adamant, so she went home to pray about the matter with her husband. Getting on her knees, she cried to the Lord, 'What shall I do, Lord?'

'Go to the prayer meeting on Thursday night.'

That meant postponing her hospital admission, but she went to the meeting where I happened to be preaching on Moses lifting up the bronze snake on the pole. All that had happened some years before came flooding back and she thought to herself, 'That was how I got healed last time. If I got healed then without knowing how it worked, now I can co-operate with God and receive again.' And she started to look towards Jesus, reaching out to Him in her spirit and really clinging to Him. Now I had no idea she was in the meeting, but just at that point I had the strangest word of knowledge I have ever had:

'It feels as though I have a six pound cancerous tumour in my womb.' I wasn't quite aware of what I was saying as this feeling was so real, a great bulge in the pit of my stomach. And then equally suddenly, the word came to me that somebody halfway back in the hall was being healed. Up shot her hand, and instantly the power of God went right through her and she lost six pounds in weight just like that.

Now her doctor was sitting next to her, and he was not amused. He came forward after the service and said,

'I like a good preacher, and I wouldn't put you in that category at all. When it comes to healing, why don't you leave it to the experts? After all, how can you heal anybody?'

'I can't,' I replied, 'I couldn't heal a fly with a headache, but Jesus can.'

Not surprisingly, he wasn't cheered up by that remark, and he urged the woman to come into the hospital for surgery the next day. She prayed about it and felt she should go in to prove to him there was nothing wrong. So she went in and he examined her for fifteen minutes with tears pouring down his face, saying,

'I can't find it! What's happened? I don't know how he did it. I don't know how he did it.'

To which she replied, 'He didn't do it, Jesus did.'

In the face of such evidence, the poor doctor had to give in and he, too, eventually committed his life to Christ.

What is it about looking to Jesus that is so effective? Again, I must emphasise I'm not talking about positive thinking or some mystical creative power released through the imagination. What I am encouraging you to discover is the redemption that is yours through the blood of Jesus:

> For you know that it was not with perishable things
> such as silver and gold that you were redeemed from
> the empty way of life handed down to you from your
> forefathers, **but with the precious blood of Christ.**
>
> (1 Peter, verses 18-19)

As I have meditated on this verse, the Lord has pointed out how Jesus' blood was shed from certain parts of His body, and each of His wounds bears a particular significance for us. In Luke 22, verses 42-43 we find Jesus praying in Gethsemane,

> 'Father, if you are willing, take this cup from me; yet
> not my will, but yours be done.' An angel from
> heaven appeared to him and strengthened him. And
> being in anguish, he prayed more earnestly, and his
> sweat was like drops of blood falling to the ground.

Jesus knew exactly what physical agony He would go through on the Cross. Crucifixions were a common sight along the roadside, and victims suffered a ghastly slow, torturing death, dying finally of suffocation after days of pushing up from the nails in the feet to try and draw breath. But His turmoil in the Garden of Gethsemane was not so much because of the physical pain He was to endure, but because He was already experiencing the mental and emotional agony of bearing the punishment for sin for all mankind, the supreme agony of complete separation from God. Terrible even for us to imagine, but for the Son of God, who had always enjoyed perfect fellowship with the Father... for the Light of the World to be plunged into utter darkness for our sake... Impossible to imagine the pressure which caused the capillaries across His forehead to burst and great drops of blood to mingle with His sweat. Apparently, there is an actual medical condition which verifies what happened and, significantly, it is only Luke, the doctor, who includes this detail in his narrative.

With this blood, Jesus was sweating away His very life and became so weak that God had to send an angel to strengthen Him before He died without ever reaching the Cross. What is the significance of the blood Jesus shed in Gethsemane? I believe one of the purposes of this particular agony was to help us find healing for emotional problems, depression, mental illness, mental handicap, migraines, and all types of brain disorder. Not that God compartmentalises healing in an 'eye for an eye and a tooth for a tooth' kind of way - but by concentrating on a specific aspect of Christ's suffering, we quicken our faith. What Jesus has done for us becomes more real and powerful as we use our imagination, or, rather, our spiritual perception, to see and understand that His pain was suffered so that we might be healed. Instead of looking vaguely at Jesus, we can zero in on specific aspects of His suffering which are relevant to our own problem;

> He was pierced for our transgressions, he was crushed for our iniquities; the punishment that brought us peace was upon him, **and by his wounds we are healed.**
>
> (Isaiah 53, verse 5)

By this shedding of Jesus' blood, God has already provided for our healing. 'It is finished,' Jesus cried out on the Cross. Nothing more needs to be done from God's point of view; we simply need to know how to receive that gift.

So, when I have a blinding migraine, I can look at Jesus sweating drops of blood in Gethsemane, and also to His head pierced by a crown of thorns, and I can say,

'Lord, I have this terrible pain in my head but thank You that You paid the price for me to be free of it for ever. Your head ached more than I could ever imagine. So I'm not going to trust in my pills, I'm going to trust in You. I'm not going to fight the devil; I'm not going to rebuke him all the time and give him all the attention. I'm just going to trust You and receive what You won for me.'

And you will be healed if you do this. You might 'die' a little because it might not be immediate, and you will have to cling on, denying your feelings and doubts, but that is what commitment is all about. Don't just glance at Jesus. **Fix your eyes on Him and don't let Him go.**

I first heard this message in 1978 from a friend of mine, Roger Price, and it started a whole new thought process in my mind. The first night I preached it, somebody came to the service with a retarded child. He could neither read nor write, he had no creative thought process, and was aggressive, hyperactive and allergic to all sorts of food. I didn't feel particularly full of faith, but I just prayed for him remembering the precious blood spilled from Jesus' forehead and asked God to heal him. There was no visible change there and then, and his parents took him home, but the next morning he started singing choruses, something he had never done before though he had been taken to church every Sunday for years. Not only that, but he came downstairs having dressed himself for the first time in his life. His parents, overjoyed, decided he must be healed and so they allowed him to eat all the food he was allergic to - with no adverse reaction at all. They sent him to school and within weeks he could read and write, and his teachers were flabbergasted. Six months later, they took him to the Children's Hospital and he passed every single test the specialist gave him. Today he loves Jesus and wants to be an evangelist.

On another occasion, I was asked to pray for the little daughter of the pastor in the house church where I had been invited to preach. Julie had Down's Syndrome and her poor physical growth and retarded mental development had caused her parents much sadness. Praying for a child with this condition isn't easy if you keep your eyes open. Cheerful though they so often are, everything about their physical aspect, their features and behaviour, makes you doubt that prayer will do any good. So I closed my eyes tightly, and tuned my inward sight to Jesus in the Garden of Gethsemane, Jesus pouring out His life at Calvary, Jesus wounded for our infirmities, and I prayed a very simple prayer.

Afterwards she was beaming so much it was hard to tell what had happened to her, but when her father bent to pick her up he nearly lifted her over his head, for instead of the dead weight she had always been because of her poor muscle control, she was now light as a feather! From that day, Julie began to improve dramatically. Next morning, she used a knife and fork for the first time. She began to reason things out and try again when things went wrong instead of giving up in frustration. She is reading now, is growing normally, and demonstrates her physical co-ordination by enthusiastically participating in games and sports with other children. This had not been an instantaneous restoration, but an ongoing healing. However, all who know the family rejoice that God is in control and working in this young life to make something of it which was not thought possible in her early years.

If we go on from Gethsemane to John Chapter 19, we find Pontius Pilate ordering Jesus to be flogged. This was a dreadful punishment. Jesus would have been strapped by His hands to the whipping post, and an instrument like a cat-of-nine-tails, with nine strips of leather ending in pieces of glass, would have lashed His back. We don't know how many times they scourged Him, but it would have been at least thirty nine, as Jewish law said forty save one, and Roman law had no limit. But what we do know is that His flesh was so stripped away that His back looked like a ploughed field, for we read in Psalm 129, verse 3, 'Ploughmen have ploughed my back and made their furrows long.'

Why did Jesus have to endure that terrible pain of having His back torn to shreds? Again, it was so that by His wounds we might be healed. His blood was shed for our **physical** healing. If you are suffering from some back problem, try picturing the torn back of Jesus, and see His blood flowing out to give you life. In fact, if you are sick in any way, always meditate on these things, or if you are praying for someone who is ill, always minister the Word to them first for,

> Faith comes from hearing the message, and the
> message is heard through the Word of Christ.
>
> (Romans 10, verse 17)

The suffering of Jesus teaches us to have faith not in the laying on of hands, not in our faith or that of a famous preacher, not in a prayer, or a sacrament or a ceremony, but **in Jesus.** It was Jesus who sweated drops of blood in Gethsemane; Jesus who went to the whipping post and endured His back being lashed raw; Jesus who had His coat stripped from Him and a crown of thorns pressed onto His head; Jesus who was thrown against a piece of wood and had nails driven through His hands and feet; Jesus who hung in excruciating agony on the Cross with a spear wound through His side; Jesus who cried, 'My God, my God, why have you forsaken me?' so that we could be healed of our rejection and insecurity. Jesus. Jesus was our substitute in every way. He was rejected so that we might know security; He was made sin so that we might have His righteousness; He was a man of sorrows so that we could have His joy; He died so that we might have His life; His body was broken so that ours could be made whole.

Just receive. It sounds so simple but some of us don't know how to receive. We only feel comfortable if we are giving or doing. We need to look at some of the ground-work we might have to do before we get to the point of being able to receive our healing.

Chapter Eight

How to Receive your Healing

Assuming you have understood the provision God has made for your physical health through His New Covenant, and seeking, with His help, to renew your mind, there are five steps which may help in preparing you to receive your healing. They are not necessarily chronological, nor even essential, because God doesn't work according to a man-made set of rules, but if followed, they will put you in a position of faith and expectancy.

1. Confess your sin

Confess your sins to each other and pray for each other so that you may be healed. The prayer of a righteous man is powerful and effective.

(James 5, verse 16)

The problem with unconfessed sin is not so much that God withholds blessing, as that a tender conscience or a feeling of guilt make it very difficult for us to expect to receive anything from God. It's not **impossible** to get healed while still walking in sin because God's grace **abounds** to us, but it is a lot easier if we obey God's commands, repent of our sins, confess any harboured resentment or bitterness, and walk in the light with God and our fellow men. The result of such action is that our prayer becomes 'powerful and effective' as we become an open channel for the full force of God's love. As a caution, I would say that we shouldn't become self-analytical and grope around for hidden sins or wrongful attitudes. If we have an honest and open relationship with God, we can keep looking to Him and His light will illuminate any dark areas in our life.

2. Praise God for your sickness

This may seem a strange thing to do, and I don't mean that we should welcome sickness, for we have already established that all illness comes from the devil. But sometimes we are so bound up with fear about our condition that we completely identify ourselves with the illness. It is as if the sickness has got us, rather than us having the sickness. 'I'm a diabetic,' we say, rather than 'I have diabetes'. And resentment about our condition or anger towards God will also make it difficult for us to receive our healing from Him.

In about 1974, I was travelling in Copenhagen and was booked to speak to some of the leaders in Denmark. When I arrived at the conference it was a shock to discover that the two other main ministries had cancelled, and that now I was to be the main speaker. Shock is probably an understatement; I was terrified! At the first seminar, I was in such a state of panic confronted by this sea of pastors' faces that I started to stammer really badly. This presented all sorts of problems for the interpreter and it was quickly decided to turn the meeting over to prayer. The meeting was a disaster from a teaching point of view, and afterwards I crawled off to a room upstairs and got down on the floor before God, desperate:

'Lord, You've got to do something; I can't cope with this.'

And God spoke to me:

'You have never praised Me for your stammer.'

I was staggered. The very thought was not only ridiculous but out of the question.

'No,' I replied, 'I don't believe in the "prison-to-praise" nonsense.'

And God said, 'That's very interesting, but you have never praised Me for your stammer.'

'No, and I'm not going to start now.'

'You've never praised Me for your stammer.'

Now when God repeats Himself at least three times, I know I'm not going to win! Either I must do what He says, or put up with the situation, because He's not going to change His mind and give an easy way out. Gritting my teeth, with everything inside me screaming out that I shouldn't be doing this, with thoughts whirling round my head like, 'The devil sent the stammer, not God, so why should I praise God for it?' I began to thank Him for my situation. I was honest with God and I think it might have sounded almost sarcastic because it seemed so ludicrous to my own understanding:

'Lord, thank You that You could have healed me years ago, but You chose not to. I thank You for letting me stammer.'

And after about twenty minutes of a **real sacrifice** of praise being drawn out of me because nothing within me felt like giving thanks, I discovered that the embarrassment, the self-pity, the resentment and the fear associated with my stammer had all disappeared. You see, my fear had been that although I knew God could heal me, yet maybe He wouldn't - because it was my thorn in the flesh, perhaps, or a Job situation. I had friends, too, who said it was because I had a ministry that I suffered this stammer - to keep me humble or dependent or something. But I also have a wife (who is very down-to-earth, and a very great help to me spiritually) and she pointed out that Jesus had a ministry and He didn't stammer!

But I had been dominated by this fear that God wouldn't want to heal me, and God's command to praise Him was a test of my submission to His Lordship. So long as my stammer and my fear ruled my life, God was restricted in what He could do in me. But after I made this sacrifice of praise, reinstating God to His rightful position as my Lord and King, all the negative feelings about my stammer left. All that remained was the stammer! But now I was a person who stammered, not a stammerer. For over thirty years my whole identity had been bound up in the fact that I was a stammerer. It wasn't just my mouth that stammered, it was my hair, my eyebrows, my big toe, everything. I was one big stammer. And through these minutes of praise, God was able to reach down into the mental and emotional problems which formed the root of my disability and start to heal me. God healed me from inside outwards, a process needing my co-operation in confession of resentment and self-pity, and in a sacrifice of praise to set me free from my fear. That healing has taken several years, but now I simply hesitate occasionally rather than stammer.

3. Build your faith

One famous preacher described this process as getting pregnant in the spirit. Faith for your healing may start as a tiny seed within you, but as you feed it, this seed will grow and grow until the unseen, hoped-for thing becomes a reality. We can feed our faith in several ways:

i)   To remove your doubts and your dependence on your own understanding, **pray and praise in tongues.** There is nothing like it for lifting up your heart and giving you joy and confidence, enlarging your vision of what God can do, and getting rid of your negative thoughts. Look at the effect praise had on Abraham:

> Against all hope, Abraham in hope believed and so became the father of many nations, just as it had been said of him, 'So shall your offspring be'. Without weakening in his faith, he faced the fact that his body was as good as dead - since he was about a hundred years old - and that Sarah's womb was also dead. Yet he did not waver through unbelief regarding the promise of God **but was strengthened in his faith and gave glory to God,** being fully persuaded that God had power to do what he had promised.
>
> (Romans 4, verses 18-24)

Praying in tongues and praising God form part of the process of renewing the mind, as we have already seen. By doing this, our spirit is allowed to control our mind, rather than our minds controlling us. Supernatural things start becoming natural to us. I was always brought up to believe that Christians could automatically hear God's voice, but if I was honest I had to admit that He didn't seem to be speaking to me. It took me eighteen months of speaking in tongues three hours a day, one and a half hours in the car to work and one and a half hours home, before I could hear God's voice. Eighteen months of washing my mind with the Spirit to get rid of all the doubts, fears and scepticism of twenty eight years of living by my human limitations. I became a Christian at the age of twenty three but it was five years later before I really started to feed off the tree of life myself, though I was ministering healing to others who were more open to God long before I personally experienced healing.

ii) **Listening to tapes and reading books on healing** will quicken your faith still further. Even if you have read a particular book ten times before, you will find something new to encourage you on the eleventh reading. Our minds are being bombarded every moment by such negative or unhelpful suggestions that it is only sensible to counteract their influence with words of faith.

iii) **Meditating on God's Word** will not only increase our faith but may also be the direct channel of God's healing when it is anointed by His Spirit. As we read in Proverbs 4, verses 20-22,

> My son, pay attention to what I say;
> Listen closely to my words.
> Do not let them out of your sight,
> Keep them within your heart;
> **For they are life to those who find them
> and health to a man's whole body.**

Meditating on Scripture doesn't mean merely reading our daily quota of verses and absorbing it simply with our minds. Nor does it mean making our mind a blank and waiting for something to drop into it. To meditate on the Word means to **chew** on it, to feed on it:

'Man does not live on bread alone but on every word that comes from the mouth of God.' In fact, the Hebrew carries the sense of **regurgitating** - taking the Word down, digesting it, bringing it back up, chewing on it again and taking it down, like a cow chewing the cud. And eventually the Word becomes part of us, just as food is converted into energy and builds our muscles, renews our body tissues, strengthens our bones.

For example, if I were going to meditate on 'by his wounds, you have been healed,' (1 Peter 2, verse 24) I would first take the words, 'by his' and dwell on them for five or ten minutes: 'Lord, thank You that all my healing comes from You; only through **Your** perfect sacrifice can I have life...' Then I would move on to the word 'stripes' and would picture Jesus strapped against the whipping post being scourged for my healing, Jesus bleeding on the Cross so that I could be free from pain... Next I would think about the word, 'you'. That means **me**! 'Thank you, Lord, that You didn't simply do this for everyone else in the world but You did it for **me**, too. Your love for me is so great; You care for me individually, personally...' Then I would spend about ten more minutes meditating on 'have been', because this is the difference between being sick and being healed: **it has already been accomplished!** Jesus did everything necessary for my health nearly 2,000 years ago. By the time I get to the word 'healed', I'm generally strong enough in faith to believe it.

Jeremiah said,

> When your words came, I ate them;
> they were my joy and my heart's delight.
> (Jeremiah 15, verse 16)

And a joyful heart is 'good medicine' (Proverbs 17, verse 22).

As Paul and Silas praised God in prison, with their backs raw from being whipped and their feet in stocks, joy filled their hearts and the power of the Lord fell with such force that it caused an earthquake. The prison doors flew open, and the jailer threw himself trembling at their feet, begging to know how he could be saved. So not only were Paul and Silas freed from bondage and eased of their physical suffering through their praise, but the father and all his family found salvation.

> Then they spoke the word of the Lord to him and to
> all the others in his house. At that hour of the night
> the jailer took them and washed their wounds; then
> immediately he and all his family were baptised.
> (Acts 16, verses 32-33)

So we see how powerful and comprehensive is the healing that lies within the anointed word.

Other verses that are helpful to meditate upon are:

> He forgives all my sins, and heals all my diseases.
> (Psalm 103, verse 3)

> For you who revere my name, the sun of
> righteousness will rise with healing in its wings.
> (Malachi 4, verse 2)

He took our infirmities and carried our diseases.

(Matthew 8, verse 17)

I will heal my people and will let them enjoy abundant peace and security.

(Jeremiah 33, verse 6)

iv) Because of the value of meditation, it is a good idea to **seek the Lord daily for a word from the Bible** for our situation. The children of Israel had to gather fresh manna each day to sustain them or else it decayed and produced worms. So we need to feed off fresh words each day and not rely on yesterday's promise because it will become stale and lose its anointing. We don't have to receive a **new** word every day but to receive it in a **fresh way.**

During the Queen's Jubilee, I had to take a healing service and just before it I developed a prolapsed bowel - not the easiest of afflictions when you have to preach for hours. I was in agony standing up, and in worse pain sitting down, so I was in real trouble. My first thought was to cancel the healing service and get myself into hospital, but then I considered that Jesus didn't do that so neither could I. Then I decided that God would surely heal me as soon as the service started, so I staggered up to preach - and endured three and a half hours of acute pain, hardly able to move. When I crawled home to my wife, I climbed into bed feeling very sorry for myself and said weakly, 'Please pray for me, darling'.

Her reply was not exactly a blessing at the time.

'There's no point. You know too much. If you are going to preach healing, you'd better live in it. Get a word from the Lord.'

Great encouragement! Well, it was obvious I wasn't going to get any sympathy so I had no choice but to seek the Lord myself.

'Lord, I'm desperate,' I prayed. 'I'm tired, I'm in pain, I'm fed up, and I feel like I'm dying. Please speak to me.' So I opened my Bible and the first verse I read just shot out of the page and hit me:

'I will come and heal you.'

This was tremendous! A 'rhema' word, a God-breathed word that flew like an arrow straight to my spirit and made my faith leap up. All the nagging doubts and fears about whether I should have been sensible and gone to hospital suddenly died. I went to sleep that night like a baby.

The next morning I woke up with the thought, 'I must be healed'. One movement and I realised I wasn't. The pain was still there and stayed with me all day. I couldn't understand why I wasn't able to live on the previous day's word. But like the manna in the wilderness, on the second day it was full of worms. Not just worms, but **snakes** of doubt and unbelief. Did I really get that from God? Was that really what He was saying? **When** would He come and heal me? It was hopeless. I had to get on my knees that evening and seek God for another word. Another Scripture fired me with faith and expectancy once more. Next morning I still wasn't healed, but now I had gone from doubt to faith, and I just had to go from that place on into deeper faith, from glory to glory, until I could receive my healing. I praised the Lord, I spoke in tongues, I sang in the Spirit, and as I was in the presence of God I said, 'Lord, speak to me again. Send me Your word.'

I could hardly believe my eyes when a verse seemed to leap from my Bible:

> Your health will spring forth speedily; I the Lord am
> your rear reward.

What a word for a prolapsed bowel! I was so filled with joy that I just forgot about my problem, and it wasn't until the next day when I was halfway across the Atlantic in a jumbo jet that I suddenly realised I had been sitting in one place for four hours and I had no pain. I couldn't tell you when I had been healed exactly, but at some point the Word had passed from my spirit into my body and brought life and health.

4. Enter into the high praises of God

Doubt and negative thoughts do not come merely from our unrenewed mind; they are often fed to us by the enemy, and one of the best ways to defeat these attacks is to **enter into the high praises of God** (Psalm 149, verse 6). When the high praises of God are in our mouths, we are taking up a 'double-edged sword' against the enemy. We are entering into spiritual warfare. For God inhabits the praises of His people, and when we enthrone Him in our praise and worship, Satan is cut down from the position of power he has usurped. The high praises of God declare to the principalities and powers of darkness that we are not under their dominion, that we belong to Jesus Christ and through our God we will do valiantly.

Now the 'high praise' of God is not a gentle chorus or a sweet melody in the Spirit. It is the people of God joining together and shouting the glory of God into the face of the obstacle. Most of us find this idea very difficult because we want to be seen as normal, decent and respectable people. Nothing too extrovert or extreme. But if we don't shout the praise of God sometimes, we can be gripped by fear about our sickness. A shout of triumph closes the door on fear and renders the powers of darkness ineffective, for its purpose is to 'bind their kings with fetters, their nobles with shackles of iron' (Psalm 149, verse 8).

I have had two wonderful examples of this recently. A pastor telephoned me and asked me to come and pray for a little seven month old baby who was in hospital on a life-support machine. He said he felt so condemned because he didn't have faith to pray for the child himself. And I had to reply that quite frankly I didn't have faith for it either, so the only thing I could suggest was to call the church together and spend two hours in high praise of God; to declare to the principalities and powers that Jesus Christ is Lord; and to put the singers out in front of the troops to inspire the army and demoralise the enemy. The whole church gathered at once and praised into the face of the devil, prophetic praise stripping him of his power in the situation and making a pathway for God to move.

Some time later I received another telephone call from this pastor who described how he had gone round to the hospital the morning after this spiritual warfare of high praise to discover all the machines switched off and the baby lying peacefully asleep. A short time later, she was at home and perfectly well. Now if I had seen with my own eyes that tiny baby wired up to machines, with tubes and drips everywhere, my faith would have died on the spot, but the high praise of God had removed all our doubts and broken the devil's hold so that God was able to heal her.

Following that event, I was up in Edinburgh where a lovely Christian lady was desperately ill with systemic lupas. She was so close to the Lord that I was a bit concerned she would just slip away to be with Him. However she didn't want to die, and so the whole church came together and praised and praised far into the night. That Sunday, she stood up in the service and testified to her complete healing and restoration, though no-one had actually prayed for her at all. Today she is perfectly fit and healthy, a spoil of war if you like, taken by force from the enemy's stronghold through the high praises of God.

5. Rest and Receive

I was travelling in Sweden some years ago and one day I was invited with another minister to a certain lady's house for coffee and cakes. On the table was a plate of cakes which looked rather like English buns - not terribly inspiring but all right if there is nothing else. What caught my eye, though, was a cake sitting right in the centre of all the scones. It was a delicious-looking cake, about four inches across and an inch high, piled high with lashings of fresh whipped cream and topped with green marzipan. This was appropriately called a 'Princess cake' and was certainly the most royal-looking confection I had ever seen. I could just imagine that delicious marzipan melting in my mouth, and closing my eyes quickly I claimed that cake in the name of Jesus. When I opened my eyes, the Swedish pastor had already reached out and taken the cake plus a couple of buns and had placed them calmly on his own plate. I was horrified. How ill-mannered could he possibly be? But I discovered soon afterwards that Swedish custom was more biblical than British custom. In Britain, we regard it as good manners to take just one cake at a time and always the one nearest you whether you like it or not. But in Sweden you take the cakes you like best and help yourself to all you want.

When I discovered this, I realised there was a great difference between claiming and receiving. I had bound that cake to the plate in the name of Jesus, but it was the Swedish pastor who had reached out his hand and taken it. Most people are like that at a healing service. When a word of knowledge comes that there is a person with an obvious and serious complaint, the individual concerned will turn around to see if anyone else has the same affliction, unwilling to claim the healing in case it belongs to somebody else. But in Africa, ten people shout immediately, 'That's me,' and they all get healed! In Britain we are so polite and reserved, but I wonder if that isn't really just a cover-up for unbelief. Are we really saying that we don't have enough faith to be healed, so we will pass it on to someone else who has the same problem?

According to Psalm 23, God prepares a table before us in the presence of our enemies. When we are attacked by sickness, God spreads a table with gifts of healing and says, 'Help yourself'. It isn't waitress-service in the Kingdom of God, it is self-service! We reach out our hand of faith and receive our healing. How do we know we have received? Well, it is rather like being pregnant. When a woman conceives, she doesn't look any different at first, but her thoughts change, and her conversation with her husband changes because they are now living with the certainty they, are going to have a family. When we receive the 'living Word of God' a seed of faith takes root within us and we have a confidence that we are going to see the fruit. So we must not simply close our eyes and claim our healing, but reach out and take the word down into our very being. When we are **claiming**, we are often striving, gritting our teeth and almost willing a miracle to happen. When we **receive**, we enter into **rest.**

I had a wonderful illustration of this a few years ago. I was speaking in a large church in America and it was very solemn and reverent - a bit like preaching in a graveyard really. I was talking about the man with the withered arm in Mark 3, and suddenly, through the hushed air, came the sound of snoring. I've had various comments on my preaching but no-one had ever gone to sleep before! At the back of the church, a young woman had nodded off in her seat and was peacefully snoring away. The man next to her was very embarrassed and, giving her a nudge, whispered, 'Sister, wake up'. Bewildered, she struggled to open her eyes - just as I was explaining that when God tells us to do something we must do it, having reached the point in the story where Jesus commands the disabled man, 'Stretch out your withered hand!' Half-asleep, half-awake, not trying to understand how it all works - the perfect position in which to get healed - the poor girl thought I was speaking to her, so she stretched out her shrivelled arm which hadn't grown since she was four and a half years old, and suddenly it started to grow and grow until it was completely straight and strong except for one little finger which was still bent over. Tears streaming down her face, she came running out to the front, crying, 'Look, look!' I didn't realise what had happened, so I simply replied, 'Yes, I've got two like that'.

'No, you don't realise that when I came in, it was just useless. One day when I was about four years old I was playing outside our house and ran in the way of my father's car as he was turning into the driveway. As a result my arm was badly crushed.'

This young woman had a non-Christian husband and she went straight home, picked up the baby with the arm that had been damaged and waited for him to come back. There was no problem at all about him receiving Christ...

Having established all these principles, we need to add that everybody will get healed in a slightly different way. And we may find it frustrating that non-Christians seem to get healed comparatively easily, while those more mature in the faith will sometimes struggle. The reason for this may be, first, that God heals the non-Christian to prove that Jesus is Lord, but sometimes heals the older Christian only when he or she proves to **Him** that Jesus is Lord. From those to whom much is given, much is also expected and it may be necessary for you to act out your faith.

Second, and linked to this, is the way in which the church is divided in a sense into three groups:

> I write to you, dear children, because your sins have been forgiven on account of his name.
> I write to you, fathers, because you have known him who is from the beginning.
> I write to you, young men, because you have overcome the evil one.
> I write to you, dear children, because you have known the Father.
> I write to you, fathers, because you have known him who is from the beginning.
> I write to you, young men, because you are strong and the word of God abides in you, and you have overcome the evil one.
>
> (1 John 2, verses 12-14)

From this it seems that God distinguishes three groups; not Catholic, Protestant and Pentecostal, but small children, young men and fathers. I don't think these are rigid categories, though, as it is possible to be a baby in one realm and a father in another, to have faith for miracles on the one hand, but to find a consistent walk of holiness and discipline hard on the other. But generally, our experience of God puts us at one of these levels.

If you're a baby in Christ, you know your sins are forgiven and you have come into a wonderful realisation of God's Father-love towards you; you are vulnerable and weak so God will feed you on spiritual milk, and you would be sensible to do everyone a favour and get your illnesses and your other problems sorted out early on because God will oblige you amazingly.

If you are a young man in Christ, you have begun to experience the power of God's Word in defeating the enemy. Instead of relying on your feelings, God has been teaching you to live by His promises and to feed off the tree of life rather than knowledge. Consequently, it may be harder to appropriate your healing because God asks you to believe you have received your healing before you feel it; you believe what God says and not what your body is telling you. This doesn't mean going around saying, 'I haven't really got cancer, I've just got the symptoms,' because you might as well say you have the real thing. We are not talking about mind over matter, but the authority of the Word of God.

If you are a father in the faith, you are not so much in the battle as in the victory. You know God not simply as Father, but as the Almighty One, the King and Creator; more than having a mere intellectual understanding of spiritual things, you have a deep knowledge of God Himself, of His thoughts and ways. If you have come to this point of maturity, you may be wasting your time asking someone to pray for you, because God may expect you to receive your healing through your communion faith with Him.

Let me give you three brief examples. I went to an Anglican church some years ago which was just on the brink of renewal. On the first evening, lots of people got baptised in the Spirit and spoke in tongues and on the second evening people began to manifest all sorts of spiritual gifts which they had never experienced before. Then on the third evening, an unsaved woman was carried into the church with a severely damaged back, hip and leg. In the middle of preaching, I gave out a word which had suddenly come to me:

'I believe God is going to heal someone right now to prove to them that Jesus Christ is Lord.'

And straightaway she found she was healed, after years of agony from an incurable condition - not only wonderfully healed, but wonderfully saved.

On another occasion, I was in a Baptist church in America where I had to pray for the pastor, who was in a steel corset because of a disintegrating spine. He had been filled with the Spirit for several years and was a mature Christian. I prayed for him and then said,

'Brother, you are going to have to act on your faith. Bend down and touch your toes.'

He looked at me as if I was mad, but after a few moments' thought, he gingerly bent down - and discovered **after** he had obeyed God that there was no longer anything wrong with his back. He was overjoyed but I felt I should warn him that after a few days he might be challenged. (That isn't always the case; beware the theology which gets blessed for three days and expects the devil on the fourth! With that sort of faith, he is bound to pay a visit.)

But sure enough, four days later, the phone rang in the early morning and a weak voice said,

'For three days my back has been wonderful, Ian, but now I'm lying in bed and I can't move. What should I do?'

'Well, do you believe you are healed?' I asked.

He mumbled into the phone, 'Er yes, I do'.

(In fact, I don't honestly think he did at that point, but he said the right thing.) So I asked the Lord what he should do and straightaway into my mind flashed a sort of cartoon picture of him doing a somersault out of bed. 'This will either kill him or cure him,' I thought. 'I'm glad I have a travelling ministry.'

'Well, brother,' I announced, 'God has shown me that you are to do a somersault out of bed.'

There was a strangled gasp at the other end of the phone and then he put the receiver on the table and there was a silence. Next I heard a thud and crash and in a moment his breathless voice came over the phone:

'Oh brother, I wouldn't have believed it if I hadn't experienced it. I'm healed!'

He was a young man in the faith: he had been tested and had overcome the wicked one, and he wouldn't be tested on it again.

I know somebody who was involved in a car crash which seriously damaged his spinal column. As he lay semi-paralysed in hospital, the Word of God came to him with a powerful anointing: 'By His stripes, I was healed.' In that moment he knew he had received his healing and over the next few days he lay there, still unable to move, speaking out what he knew in his heart: 'By His stripes, I was healed.' His testimony now is that for five days, his body told him that he was paralysed, but at the end of that time it finally submitted to God's Word, and he was completely restored to strength. This man had earlier proved healing in another dramatic way. He himself was a well-known preacher, a real father in the faith, and one summer he was holding a large evangelistic tent crusade. While he was helping to take down the huge tent, he slipped and broke his ankle. He actually heard it crack, pain shot up through his foot, and his ankle, swollen like a balloon, hung limp and useless. Refusing medical help, he lay on his bed and talked with God:

'Lord, you know I'm the only one who can take this tent down. Just speak to me and give me a word. That's all I need, Lord. A word from You is quite sufficient.'

And God said to him, 'Immediately his feet and ankle bones received strength'.

So he thought, 'That's a wonderful word, Lord. Thank You.'

And he put his foot on the ground - to find searing pain shooting up his leg, so he quickly put it up on the bed again.

'Lord, say something else. This is too much.'

And God replied, 'I said, "Immediately his feet and ankle bones received strength." '

The man thought about this for a while, and then asked hopefully, 'God, aren't you going to say anything else?'

And God said, 'No. "Immediately his feet and ankles received strength." '

Now, as I said, this man was a father in the faith and I wouldn't necessarily recommend anyone else trying this unless they are as sure of God as he was.

'Lord,' he said at last, 'I know that You spoke. My spirit witnesses with Your Spirit that I've heard from You. So unless You stop me (and I'm **very** open for You to stop me, Lord), I'm going to count to ten and then I'm going to jump out of bed onto my broken leg. Now if You

Chapter Nine

Some Major Reasons why People are not Healed

In discussing the physical aspect of healing, we must remember that God's prime concern is wholeness. The Holy Spirit comes into our spirits at the new birth, restores our souls through many different dealings, and also quickens our mortal bodies. We know that **God** wants us to enjoy all His benefits, so what is wrong when people we pray for are **not** healed? Sometimes we may feel full of faith, the anointing of God seems to be with us, and there is even a powerful sense of God's presence, yet the sickness remains. Most of us just withdraw, and conclude that perhaps it wasn't God's time, or maybe it wasn't His will. Usually, though, we feel we have failed somehow, and the experience makes us reluctant to ask God why we have not received physical healing. I used to just accept that I didn't understand, but several years ago I felt I should seek God for specific reasons why some people are not healed, and He gave me eleven main ones.

It's not good enough sending people away with the old cliché, 'You didn't have enough faith'. If we have real love and compassion for people who are suffering, if we have genuine concern for the health of the Lord's body, we will give them support and encouragement; we will provide shepherding and counselling for them; and we will see it through, if we can. Now I'm not suggesting that we should cross-examine people as if they were being interrogated. That can be unhelpful at best, and dangerously destructive at worst, leading people into introspection and condemnation. But with wisdom and discernment, we can fit the right key into the lock and allow God's power to flow to them. In the course of our ministry we have experienced that the most common blockages that prevent healing taking place are:

1. Fear

Fear can present a blockage to healing, and it may take several forms. Some people are afraid that if they trust themselves to God for healing and it doesn't work, they will lose what little relationship with Him they feel they are clinging to at the start. Having been let down by others in the past, they fear being hurt by God in the same way, and so to protect their vulnerability, subconsciously they do not give themselves wholly to God. If these people are able to receive His love, they can be set free from the fear of opening themselves up to Him.

For others, the deepest fear is of the sickness itself, and ultimately, of death. They diagnose their symptoms as being those of a serious illness and do not even respond to assurances from the doctor that the complaint is minor. Some people are dominated by a fear of cancer and interpret every ailment as the 'Big C'. And others receive doctors' verdicts as death sentences, and are so afraid they are going to die that they cannot receive the word of life.

There are perhaps three ways of getting rid of fear. The first is to receive the peace of God through His Word:

> God did not give us a spirit of fear, but of power, of love and of a sound mind.
>
> (2 Timothy 1, verse 7)

To be honest, I find very often this alone doesn't work as the person is usually so bound up with fear that he finds it impossible to respond to the Lord. In which case, it might be necessary to cast out a spirit of fear, and this may be successful - unless, perhaps, the person is a very mature Christian! Then there isn't such a simple solution. Or, at least, it is simple in a sense but it requires much more effort and self-denial, as this illustration shows.

Whilst we were travelling and ministering in America, having had numerous meetings, we arrived at the house of some good friends feeling tired and looking forward to some rest and relaxation. It is often at these times that the devil seeks to attack our minds and our bodies. Rosemary recalls:

I was having a shower when I noticed a lump in my breast that took me by surprise. Could it be just a benign cyst or was it a malignant growth? Immediately a conflict began in my mind: God's Word versus the enemy's thoughts and fears. Pictures of hospitalisation, bouquets of flowers, even death suddenly loomed in my mind. At least I would become the centre of everyone's attention but I also had the thoughts of how my family would cope without a wife and mother. I decided this was no place to fantasize, this was reality. I had proved the healing power of Jesus before and He had never let me down, but now I needed living faith again. I decided to tell Ian and that together we would stand against this attack on my body. We agreed together in accordance with Matthew 18, verse 19.

That night I lay down in bed but sleep did not come easily; I knew the truth of 'By His stripes I was healed' and 'Jesus Himself took all my infirmities and carried away my sickness' but I had to bring all my thoughts and Satan's lies into subjection to the Word of God. I began by thanking God for healing me nearly two thousand years ago and saying to myself, 'Surely goodness and mercy shall follow me all the days of my life' (Psalm 23).

Then as I was putting my thoughts on Jesus, I heard Him speak to me. Just what I needed! He said, 'I love you too much to let that deadly sickness happen to you'. That settled it for me, God's breathed word was my final authority! I said, 'Thank You Lord' and refused to think any other thoughts as I fell asleep. In the morning I refused the natural inclination to touch my body and feel for the presence of the lump. I did this deliberately so that my senses would have no room for doubting, thereby allowing my faith to grow stronger. You can tell when you are through the crisis of faith because you no longer want to look at your body 'to see' if you have been healed. You look because you know! **We** do not have to get rid of a physical problem, for as we receive the Word of God it does its own work, becomes flesh in our experience and heals us. Jesus' stripes have paid the price for our healing and when we stop being occupied with our sicknesses, realising God's love for us, the Holy Spirit brings to reality what we are believing for.

After a week or so had passed I accidentally prodded myself where the lump had been and discovered that once more Jesus had triumphed as there was no sign whatsoever of the lump. Faith in God's Word always works and brings results.

Rosemary's experience illustrates the third way to get rid of fear, as found in Ephesians 5, verse 20:

...always giving thanks to God the Father for everything, in the name of the Lord Jesus Christ.

We discussed the power of praise in a previous chapter and it really is the way out of the prison of fear. Many of us realise that truth, but applying it is much harder. We read in Ephesians 5, verse 14:

Wake up, O sleeper, rise from the dead and Christ will shine on you.

Most of us know that waking up doesn't present too much of a problem, but **getting** up is another matter.So it is with spiritual truths. After we have realised the truth of God's Word, we need to **walk in it,** and **then** Christ will give us revelation - we will see the fruit of our faith in our experience.

In the same passage, Paul goes on to say that we must 'redeem the time' or make the most of every opportunity. Don't wait until your sickness is terminal before you seek prayer because time is always against you - 'the days are evil'. At the first symptom, pray and get ministry, because if you leave it, and try the doctors, try the health food shop, try the chemists, by the time you get to God your condition is desperate and you are terrified.

So if this is your problem, if you are full of fear and no-one seems to have any answers or any hope, don't waste time wondering what the will of God is. His will is stated clearly in the next verse in this passage:

> **Be filled with the Spirit.** Speak to one another with psalms, hymns and spiritual songs. Sing and make music in your heart to the Lord, always giving thanks to God the Father for everything, in the name of our Lord Jesus Christ.
>
> (Ephesians 5, verses 18-20)

It says in Proverbs 23, verse 23 that we should **buy** the truth, so there is a price to be paid for walking in God's ways. It will mean denying your natural mind, denying your feelings; it may hurt your pride. Praising God for your problem means dying a little for it is only in losing your life that you come into His.

2. Misbelief

A misbelief is something you believe that has no foundation and truth. For instance a man might say, 'I believe God has given me this illness as a thorn in the flesh'.

Well, I would reply to him, 'Really, brother? Fantastic! Let me sit at your feet.'

He might not have expected quite that reaction so I would explain to him that Paul had a thorn in the flesh and he wrote a large portion of the New Testament. Not only that, but the thorn, the messenger of Satan (probably a person not a physical affliction anyway, but we won't go into that here) was sent to him to stop him being too proud of the fact that he had been transported to Paradise and heard 'inexpressible things', 'surpassingly great revelations'. So it would be fair to say that **most** of us don't qualify for a thorn at all.

Another misbelief is that 'God is teaching us something through this sickness'. Well, that may be a gracious by-product, but it is the Holy Spirit who is our teacher, not Satan, who is the author of all sicknesses. If we hold this misbelief, then when illness strikes, instead of taking authority over it and standing on our Calvary covenant, we go into ourselves and start wondering, 'What is God showing me? What have I done wrong? What new revelation is God trying to give me?'

By the time I find out, I'm almost dead. Because if we look inwards, we will always find something wrong, and the devil will keep feeding us new problems - this could be sorted out, this should be adjusted. But we are told to look to Jesus. If we have this misbelief, we may never get to the point of being able to receive prayer, because we will never be sure if God has finished showing us all His deep truths.

I went to see some good friends in the United States, and a bad 'flu bug was going round. The pastor's wife had been in bed for three or four weeks and was quite ill so I went along to see her. Going into her room, I said, 'I've come to pray for you'.

But she didn't seem to hear.

'Oh Ian,' she cried, 'I don't know what the Lord is saying in all this'.

'I do,' I replied. 'Nothing!'

'How can you say that?' she asked angrily. 'You're far too simplistic.'

'Well, I believe Jesus was,' I had to answer. 'Every time He met the devil, He had one word for him: "Go!" A very simple approach. And every time somebody was sick, He healed them. A very simple approach. God isn't teaching you anything - except how to get well.' But she was so convinced that she should be learning something more profound that, sadly, I had to go away without praying for her.

I've heard other people say that their sickness is a symbol of a problem in the Body of Christ: if I have a bad toe, perhaps it means that the church isn't walking right. Or, there is still sin in the Body of Christ, and my illness is a reflection of it. Yet there is no scriptural pattern for these claims.

Someone else might say, 'I've sinned, brother Ian, and God is burning the sin out of me'. No, the **devil** pays his wages, and he is the most faithful employer in the world. The wages of sin is death, but the gift of God is eternal life through Jesus Christ, our Lord. God doesn't pay wages, He gives gifts. The devil makes people sick, but God sent Jesus to heal them. A girl once came to me for prayer but insisted that she couldn't be healed as she had venereal disease.

'Why can't you be healed?' I asked. 'Have you repented?'

'Oh yes,' she replied, 'years ago, but I can't be healed; it's incurable.'

When I explained to her that God didn't hold our past against us, that once forgiven it was forgotten by Him, and that Jesus had triumphed over the devil by dying and rising for us, I was able to pray for her and she was healed. Soon afterwards she conceived and gave birth to a beautiful, healthy baby, which was a miracle in itself.

To believe that your illness is inherited is another common misbelief. We touched before on the verses in Ezekiel 18, verses 1-4:

> The Word of the Lord came to me:
> 'What do you mean by quoting the proverb about the
> land of Israel:
> "The fathers eat sour grapes,
> and the children's teeth are set on edge"?
> 'As surely as I live,' declares the Sovereign Lord,
> 'you will no longer quote this proverb in Israel.'

Now I know there is hereditary disease, but we shouldn't treat it as a curse, the result of our great great grandmother having wandered round London on the end of a broomstick. If we think like this, we do away with the efficacy of the new birth; we are denying the power that is in the blood of Jesus. We don't need healing but **revelation**, for Jesus took His blood up to heaven, presented it before His Father, and sprinkled it on the mercy seat of God. And the blood of Jesus speaks to God of better things than the cry of the law, the blood of animals that was sprinkled on the mercy seat of the Old Covenant. I am justified by that blood; I am born again by that blood. I am not who I thought I was! I may look the same, but inside I am a new creation. So I cannot inherit a disease from my parents because the old me has died. And I cannot blame my sickness on the sins of my family and ancestors because according to Ezekiel 18, verse 4, every man dies for his own sins.

So-called hereditary illness is complicated by a double-barrelled fear. The first is that you are afraid you'll pass it on to your children - and that is an open door for a spirit of infirmity to get into them. The second is that you are frightened that you can't be healed because it's not your problem but somebody else's, such as your grandfather or your mother. What we must realise, to break out of this fear, is that the devil is a master liar, and he impersonates the same disease in you as your father, for instance, had. So the truth is that you are not really **inheriting** a disease; rather, you are having manifested in your body by an evil spirit the symptoms of the same affliction. But if the devil can deceive you, he's really got you because you will be praying for the wrong thing.

3. Scepticism and unbelief

It is sad that there is such tremendous scepticism in the body of Christ: 'I'll believe it when I see it.' And even when they do see it, they give all sorts of explanations why it might not be the work of God. If you are sceptical, God will never heal you. Jesus never wasted time on sceptics; He just ignored them. For scepticism hides an 'evil heart of unbelief' as the Bible puts it. It is the enemy of faith. Our problem is often not that we need more faith, but that we need less unbelief so that our faith can work properly. Look at the episode in Mark 9 of the man who brought his epileptic son to the disciples for healing, but they were unable to drive out the evil spirit.

'Oh unbelieving generation,' Jesus reproached them and turned to the father of the boy. Jesus could see that the disciples, confronted with the sight of such a serious affliction (the boy had been suffering from this violent condition from childhood and he was scarred from throwing himself into fire and into water,) were overwhelmed by their unbelief. But evidently, instead of admitting it, they had tried to pray for the boy even though they didn't really believe it would work. Perhaps Jesus perceived in the boy's father a greater degree of openness and honesty. Less pride too, possibly. He was desperate, after all, and Jesus was now his only hope:

'If you can do anything, take pity on us and help us.'
'If you can?' said Jesus. 'Everything is possible for him who believes.'

Straightaway the man saw what his problem was for:

Immediately the boy's father exclaimed, '**I do believe; help me overcome my unbelief!**'

His unbelief, nurtured every day by the terrible sight of his son so afflicted, was preventing him from exercising his faith. Jesus confirms this, for in the same incident recorded by Matthew, after casting out the evil spirit with a single command, He tells His disciples why they have been unsuccessful:

> 'Because of your little faith. I tell you the truth,
> if you have faith as small as a mustard seed, you
> can say to this mountain, "Move from here to
> there," and it will move. Nothing will be
> impossible for you. But this kind does not go
> out except by prayer and fasting.'

This translation is rather confusing because on the one hand Jesus rebukes them for only having little faith, and then, on the other, He says faith as small as a mustard seed is sufficient for great miracles. The point Jesus is making is that our faith need only be like the tiny mustard seed, which, under the right conditions, grows at an amazing rate and reproduces prolifically, and the right conditions for our faith to grow like that is in the absence of the weeds of unbelief.

There is only one way to kill these weeds, Jesus says, and that is by prayer and fasting. I am convinced that 'this kind' which He refers to is not the evil spirit but the disciples' unbelief. So when you fast and pray, you are not increasing your faith but getting rid of your unbelief, breaking the hold it has on your faith being exercised. In Isaiah 58, we read,

> Is not this the kind of fasting I have chosen:
> to loose the chains of injustice
> and untie the cords of the yoke,
> to set the oppressed free
> and break every yoke?

(verse 6)

Fasting breaks the yoke of your unbelief so that you are able to share what you have with those in need (verse 7). Just like Peter and John with the crippled man at the Beautiful Gate, we speak the unhindered word of faith to bring life and healing.

> Then your light will break forth like the dawn,
> and your healing will quickly appear.
>
> (verse 8)

I remember a story recounted by a well-known preacher who went to Australia to speak in a number of meetings. In the healing time at the end of one service, a man came up to him for prayer, and this minister took one look at him, and said,

'I'm not going to pray for you, brother. You're full of unbelief. Go away and fast and come back tomorrow.'

I should think the man was too astounded to argue but he went away and, sure enough, next day he was there again in the healing line. Imagine his amazement when the preacher said,

'Sorry, I'm not praying for you. You didn't fast, did you?' Red-faced, the man admitted he hadn't. Two nights later, and perhaps a couple of inches thinner, he stood before the preacher once more to be told,

'I don't need to pray for you now. You are healed already.'

And in that moment, he was.

4. Pride

The Bible says God opposes the proud (James 4, verse 6) and will not walk with them. But it is no good praying, 'Lord, please humble me,' because we are told to **humble ourselves** under the mighty hand of God. Some people are ashamed to admit they are sick because they feel it is admitting to failure, and to a lack of spirituality. This is basically pride, and if we have this attitude we cannot receive anything from God, for we feel that everything we have achieved is by our own efforts, and our present situation is because of our own weakness. We need to learn dependence on God in whatever state we find ourselves, whatever our natural abilities.

I discovered how full of pride I could be through my own physical problem, my stammer. Every time I felt out of my depth in a healing situation, I couldn't have stammered if I tried; every time I thought I could do it alone, I couldn't put two words together without tripping over them.

Pride can also infiltrate our motives in seeking healing. We say it is for the glory of God, but a part of us wants to be healed, or to pray for someone else's healing successfully, in order to prove our spirituality and to draw attention to ourselves. This is more likely to be a problem if we aren't too seriously sick; there is no leveller of pride like desperation. We are usually willing for anything then.

5. Occult Involvement

There is absolutely no doubt that dabbling in the occult will present a blockage to healing. Conscious and deliberate involvement in the works of darkness will certainly block God's power, but so also might unwitting participation in less obvious Satanic practices - ouija boards, tarot cards, fortune telling, astrology, drugs, yoga, T.M. and even some forms of alternative medicine. Repentance and renouncing of these involvements may remove the blockage straightaway, but unfortunately they may have inflicted worse problems on us than our sickness. We will certainly have exposed ourselves to demonic interference and we may need the ministry of deliverance. Not only this but various areas of our lives may seem, or actually be, cursed. This is illustrated graphically in Isaiah 47, verses 9-15:

> Both of these will overtake you in a moment, on a single day: **loss of children and widowhood.** They will come upon you in full measure, in spite of your many sorceries and all your potent spells.
>
> You have trusted in your wickedness and have said, 'No-one sees me'.
>
> Your wisdom and knowledge mislead you when you say to yourself, 'I am, and there is none besides me'.
>
> Disaster will come upon you, and you will not know how to conjure it away.
>
> A calamity will fall upon you that you cannot ward off with a ransom.

> A catastrophe you cannot foresee will
> suddenly come upon you...

God loathes spiritism and occultism. He said, 'You shall have no other gods before Me'. By messing around in the realm of darkness, we are giving Satan power and authority over us. Although he pretends to give with one hand so that we are lured into his kingdom, he is robbing us with the other, yet so subtly that we don't realise that he is the cause. I have counselled so many women who have had miscarriage after miscarriage; they have been prayed for that their womb will be strengthened and that the pregnancy will be blessed, but still they have gone on losing their unborn children due to previous occult involvement.

In the firemen's strike some years ago, there was a tragic fire in which two little children died. There were horrific pictures of the children appearing at the top of the house just before they were burnt to death. Some months later, I was preaching in a nearby town on Isaiah 47 (I hadn't understood at all why the Lord had directed me to preach on this passage), and a woman broke down and came sobbing to the front of the meeting. She said she was the mother of the children who had died.

'I am a spiritist medium,' she confessed through her sobs, 'and I cursed God for that fire, but now I see why it happened.'

She repented and God gloriously saved her that night, setting her free from all effects of her evil practices. But she had still lost her two little children. There is a terrible price to pay for involvement in the occult.

Don't think, either, that because you didn't take the occult practice seriously, it didn't have any effect. It's rather like being exposed to radiation: you don't always see any outward sign, but, deep inside, its insidious damage is being done, causing mutations in cells which may manifest themselves as cancers many years hence. Even if you went to a fortune-teller once, just as a joke, beware. They tell you enough truth to catch you - and then either you become dependent on them or you try to manipulate events and people to bring about or avoid what was foretold. You become dominated by curiosity or by fear. Either way, it is a curse, but Jesus gives us a promise of freedom and blessing.

6. Sin

We have discussed this earlier so I will just summarise. If you are practising sinful habits, you will probably have difficulty getting through to God, because if our heart condemns us, we have no confidence towards Him. Some people have a rather dull conscience, and it may be possible for them to relate to God and receive His blessings, but most of us don't expect to receive anything when we know we are disobeying and grieving God.

Never look inwards, look up at Jesus because when He **convicts** of sin, it is with His finger pointing specifically to the problem. When we are under the condemnation of the devil we feel a heavy hand, hitting us and crushing us flat. When God's Spirit points out our sin we know it is right because we have a witness inside, and since He shows it to us in the light of Calvary we know we can confess our sin and be cleansed of it straightaway, going on to receive our healing.

7. Despondency and Dismay

You've been prayed for a multitude of times, you've had more hands laid on you than you've had hot dinners, and still you are not healed. You can't bear the thought of being prayed for again. I can understand you will be feeling despondent and dismayed. The people of Israel must have felt much the same as they stood at the entrance to the Promised Land at the beginning of the book of Joshua. After forty years of wandering in the wilderness they hear that Moses, the great leader, the one they had always depended upon, has died. Fear, despondency and dismay overwhelm them. After all they have been through, they feel too crushed now by this last blow to overcome the final hurdle. They are on the point of giving up - when the Word of the Lord comes to them through Joshua:

> 'Now then, you and all these people, get ready
> to cross the Jordan River into the land I am
> about to give to them - to the Israelites. I will
> give you every place where you set your foot as

I promised Moses... No-one will be able to stand up against you all the days of your life. As I was with Moses, so I will be with you, I will never leave you or forsake you.

Be strong and courageous, because you will lead these people to inherit the land I swore to their forefathers to give them.

Be strong and very courageous. Be careful to obey all the law my servant Moses gave you; do not turn from it to the right or to the left, that you may be successful wherever you go. Do not let this Book of the Law depart from your mouth; meditate on it day and night, so that you may be careful to do everything written in it. Then you will be prosperous and successful. Have I not commanded you? **Be strong and courageous. Do not be terrified; do not be discouraged, for the Lord your God will be with you wherever you go.**'

(Joshua 1, verses 2-9)

Three times God says 'be strong and courageous'. There is no way out. God tells us, if we want to go into the promised land, that we must put some steel in our will and act like the victors, not the vanquished.

Time and again through the New Testament, there echoes the cry '**stand firm,**' and having done all, **stand**. The idea of the world is, if you can't cope with life, turn to religion; or if you can't succeed at any other job, become a minister! What a reputation. Obviously the church will, and should, bring in the lost, the weak and the needy, but once they have made Jesus Christ their Lord, the weak hands and feeble knees ought to be getting strengthened.

Whatever we say about life not being a bed of roses as a Christian, many of us still do not expect to have to fight for anything, as if there wasn't a devil trying to rob, usurp and destroy at all. God promises to be with us every step of the way, so instead of giving up when things don't work out and saying, 'I won't try again,' why not get aggressive with the devil and refuse to give up? We need to get righteously angry about the territory the devil has stolen from the church. When we get some spiritual adrenalin going, we start fighting and it's the despondency and dismay which are put to flight. Resist the devil and **he** will flee from you. Rejoice in the Lord always, and again I say, **rejoice.** You can't be dismayed and joyful at the same time. Rejoice, and you will enter the promised land. Rejoice, and the walls will come crashing down.

As a footnote, let me make clear that I'm not talking about **striving.** We strive when we don't know what God's will is, and when we feel we're on our own. But when we are called to be strong and courageous in fighting our enemies (the forces of darkness) and entering the promised land of health or any other blessing, we are assured that God will never leave us nor forsake us; nothing will be able to stand against us. And though we may have to fight several battles to get there, we should never lose heart, because He has promised we **will** inherit the land.

8. Self-Pity

Not a very glamorous problem, this one, but we find it surprisingly often at the root of our attitude towards our sickness and healing. Poor me. Why is life always so hard for me? Why should I be the one to suffer all this pain? Unfortunately, it's only a short step from there to the accusation, 'God, why did You allow this to happen to me?' and then we find we are letting in anger, resentment and all their attendant problems. Or we simply become so absorbed by our own condition, obsessed by our symptoms, that we actually start to enjoy our illness in a morbid sort of way.

In the early days, if I got sick, I would come home and be ill there. After all it wouldn't look good to be sick while I was out preaching about healing. In fact, I was usually healthy 'on the road' because as long as I was preaching healing, I lived in it. But when I stopped, I would let my guard down and the devil would make me sick. When I got safely home, I would decide I was really sick and, well, I deserved a day in bed anyway. My wife would ask, 'Shall I call the elders?' and I would hastily say we shouldn't bother them as they were so busy.

'Just draw back the curtains, darling, so that I can see the sunshine,' (lying back feebly on my pillows), 'and don't let anyone come round today. I need some peace and quiet.' It didn't seem so bad to be sick after all, and just as my wife was going out of the bedroom I would say,

'Darling, I've just had a vision. I see a lunch tray with...' And by this time, her patience would have run out, the bedclothes would be on the floor, and I would be exercising my faith or dying of pneumonia.

I remember the first time I preached about healing. I woke up next morning with the most violent stomach pains I have ever had in my life. I thought I was dying. 'It's not fair,' I groaned. 'I didn't mean to attack the devil like that. What sort of reward is this for preaching the Word?'

Rosemary, my wife, wasn't exactly sympathetic, however. 'Get up,' she said.

So up I got and staggered round the bedroom, muttering, 'By His stripes, I was healed. By His stripes, I was healed.'

God let me walk around that wretched floor for forty five minutes and then He spoke to me:

'Do you **believe** that by My stripes, you were healed?'

'Yes Lord,' I said.

'Well stop **trying** to get healed then.'

And as I relaxed and looked to Him, I was healed, just like that.

'Lord,' I protested, 'why did you wait for forty five minutes?'

'I was just bringing a little death to self-pity,' He replied. 'I could have healed you the minute you got out of bed, but you were so full of self-pity that it was more important to get rid of some of that first.'

Three quarters of an hour walking round in agony shows that God meant business as much as I meant business - though I was just about to get back into bed so maybe that's why God thought He had better give me a victory! But He hates self-pity because we are putting ourselves on the throne, ourselves at the centre of the world; we are considering ourselves instead of denying ourselves; we are pushing God out.

9. Apathy

I believe apathy is one of the national demonic principalities of Great Britain. Over so many things, people say they are not bothered, they don't care. There is no sense of urgency about most of what we do. Bored or dissatisfied with our lot, we still haven't got the energy or inclination to do anything about it. And this apathy has infiltrated the church too. When people come forward for healing, I sometimes ask them a few questions: Have you prayed for yourself? No. Have you fasted? No. Have you sought God with all your heart? No. Have you read the Bible this month? No. Have you been to church this week? No. What have you come for? Healing. Do you really want to be healed? Well no, actually it's rather nice being off work. People seldom admit this, of course, but you can tell by the shifty look and the change of subject that this is the real answer. It's hard work being healthy. Have you ever reflected that living in health means never taking another day off work?! Most of us enjoy a good lie-in, and we lie wallowing on beds of self-pity, fear, dismay, misbelief...

Jesus healed many people who were carried to Him on stretchers, or lying helpless on the ground and His command was usually not 'be healed,' but 'rise up,' 'stand,' 'take up your bed and walk'. He could see that before they could walk physically they had to rise up in their spirits first.

No wonder Jesus said to the man who had been ill for thirty eight years lying by the pool of Bethesda,

> 'Do you **want** to get well?'
>
> (John 5, verse 6)

What is at the back of the man's answer?

> 'Sir, I have no-one to help me into the pool
> when the water is stirred. While I am trying to
> get in, someone else goes down ahead of me.'
>
> (verse 7)

Notice he doesn't reply to Jesus' question directly. He seems keen to make excuses, to put the blame on other people, but there seems a certain amount of self-pity and probably apathy and laziness too. If he was healed, he would have to leave his security (he must have been quite a local personality if he had been lying there for thirty eight years...), leave the money he received by begging for alms, and face the difficulty of trying to get a job and earn his keep after a lifetime of dependence. So Jesus gives him the short, sharp, shock treatment: 'Get up! Pick up your mat and walk.'

That's not the tone you generally use to someone who has been earnestly, whole-heartedly, courageously seeking healing for years. I should think the man leapt up as if he had been stung. He was healed the moment Jesus spoke but he wouldn't have known it until he made the effort to get up. That Jesus was reprimanding him slightly is borne out by His comment when He finds him at the temple later that day:

> 'See, you are well again. **Stop sinning**, or
> something worse may happen to you.'
>
> (verse 14)

Now a man who has been crippled for thirty eight years doesn't have much scope for active sin. But Jesus could see his thoughts and warned him against the apathy which had kept him an invalid for so long.

10. Rebellion, Resentment, Anger

I have treated these together as generally all three are present at the same time. We are all aware that there are various streams, denominations, fellowships and other groups that make up the 'body' of Christ around the world. Sometimes these different fellowships co-exist quite happily, but there are many sad examples of rebellion, criticism and hurt which can cause great stumbling blocks to the spiritual growth of the individuals and fellowships involved.

If I go to minister to a group which has broken away from another one, I encourage them to pray to make sure there is no rebellion in their hearts. It may have been that God desired the break in order to do something different with them or simply to bring growth, since most organisms grow by cell division. But occasionally the split has come because of personality clashes, or because certain individuals have found it impossible to submit to the leadership of the church, or because the elders have refused to delegate responsibility or to accept new ideas. A lot of hurts are incurred in these situations. I usually ask the group to pray in tongues, thinking of the leadership which gave the left foot of fellowship or whatever, and to keep on praying in tongues until they have nothing but love in their hearts for those concerned. You can never build if there is rebellion in the camp. The group will splinter and split and splinter again.

Normally, we don't use the word 'rebellion' - that indicates sin on our part. We call it 'hurt' - that sounds much nicer and anyway, it puts the blame on someone else. 'I've been desperately hurt by those brothers. They have treated me so badly.' What we really mean is that we are furious with them, and we think they were completely wrong anyway. We are hiding our rebellion and anger under the mask of hurt, and hurt is only a form of self-regard, self-love and pride.

An experience in Denmark brought all this home to me. I was speaking at a conference in Copenhagen with other ministers, among whom was an internationally-known charismatic figure. After he had preached, I went up to him and told him how much I had enjoyed his ministry.

'Who are you?' he asked, extending his hand cautiously.

'Ian Andrews,' I replied, knowing that would mean nothing to him.

'Where in England are you from?'

'From South Chard,' I answered innocently, and he dropped his hand as if I had leprosy.

'People like you ought to stay at home,' he spluttered furiously. 'You bring division wherever you go.' And he marched off.

Now I was hurt - I thought. In fact, he had triggered off a deep feeling of resentment in me because he represented the establishment that I despised. Angrily I thought, how can God put him as a leader? He preaches all about the love of God in the meeting, and then he does that to me. I got into bed that night seething with 'righteous indignation'. And God said to me,

'Pray for Brother so-and-so.'

'Sorry, Lord, I haven't got time. Must get some sleep.'

'Pray for Brother so-and-so.'

I was so amazed, or outraged, by this idea that I got out of bed at past twelve o'clock to sort this one out.

'Lord, how can he be a leader? Do you know what You're doing, putting him in authority? Of course, he doesn't really have authority, not spiritual authority; he just has an ecclesiastical position, and there's a great difference…'

As I ranted on, I gradually realised God wasn't taking any notice.

'I want you to pray for him,' He said.

I still couldn't take Him seriously:

'Oh, Lord. Bless him with a brick.'

He wasn't amused.

'That's not what I want you to do. Bless those who curse you. Love your enemies. Live at peace with all men.'

'But I **can't** pray for him,' I argued, hoping to get some sympathy.

'Yes you can. Pray for him in tongues and picture his face.'

I had run out of arguments. So with a desperate effort of will, I started to pray in tongues and I had the most wonderful experience. The love of God was shed abroad in my heart by the Holy Spirit with such power that I felt a tremendous love for this man. My judgmental attitude disappeared, my criticism left, and my fear vanished. I had felt crushed by that man's rebuff and it had left me wounded and anxious, as well as angry.

About a week later, I was checking in at the airport in Copenhagen and who should I see in the line three places ahead of me but this brother. Normally, if you meet someone who has really hurt you, you have a churning sensation inside. But I didn't feel anything like that - only goodwill. So I went up to him and tapped him on the shoulder.

'Good to see you again, brother,' I greeted him. 'How did the conference go?'

He looked uncomfortable, and muttered, 'Very well, thank you'. Picking up a copy of *The Times* he opened it and held it up like a protest banner (which I suppose it was!) so that I couldn't speak to him anymore. But it didn't worry me at all. I can meet him now quite happily because God has set me free. So if people don't speak to you, that needn't put you out of fellowship with them. Refrain from judgement and preserve your spirit in love by praying for them in tongues - then you will find no problem in receiving from the Lord.

Obviously, the list of blockages to healing which we have been through in this chapter is not exhaustive; one or two others were mentioned earlier in the book, and doubtless you will be able to think of more. But one final problem is so pervasive and profound that it needs a chapter of its own to discuss it fully, and that problem is rejection.

Chapter Ten

Rejection

In 1967, I asked God to heal me of everything that was wrong with me. That was a rather foolish prayer, and not surprisingly, nothing seemed to change until 1976 when Rosemary and I bought a lovely old thatched cottage in Chard. At least, it was potentially lovely, but it needed completely renovating. I've never felt interior decorating was my calling, but Rosemary surveyed the dereliction inside the cottage with enthusiasm.

'No point in putting any more wallpaper on these walls,' she said cheerfully. 'We'll have to strip them down first.'

I would have been happy just to paint the wall again, but I could see Rosemary had got that gleam in her eye which meant she intended to do a 'proper job', so we set to. After soaking the wall, we peeled off the paper, to find another layer underneath. So we scrubbed away at that, only to find another floral creation underneath - and another - and another. We went through five layers before finally the plaster fell away under the strain. And if God hadn't spoken to me then, I wouldn't have spoken to Rosemary for months:

'That's what I'm doing to people's lives,' He said. 'I'm not interested in just patching something up. I'm pulling it all down until we reach the solid rock. And that's what I'm doing in your life. The day you asked Me to heal you, I started.'

'It doesn't look much like it, Lord,' I replied darkly.

'But remember Jeremiah,' was His reply. 'I told him to **uproot and tear down, to destroy and overthrow, and then to build and plant**. It's taken all these years to clear the ground before I can sow and build.'

So that's what He had been doing. I wish He had told me. I had spent years struggling through doubt, fear, insecurity and anger because I had interpreted all that happened as God not caring, rather than God loving me. Through this incident, He started to show me what was at the root of all my sense of failure and hurt. Rejection. And I am convinced, years later, that this is the main reason why some people do not receive their healing.

Why should rejection be such a common problem? I think there are several reasons. **First**, people of my age are paying the price of the Second World War. For so many children, their father was away fighting during the most formative years of their life, and either never came back, or returned a stranger, sometimes unable to re-establish a deep relationship with his children. **Second**, with a divorce rate of at least one in three, higher in the United States, the family structure is breaking down. Children are growing up in an atmosphere of insecurity, without models of faithfulness, loyalty and morality on which to base their own lives. **Third**, we live in a culture where demonstration of emotion or affection is not generally encouraged. Unlike the Continentals, for example, our national characteristic is reserve and understatement. Our public school system has perpetuated this so that many adult relationships of people with that upbringing suffer through a difficulty in expressing feelings. A lack of communication breeds hurt, insecurity and rejection. **Fourth**, more and more children are being brought up by child-minders or left at playgroups and nurseries all day while mothers work. Whatever the reasons for this situation, it is a sad fact that many children lack a sense of stability and reassurance, as insufficient attention and love is given to them to build up their self-esteem. And the list goes on.

I was born in 1939, the first of two children, and my impression during the first six years of my life was, 'My father doesn't love me'. He seemed to be always busy or away from home and when I did see him he was pre-occupied with his own problems. I wasn't badly treated or neglected physically, but such a lack of affirmation and attention made me grow up feeling like an orphan. For I do believe that it is the father who unlocks the emotional life of the child. A mother's love is natural and instinctive; there is normally an immediate bond between mother and child at birth. But a father who loves his child is able to develop it to the fullness of its ability. He will encourage the child to help him dig the garden; he will take an interest in the little child's games, projects and hobbies; he will spend time just talking, listening, encouraging; he will build up the child's self-respect, confidence and security; he will be there for a hug and a cuddle, as a counsellor and a shoulder to cry upon.

My own reaction to the absence of all these benefits was made more negative by school and church experiences. Handicapped with a terrible stammer, I vividly remember being told impatiently by the teacher at the age of seven, 'It's no good asking you for the answer, we'll be ten minutes waiting for it to come.'

She might as well have taken a stick and caned me - in fact, that might not have damaged me as much. At Sunday School, I was taught that we were made in the image of God. The idea horrified me. Looking at my puny frame, my knock knees and my hopeless stammer, I quickly concluded that God must either be very weird or have a sadistic sense of humour.

The irony of the situation was that inside this pathetic exterior, I had plenty of will-power and ambition. My heart's desire was to be a barrister, and in my mind's eye I could see myself standing up in court dazzling everyone by my brilliance. Actually, I think there was an unhealthy aspect to this dream as what I really wanted was an outlet for all my bottled-up anger and resentment which overflowed in a fluent and biting sarcasm. It is strange how insecure people are often the most proud and critical. I could reduce people to tears with a few words and I thought I would make a marvellous counsel for the prosecution, wringing confessions out of sobbing defendants with my blistering attacks. The only time I didn't stammer was when I was angry. Part of me, too, wanted to be an actor, and I think this stemmed from a desire to escape from all my failings and inhibitions, and win admiration and praise. In reality, of course, I couldn't put two words together without falling over them, and everyone said I was wasting my time thinking about the legal profession. In the end I settled for accountancy, but this compromise only increased the chip on my shoulder: I felt that life (or God?) had treated me badly.

I had met Rosemary in my late teens. She was a nurse and we met at a church dance, though neither of us had any sort of faith at all. We started going out with each other straightaway, and though it sounds terrible to say, I think one of the reasons I was attracted to her was that she was even more timid and insecure than I was, and I could dominate her! (That was my fatal mistake: inside that mouse was a lion trying to get out, and we had some big clashes later on when she refused to lie down and be trodden on. In fact, in the years to come, Rosemary proved to be the strong one with the unshakable faith and confidence in God.) We got married quite young when we were about twenty one and I was just finishing my accountancy training.

We went to live in London where I got a job as an accountant in the city and Rosemary worked for British United Air Ferries as a receptionist. A friend of hers at work pestered Rosemary for months to go along to an evangelistic group at Westminster Chapel and eventually Rosemary gave in and dragged me along with her. In 1963, through evangelical books and tracts, and through the preaching of Martyn Lloyd-Jones, Rosemary and I became Christians, but we only made an intellectual sort of commitment. We were told we had to come to a decision by a certain Sunday, and we simply concluded that, weighing up all the evidence, God probably did exist and the Christian life was the best one to lead.

We wanted to have our own home and two years later we bought a house in Fleet, the nearest place to London we could afford. We commuted into the city but it was too far to go to church meetings so we went to an Anglican church in Reading and then a Baptist church in Farnborough just down the road when our son Stephen was born. During this time, we came into contact with people who had another dimension to their Christian lives, people with joy and power in the Holy Spirit. We started to seek something more in our faith and began to discover the excitement of God speaking to us. Rosemary in particular, through problems with her pregnancy and our son's birth, found God's Word was life and joy and strength to her. I was generally more cynical and pessimistic!

Some ministers from a church in South Chard, Somerset, which was experiencing the most wonderful revival and growth, visited us at Fleet, and made many of us curious to know what was going on down there. We went along one weekend and couldn't believe our eyes. The move of the Holy Spirit was equal to anything we had ever read about. At meetings people were being knocked to the floor under the tremendous presence of God, miracles were happening and there was an abundance of joy and love. Ordinary people, even young Christians, were living by faith. In fact, giving up everything and working for the Lord almost seemed to us part and parcel of being baptised in the Holy Ghost.

We started to travel from our home in Hampshire to South Chard each weekend. We also opened our home for meetings and hospitality for anyone in need. Soon we were baptised in water and a man who did not know anything about us gave an incredible prophecy over me. Unaware that I stammered badly, he said that I would walk in righteousness and power, pull down the strongholds of Satan and see many mighty miracles in the Name of Jesus. Everyone in the church began cheering when they heard those words, but we had little idea of how this could possibly come to pass. In fact God had to show us that we must not act to bring prophecy to pass by our own efforts, but that He would do it all by His grace.

It was during this time that Rosemary had a life-changing experience when she was filled with the Holy Spirit. As a child she was dominated and crushed by an overbearing and sometimes violent father. This had caused her to become very introverted and she lacked any form of confidence. Her life was full of tension and embarrassment, due to having a father whose lifestyle made him the talk of the town. As a result, communication and love were completely unknown to her, and repression and terrible fears were the norm.

The thought of giving her life totally over to God simply accentuated these fears and she felt certain that God, like her father, would only punish her and take things from her. Life had been very traumatic. Full of rejection and looking for love, she was easy prey for the devil. The emptiness inside just could not be filled, and owing to a life of suppression she found it very difficult to communicate with people.

The pastor at Chard was a very gentle and sensitive man who showed Rosemary the love of Jesus for the first time. She thought that God would send her to Africa as a missionary to live in a mud hut somewhere, and had no idea of what God was really like. The pastor asked her to make Jesus Lord of her life - past, present and future - including her childhood experiences. This was quite a difficult decision and she needed a few hours to make up her mind. Finally she asked for prayer, and out loud she gave her life into God's hands, asking Him to take over. She just sat there breathing in the presence of God - she couldn't see or feel it, but the pastor said it was there! At some point the Holy Spirit came and lifted her off the chair onto the floor, where she began to be filled with the Holy Spirit and shout, yell and sing at the top of her voice, as well as shouting in tongues. Then the laughing started. It grew inside until she was bursting, and started rolling all over the floor. (Had she known what was to happen she says she would have hung on to her chair)!

Suddenly Jesus appeared in the corner of the room. He had wonderful eyes and was full of joy and full of life. He just said, 'It's Me' and she began to laugh again, as if she was drunk with new wine. Then He said, 'I love you, I accept you, and I can't find anything wrong with you'. It was as though the words He spoke went right into her and she felt clean and free from condemnation, wanting to love everybody. For what seemed hours or days she couldn't speak in English, so much did this heavenly language keep pouring out.

Needless to say, it totally transformed her life. From being a terrified introvert she became full of confidence and joy, knowing without a doubt that God loved her and wanted to bless her. Her faith was strong in God. If the family needed anything, from the evening meal to new clothes, she just prayed it in. People called round with the very object we were in need of; cheques for the exact amount she was needing would come through the letter-box. She told anyone and everyone about the Lord, and prayed for all sorts of sicknesses and problems. It was impossible to dampen her joy (and I confess I did try many times) because she just gave thanks for every difficulty and setback, trusting that all she had was God's and all He has was hers, so He would provide.

Now, it's not necessarily very easy living with someone like that - particularly when you haven't received anything like such an outpouring and assurance of God's love yourself. And what bothered me more, I still stammered just as badly. There were a lot of tensions and difficulties in our marriage at this time, mainly because of my inner resentment, yet despite these, we felt our life was about to change direction dramatically. In the same week God told me that I was going to lose my job (through an incredible verse in the Bible about God severing men out of employment to pass through the land), and He showed us we should move down to Chard. Two days later, I was made redundant.

That morning as I drove to work, I heard the audible voice of God for the first time in my life. I nearly drove off the road:

'You will work at the Taunton XYZ Company.' (Not its real name!) I had never heard of the firm. In fact, I had no idea if it even existed, so when I got home that night I looked it up in the telephone directory.

And there it was in black and white! I wrote to them straightaway, asking if they had any vacancies, and they replied that a position would shortly be available. I was granted an interview and given the impression that the job would be mine. Then a week later I received a formal letter notifying me that I would **not** be given the position. Like Hezekiah I spread the matter before the Lord, knowing that God had already spoken to me about working with that company. Some weeks later, I noticed that they were advertising for a financial manager, so I re-applied. It was then that I received a letter from the director, saying that the job was not being offered to me because of my stammer. All I could do was spread the letter before the Lord again and the Lord said, 'Write and tell them that by My stripes, you are healed.'

With a sinking heart, thinking that this was bound to spoil any chance I had of getting the job, I obeyed. Immediately I got a phone call from the boss asking what I meant. I started stammering and spluttering all over the place, but fortunately he said, 'I think this must be a bad line. Could you come for another interview?'

We got in all the prayer reinforcement we could this time - and when I went to the interview, I couldn't have stammered if I had tried.

'Well, Mr Andrews,' the director said, 'it's remarkable, but your speech problem really does seem to have improved greatly. We would like you to come and join us straightaway.' But as I drove home I didn't feel elated.

'Now you've done it, Lord. As soon as I arrive on Monday morning and stammer over trying to say "hello", they'll give me the sack. And You're going to look pretty stupid.'

God, however, told me that was His problem, not mine, and the miracle happened. From nine o'clock in the morning until five thirty at night for the whole time I worked for that company I hardly stumbled over a single word.

But God didn't let me stand still for long. Five months later, the company was forced to make several redundancies and I was among them. It was depressing. Getting a job with a stammer like mine wasn't easy and I decided I'd had enough of it. I started a fast and I meant business.

'I'm going to fast until You heal me, Lord, and if You don't, they can write on my tombstone that I died trying to get healed.'

But after several days, God managed to make me see that I wasn't on a fast, I was on a hunger strike. Then He spoke to me very clearly once more:

'I have called you to preach the gospel and heal the sick.'

I suppose I should have been overwhelmed, thrilled, excited, grateful at such a promise. But to be honest it didn't please me at all. The last thing I wanted was a healing ministry. Whoever heard of a preacher with a stammer? It sounded like a rather sick joke. But maybe I could do some bargaining:

'Heal me first, and I'll go.'

The answer came like the slam of a prison door:

'No, go as you are, and everyone will know who the healer is.'

'That's not fair, Lord,' I protested.

'If you want what is fair, you can go to hell,' the Lord replied.

You can't argue with that.

There followed a gruelling year which became a training ground for the healing ministry which was meant to be emerging. For the first six months I was on the dole, and then the church encouraged us to walk out in faith and trust the Lord to support us. Live by faith!

(I have to admit it, I had perfect faith for bankruptcy. It was Rosemary who kept us going in those early days with **her** wonderful faith.)

If I hadn't been thrown into praying for the sick I don't think I would ever have done it. What happened was that a friend of ours was going to America for some months and he felt we should borrow his car, and literally get on the road.

'If you're going to work for Father, Son and Holy Ghost Unlimited,' he said, 'you'd better start doing some work. Here are the keys and £10 for petrol. Off you go, and if you come back, you're in the will of God.'

Marvellous! Discipleship, they called it. If you come back, it's God and if you don't, goodbye! Still, I didn't have much choice, even though I could see myself disappearing into the sunset and never being seen again. But there happened to be a Catholic lady in the car with us and after dropping my friend Harry at the airport, I took her on to see a friend, a Southern Baptist from the USA, in Gerrards Cross. They politely asked me to stay for a cup of tea before I drove on, and over tea and biscuits, I explained that I had been called by the Lord to travel round the world, preach the gospel and heal the sick. They clearly thought I was absolutely mad, and urged me to go to theological college first, get financial sponsors and get organised in a sensible fashion. Then they asked if they could pray for me and I thought it was better to let them than to try and argue with them. But as they were praying, God spoke to me and said, 'One of these ladies has got a kidney problem. Pray for her.'

I sneaked a glance at them. They both looked healthy and that was a relief because I would have found it a terrible problem if the lady concerned had **looked** really ill.

I had only been properly 'launched' into the healing ministry for a few hours but I knew I had to pray for her if I wanted God to provide for me. Summoning all my courage, I asked them which one had the kidney problem. I was secretly relieved again when it turned out to be the Catholic lady as at least Catholics have always accepted healing doctrinally. She was so startled by my question that she nodded mutely when I offered to pray for her, and so we closed our eyes. I have to confess that I had almost total confidence that it wouldn't work but I just felt I had to be obedient to the Lord. I laid my hand on the lady's head and desperately tried to remember every prayer for the sick I had ever heard, and all the teaching I had learnt, and then I threw it all together: I rebuked the devil, I cast out spirits of this and that and prayed in other tongues, I pleaded the blood and I commanded her to be healed ... and I felt absolutely nothing. 'I'm just not spiritual enough for God to use me,' I thought despondently. So I took my hand away and turned around for what I was sure would be spiritual counselling from the Baptist lady - only to find the Catholic lying absolutely still on the floor like a dead person and the other woman staring with eyes like saucers, as if to say, 'What have you done to my friend?' Well I hadn't a clue, so I quickly picked up my coat, said my goodbyes and drove off. (It's a real advantage having a travelling ministry; you can always leave before the trouble starts!)

But six weeks later, I received a long letter from this Catholic lady saying that she had been suffering from a terminal kidney condition and had been given only a short time to live. She had been to Lourdes, she had done penance and she had visited Rome and kissed every step to the door of St. Peter's, but nothing had improved until the day we prayed. From that moment she was completely healed and the doctors had discharged her, mystified. I didn't tell her I was too. But it made me realise that it wasn't **my** faith doing the healing but His power working through me.

So this was my first experience of healing. Soon afterwards Rosemary, the baby and I went off to Sweden to minister as someone in our church had some contacts there. We stayed there for about three months, mainly because we couldn't afford to come home again!

For several more years, it seemed as if we struggled on living on the knife edge of bankruptcy, and although the Lord was doing some amazing things in the meetings I spoke at, I still had no assurance of His love and leading. Every time I got up to preach I would be terrified that the Holy Spirit wouldn't turn up; hundreds of people would get healed and I would ask them, 'Are you **sure** you're healed? Haven't you even got just a bit of pain left?' I was constantly hounded by feelings of anxiety and fear, and I think deep down I felt that my calling was a sentence, not a gift.

To make things worse, we arrived home from our travels on several occasions to find that the people who had been living in our home had left us a damaged kitchen, dirty carpets or smashed china. Rosemary, as usual, was able to praise God through all this, but it didn't do anything for my sense of rejection and anger.

Eventually, in 1976, I was invited to speak at a retreat centre in Canada for French-speaking Roman Catholics. I was dreading it. How did I manage to get myself into this situation? With my church background they were bound to reject me, and anyway, I was still stammering badly. What could I speak to them about to make them sympathetic to me? How about Mary? That was bound to bless them...

I had been asked to come along at four o'clock in the afternoon to pray for the sick in a hospital wing of the convent. Looking round at the chronically sick people, I felt my faith sink to my boots, and I prayed for them with almost perfect faith that nothing would happen.

Then I made my exit as soon as possible, without waiting to see what was the response to my prayers. In the church, we waited in vain for the interpreter to show up, and eventually had to start without him.

After a few minutes of preaching in monosyllabic English, I began to realise that my idea of Mary and theirs were rather different, and the more I spoke, the bigger hole I dug for myself. In about twenty minutes I had dug a grave, so the priest put us all out of our misery by standing up and giving the benediction. Just as he did so, God gave me a three-dimensional vision, as vivid and real as the congregation in front of me. Suddenly I could see a man lying in hospital under a great white sheet, which I assumed was an oxygen tent because I had never seen one, and I knew he had had three coronaries and God had healed him.

I didn't know what to do because the meeting was closing so I went over to the priest and said, 'Excuse me, Father, but I have a vision'.

The poor man looked rather vexed, and muttered something about this being highly irregular after the benediction, but to his credit, he asked if I would like to give it. It seemed to me I had very little credibility left to lose so I might as well do so, and if it was right, God would get the glory. So when the priest had got everyone's attention again, I described what I could see.

Instantly, two French nuns grabbed tambourines and started to jump up and down, praising God and crying, 'That's Mr. so-and-so we've been praying for!' 'Hallelujah,' I thought, 'it looks like something's happened anyway, but I'm not staying to find out.' The next day I returned as planned to England.

But I couldn't escape the fact that I felt angry and bitter towards God, hurt and rejected by the way He seemed to have let me down and then humiliated me, first at the hospital wing, and then in the meeting when I had to preach. When I got home I found a convention in progress on the theme of God's love. It seemed the final twist of God's peculiar sense of humour and, unable to bear it any more, I stood up in front of everyone and said,

'If God loves me, He has a very funny way of showing it. I've been asking Him for six years to heal me, and I thought He promised to do it if I preached and did His will. Quite honestly, I might as well throw the whole thing in.'

There was a deathly silence; everyone looked away, embarrassed. I turned round and walked out.

Next day, the pastor called round and he got right to the point. 'The trouble with you,' he said, 'is that you don't **know** God loves you, except intellectually'.

(No prizes for stating the obvious, but in fact if you had asked me if I thought God loved me, I would have said, 'Of course'.)

'You believe He will bless everyone else,' he continued, 'that's why you're happy to minister to the sick, but you don't believe He is bothered about you. You can't really trust Him or receive anything from Him. What you have is a spirit of rejection.'

He said a lot more, all of which seemed to open me up like a surgeon's knife, cutting right through to the problem underneath, and then he prayed for me. I was gloriously released from my anger and sense of rejection and for the first time in my life, I began to feel God's personal love for me.

Several weeks later, I got a letter from Canada:

> Dear Mr. Andrews,
> Last time you visited Canada, someone was raised
> from the dead. We would like you to come and talk
> about it on T.V. and radio...

I replied drily that if someone had been raised from the dead I would have remembered it, and there was obviously some mistake. Perhaps they meant Brother Andrew from Holland...? Then about a fortnight later, I got another letter saying the same thing from a different church, asking me to go over to Canada and speak. I decided I would have to go and see what all the confusion was about.

I was amazed to discover that the man I had seen in the vision had, in fact, been lying dead under a sheet. Suddenly he sat upright and started speaking in tongues, so the hospital sent him home. Now his next door neighbours had just heard he had died, so they were somewhat surprised to see him cutting the lawn! The news spread like wild fire, and quite a Catholic community started up through that one healing. The Catholic Retreat Centre asked me to come back to speak to them, and that would have been fine, except that once more I was asked (groan) to pray for the sick in the hospital wing. When I arrived at four o'clock, I was immediately handed a cup of tea, shown a chair and treated like an honoured guest. Then reality hit when they asked me to come to the ward again. But when we got there, I could hardly see a bed occupied. Apparently, almost everyone had been healed on my last visit! By this time, I felt I was in a dream, and when six hundred people turned up at the meeting that night and dozens received salvation and healing I was past the point of surprise. Maybe God did care after all.

From Canada I went down to speak on a T.V. chat show in front of several million viewers in Chicago. Part of me would have loved that public opportunity to speak, but the rest of me was absolutely terrified. With my speech problem, I was bound to look ridiculous and any doors which were opening up for me would be sure to shut pretty quickly. In fact, it rubbed on a sore spot because I felt God would make a fool of me again, so I rebelled against it, and decided as it was a cold, hard winter the best way out was to pray for snow so that I couldn't make it to the studio. (It started snowing the moment the programme finished and stopped only five days and fifteen feet later!)

There was no way out so I presented myself at the studio like a man going to an execution. I was made up, and then told that when my cue came, I should run down the steps, sit in the chair, and say, 'Praise God!' Now the chat show was going out live, and I was to be the guest from 9.30-11.00 a.m. Unfortunately no-one had told the host of the show that I stammered. I ran down the stairs, managed not to fall over, the cameras zoomed in on me, fear hit me like a bullet, and I burbled,

'Ppppppppr…'

The interviewer gaped and made frantic signs for the camera to swing on to him.

'Mr. Andrews, I gather you have spoken at a conference of twenty five thousand people and there have been some spectacular healings. Would you like to tell us what is happening there?'

The cameras came back to me, and I was still trying to say 'praise'. The first few minutes were a nightmare. I think both of us wished the floor would open up and swallow us. I felt as if God had completely deserted me, and in desperation I cried out to Him, 'God, please **do** something!' From that moment I couldn't have stammered if I tried. The anointing came down and I began to speak fluently and confidently. My host hardly knew what to make of it:

'Er, Mr. Andrews, when you came on, you appeared to have, um, a speech problem, and now you don't. Would you like to comment on this?'

All I could say was that they had seen my humanity and my

weakness, and that it had obviously been God who had done those miracles at the conference. For the rest of the programme I was able to testify to His power and love without any hesitation whatsoever. And as soon as we came off the air, the phones started ringing, and hundreds of people called to say they had been saved or healed through what I had said.

It was fantastic - for everyone except me. I was still devastated by that sense of abandonment and humiliation at the beginning of the programme. I went back to my hotel room, lay on the floor, and felt a tide of rejection flow over me again. I couldn't pray, I wondered how I could possibly carry on ministering, and all my faith for healing seemed to have gone. I didn't expect to hear from God, but nevertheless through all my hurt came His voice - with an extraordinary message.

'You are going to meet someone with an orphan spirit.'

A what? I had never heard of such a thing. And anyway, what an irrelevant thing to say at a time like this. Still, I couldn't be bothered even to question it.

The next day I travelled on to another church. I had been invited to stay with the pastor, and as I walked in the door, his wife took one look at me and broke down and wept. I had provoked some strange reactions in the past but no-one had ever burst into tears after one glance! However, it was as if a tap had been turned on. Without my saying a word almost, she poured out her story, telling me her father had just died but she was glad he was dead because he had beaten her repeatedly as a child if she wasn't perfectly behaved, and she had hated him all her life.

'And the last thing I want to hear from you,' she sobbed bitterly, 'is that God loves me and wants to be my Father.'

Instantly God spoke to me: 'There's your orphan spirit.'

'It can't be, Lord, she had a father.'

'So have orphans,' God replied, 'but she has never been fathered. And neither have you.'

This was too much all in one go. It was late and I just suggested that we shelve it for the night and talk the next morning. In the meantime, I knew I had some business with God.

As I lay in bed that night, God began to speak right into my heart.

'You know My lordship, but you don't know My fatherhood. Your prayers for others are answered but how many prayers for yourself are?'

The Lord was putting His hand on the very centre of my deepest wound. All these years in the ministry and I had never had any confidence at all that God would look after us. It was Rosemary who had kept us alive; she who prayed for money to pay the mortgage, for the washing machine to be mended, for bills to be met. All I had faith for was bankruptcy. I never seemed to pray successfully for our own needs, but everything Rosemary prayed for came in. It was infuriating! I remembered how I was told after I was baptised in the Spirit that I should pray to the Father rather than to Jesus. But this had created a negative situation for me, because our concept of our heavenly Father is based on our earthly one, and God consequently appeared to me as someone who was too busy and remote to have time for me. When I tried to look at God in that way, I was dominated by feelings of insecurity and anxiety. Consequently, in those years of ministry, when God asked me to do anything - preach or pray for people - I didn't get butterflies in my stomach, I had a flock of vultures.

That night, as I laid all these things before the Lord, confessed them and asked for His deliverance and healing, I was wonderfully set free from that orphan spirit. The next morning, in the light of what had happened, the pastor prayed with me that any vacuum left by the orphan spirit would be filled with God's Holy Spirit of 'adoption' or 'sonship' (Romans 8, verse 15) by which we cry 'Abba, Father'. As he did so, I **knew** as I had never done before that I was God's child and that He loved me as His son, for I seemed to feel Him put His arms around me and say, 'Son, I love you'. What a sense of security and peace filled me. From that day I have never again had a trace of nervousness when I get up to speak and my stammer has disappeared except for the odd hesitation, but this doesn't bother me as I know my Father loves me. What happened to me was what Paul described in Ephesians 3, verses 14-19:

> I pray that out of his glorious riches he may **strengthen you with power through his spirit in your inner being** so that Christ may dwell in your hearts through faith. And I pray that you, being rooted and established in love, may have power,

together with all the saints, to grasp how wide and
long and high and deep is the love of Christ, **and to
know this love** that surpasses knowledge - that you
may be filled to the measure of all the fullness of
God.

We then prayed for the pastor's wife together and she, too, was
delivered of the orphan spirit and came into a glorious experience of
God's Father-love.

With this wonderful revelation, I went into the church meeting to
preach. At the end a girl stood up with a disfiguring hare-lip and cleft
palate. She explained that she had never had faith for healing before
but today she had a glimmer of hope. Then she broke down in tears,
and described the tragic way her father had always refused to walk
beside her as a child because he was embarrassed and ashamed by the
way she looked. Her sense of hurt and rejection were obvious. I
explained to her that first she had to forgive her father for the way he
had treated her. This she did, and then I prayed for her.

The next day, at a larger meeting, I was preaching on 'By His
stripes, we are healed,' and again this girl stood up in front of the
congregation and simply said, 'Look what God has done to my mouth'.
The hare-lip had closed over, the structural disfigurement of the cleft
palate had disappeared and she stood laughing through her tears, a
beautiful young woman. Apparently, for years people had prayed for
her unsuccessfully and had assumed it was her lack of faith, but, in
fact, the blockage had been in her because she felt she wasn't pretty
enough, good enough, worthy enough. She had never known a father's
love.

That evening, I spoke on something God was revealing to me
through my own healing experience. He had shown me that there were
three degrees of knowing God's love:

1.   Because the Bible tells me so.
2.   Because He answers my prayers.
3.   Because I feel Him loving me.

Suddenly a girl at the back of the church started to scream and cry,
stumbling forward to where I was standing. By the time she reached
the front, her make-up was smeared all over her face from her tears,
and she was a pitiful sight. Oblivious of everyone else, she explained

that she was a prostitute and as she was walking past the church that evening, trying to pick up a client, she had suddenly heard a voice say, 'Go in'.

Not knowing really what she was doing she had opened the door and been riveted by what I was saying about God's love. It had seemed as if God was speaking specifically to her. A hater of men and God, she told an horrific story of how her father had committed incest with her at an early age.

Emotionally damaged, she was later seduced by a church pastor at the age of fourteen. Turning to another church, she was made pregnant by the choir leader at the age of eighteen and she had an abortion. From then until now, at the age of twenty three, she had wanted to destroy men and that was why she had become a prostitute. All this was said over the loudspeakers, so caught up was she in her pain and anger. Gently, I explained that God could heal all those scars and give her a new life if she would first forgive her father, the minister and the choir leader. There was a long pause and I watched her digging her sharp, painted nails into the palm of her hand. Then through gritted teeth, she muttered, 'I forgive them'. Instantly, the power of God just knocked her to the ground. Then, after a few minutes, she jumped up, and with all the joy and openness of a young child gave me a big hug! Three or four years later, I heard that she married and was wonderfully settled with a secure home and children.

A day or two later, I flew home, now with a new realisation of the importance of parents, and particularly fathers, giving a sense of security and worth to their children. So when my son Stephen said to me rather wistfully, 'Couldn't we spend some time together, Dad?' I didn't give him the usual 'I'm-too-busy' brush-off. Instead we sat down and discussed what he would most like to do.

'Golf,' he replied without hesitation.

'Great,' I agreed, wondering how we could afford it. Doing an accountant's lightning calculation, I realised it would cost us about £500 to join the local golf club and get us both kitted out with clubs and bags. And we had literally not a penny in the bank. That night I prayed with a new confidence that God would provide us with the money to join the club and buy our equipment. The next day a cheque arrived from a London church for £500, with a note saying, 'Strictly for **private** use'.

Since all this happened, I have found that time and again the main reason why people are not healed is because of rejection or an orphan spirit, rejection stemming from a broken relationship within or outside the family, an orphan spirit arising only from a breakdown between parent and child. In both cases, the path to healing starts with repentance and forgiveness because there is nearly always resentment and anger underneath the hurt.

Some years ago, I was speaking in the north of England when a woman I later discovered to have terminal cancer suddenly interrupted angrily,

'I've come here because I was told it was a healing service so why are you going on about rejection?'

I explained that she would see the relevance if she listened a bit longer and she subsided into her seat, only to leap up a little while later, this time in tears.

'My husband left me for a younger woman eighteen months ago when I was fifty two,' she wept. 'When I looked in the mirror, I hated myself and I hated him.'

Six months later, she developed breast cancer and had to have radical surgery. Her resentment grew. Six months after that a tumour developed in her other breast, then secondaries elsewhere. She knew she didn't have much time left but she didn't care. No-one loved her anyway. But now she said without prompting:

'I know I have to forgive him.'

And she did. Like the others, she fell to the ground under the power of the Holy Spirit and when she stood up, all pain had disappeared.

(Incidentally, in case you think people fall on the floor every time I pray for them let me say that as far as I am concerned, if it happens, that's fine, but I don't necessarily expect it or encourage it. But with rejection it does seem to be a common occurrence, as if this is such a deep hurt that often only deep surgery under the anaesthetic of the Holy Spirit is the channel through which God's healing can flow.)

One of the saddest things about rejection is the person's sense of the wasted years of childhood or marriage, the bitter sense of regret that the time is gone and can never be redeemed. Not only were those years diseased and bitter, but they blighted all future relationships and events. But God gives hope and a glorious promise:

> I will restore to you the years which the swarming
> locust has eaten, the hopper, the destroyer, and the
> cutter, my great army which I sent among you. You
> shall eat in plenty and be satisfied and praise the
> name of the Lord your God, who has dealt
> wondrously with you. And my people shall never
> again be put to shame.
>
> (Joel 2, verses 25-26)

All those years are not lost and wasted forever! God will not only heal the effects of those early hurts but He will redeem the time, give you back the joy, the security and the love you thought you could never know. Never again will you have to feel ashamed; never again will you consider yourself worthless, or unlovable; for God has made you **His** child. He dwells inside you by His Spirit so that you can call Him, 'Abba,' Daddy, and you have the identity and security of belonging to His family forever. This was the wonderful revelation Jesus brought, that God was no longer the unapproachable El Shaddai, God Almighty, but **Our Father.** Hallowed be His name!

PART THREE

How to Pray for the Sick

Chapter Eleven

God's Government in Healing

The Corinthian church was obviously wonderfully blessed with spiritual gifts. People were getting saved, healed, delivered; preaching, prophesying, teaching; working miracles, healing the sick, speaking in tongues...

There was a lot of enthusiasm and there were many spectacular happenings. But maybe there was also a bit of confusion and fear, even envy and criticism, too. As young Christians, they all needed some guide-lines as to the exercise of spiritual gifts, and in 1 Corinthians 12, Paul gives some basic teaching on the purpose of these gifts and their importance in the context of the body of Christ, and in particular, the local community of believers. Paul is very concerned that there should be neither pride nor inferiority, emphasising that a body is made up of many parts, even the most insignificant member being of vital importance to the whole. But he also sees the importance of these parts working in harmony, with the body taking its orders from the head.

> There are different kinds of gifts, but the same Spirit. There are different kinds of service, but the same Lord. There are different kinds of worship, but the same God works all of them in all men. Now to each one is the manifestation of the Spirit given for the common good.
>
> (1 Corinthians 12, verses 4-7)

There is a whole variety of gifts, service and working, so how can those all be brought together into some sort of order? In Isaiah 9, verse 6, we read an interesting verse:

And the government will be on his shoulders.

Where are the shoulders? On the body. So the government of God's Kingdom will be in the body of Christ, in the church. The church will provide a Spirit-inspired administration of God's gifts. The rest of the chapter is devoted to the operation of this governing structure.

> Now you are the body of Christ, and each one of you
> is a part of it. And in the church, God has appointed
> first of all apostles, second prophets, third teachers,
> then workers of miracles, also those having gifts of
> healing, those able to help others, those with gifts of
> administration, and those speaking in different kinds
> of tongues.
>
> (1 Corinthians 12, verse 28)

Now verse 29 is crucial:
'Are all apostles?'
The answer is clearly, 'No'.
'Are all prophets?'
'No.'
'Are all teachers?'
'No.'
'Do all work miracles?'
'No.'
'Do all have gifts of healing?'
Following Paul's logical argument, the answer must again be 'No'. Is Paul suggesting, then, that only some people can pray for the sick? Well, yes and no! First of all, Paul seems to be making a distinction between ministries and gifts. He doesn't say, 'Do all prophesy?' It may be that many people in that Corinthian church had that spiritual gift but they were not all considered prophets. A person with a ministry is someone anointed by God, (that is with a recognised spiritual authority) to exercise a gift consistently and regularly as part of the work of building up the church. In the first part of verse 28, Paul establishes three ministries: apostles, prophets and teachers. In Ephesians Chapter 4, evangelists and pastors are added to the list. All the other gifts are open to everyone as well as being employed by those

with any of the five ministries. So healing - like working miracles, helping others, administration, speaking in tongues, interpretation, faith, wisdom, discernment - is a gift we may manifest from time to time, along with other gifts, for the edification of the church. This is confirmed by Jesus when He commissions His disciples after His resurrection:

> Go into all the world and preach the good news to all creation. Whoever believes and is baptised will be saved, but whoever does not believe will be condemned. **And these signs will accompany those who believe**: In my name they will drive out demons, they will speak in new tongues; they will pick up snakes with their hands; and when they drink deadly poison, it will not hurt them at all; **they will place their hands on sick people, and they will get well.**

So anyone who **believes** may exercise miraculous gifts, but in reality, as Paul observes, not everyone does believe. There are certain people who definitely **should**, though, and these are those with the five-fold ministries. Healings and miracles, we read in Scripture after Scripture, accompany people God had called to these roles. It seems, then, that there are two ways of praying for the sick:

1. Out of our faith ('those who believe').
2. Out of our God-appointed position of responsibility in the church.

What a difference it would make if people in these offices realised that God has promised that healing will be a natural extension of their ministry; instead of wondering whether they have enough **faith** to pray for someone to be healed, they would know they have **authority** to do so. God has **appointed** and **empowered** them to manifest this gift in the course of fulfilling their particular role of leadership.

So in a sense, a healing ministry, in isolation from any other spiritual office, doesn't really exist. Those who are called 'healers' are either people who have a strong degree of faith in the God who heals and is able frequently to bring His gifts of healing to sick people; or they are apostles, prophets, teachers, pastors or evangelists who exercise the healing ministry as part of their responsibility towards the body of Christ, and have been labelled 'healers' by people whose eyes are caught more by this spectacular element in their ministry than any other. Over the years, God has increased my faith in His ability to use me as a channel of His healing, and there have been many instances when He has actually given me a **gift** of faith which has enabled me to bring His healing in situations which would normally be way beyond my everyday, personal faith. But basically, I have been called to preach the gospel and to teach, and people get healed in my meetings partly as a by-product of receiving that ministry. It is the anointing on my spiritual office which gives me the authority and power and confidence to pray for the sick. Realising this, there is no excuse for people to look to me and think that I have some tremendous healing power, because I am as weak as everyone else. God is the one who heals through the structure He has ordained in the church and He is not dependent on the ability of man, but on a person's openness and commitment to His purposes.

Let us look more carefully, then, at **who** has gifts of healing. And notice it is plural - **gifts** of healing(s) implying that healing is not a power which we possess, but a new gift of health given individually to every sick person. The gift is for the one who is ill, not the one who prays.

1. Apostles

Paul considered that his own main ministry was that of an apostle, though he was undoubtedly an evangelist and a teacher as well. In 2 Corinthians 12, verse 12, we read:

> The things that mark an apostle - signs, wonders and miracles - were done among you with great perseverance.

We know from his own testimony, and from Luke's record in Acts, that one of the miraculous works Paul did was healing. Many of the men I have spoken to who are apostles have suggested that church-building is their sign: the charismatic groups and fellowships they have established are seen by them as the sign or wonder that validates their ministry. But I suggest the church-building should be their **fruit** not their sign. Building churches is what they are **supposed** to do; but there is an added dimension of performing miracles to attest this ministry. A true apostle **should** establish churches and bring in the kingdom, and Jesus said the kingdom of God was near when He healed the sick, cast out demons and worked miracles. So when an apostle seeks to establish a church in a community, he should proclaim the coming of the kingdom by healing the sick and working a few miraculous signs, preaching the word with signs following. By doing this, he establishes spiritual authority, the lordship of Christ mediated through his ministry, and the people will be much more likely to listen when he goes back to preach next time. His kingdom authority will draw out the other ministries and he will then be able to encourage these people in the exercise of their governmental gifts which will ground the church in God's order and righteousness. So to these apostolic brethren I say, 'Next time you go to an area, offer to pray for the sick. Don't wait for a word of knowledge. Pray for them because you already have gifts of healing for them in your spiritual office.' One or two men have gone off and done this, and some mighty things have happened because they have had confidence that they have something to share that's not dependent on their faith.

2. Prophets

God has always wanted to make His will known to His people in order to draw men and women, nations and peoples back to Himself for their benefit, blessing and security. For this reason God raised up prophets who would lead God's people out of their enemies' hands and into the purposes of God for their time and generation. The Old Testament prophets had an unusually difficult task persuading the people to believe their words and in turn believe in Jehovah as the only true God. They certainly suffered their share of rejection and had to maintain a clear line of communication from God. To show His reality and presence, God graciously attested to the prophets' words with powerful signs and wonders. The prophet was in one sense a sign pointing to an invisible God who wanted to make Himself known to His people.

Elijah and Elisha called down fire from heaven, transformed poisonous food and water, provided for the widow in time of famine, fed one hundred people on twenty loaves with food to spare, cleansed the leper, raised the dead, and more. They brought the power of God to bear in every type of situation whether in the material, physical or spiritual realms.

When Jesus came along and declared Himself to be a prophet He was believed because of the miracles that He performed. The signs of a prophet were upon His life so that when Jesus raised the widow's son from the dead everyone was 'filled with great awe and praised God'.

> 'A great prophet has appeared among us,' they said.
> 'God has come to help his people.'
>
> (Luke 7, verse 16)

Jesus was accepted by some and rejected by others, just like all the prophets before Him. So when He came to His own home town, 'He had no honour and did not do many mighty miracles there because of the lack of faith' (Matthew 13, verses 57 and 58).

Many of the people only saw Jesus as being Joseph the carpenter's son and thereby rejected the benefits He came to bring.

Jesus as the prophet and King spoke the word and it came to pass: water was turned to wine, the hungry were fed, the demonised were set free and the dead were raised, showing that the Kingdom of God had come.

The words of the prophet are truly in deed and power and the same signs should accompany a prophet's ministry as he proclaims the will of the Lord.

3. Evangelists and Teachers

An evangelist preaches to the unsaved and proclaims the good news of salvation through Jesus' death and resurrection. A teacher preaches to the saved, being able to communicate revelation truth from the Word of God in a simple manner. They have in common this fact, that they both preach the Word - which God promises to confirm with signs and wonders following. In the Early Church, the same man would often be fulfilling the two functions since new converts would have no other source of teaching.

Again and again in the New Testament, we see the miraculous (and that undoubtedly included healing) accompanying preaching of the Word. Paul, in fact, seemed to think it was the essence of proclaiming the gospel of Christ:

> I will not venture to speak of anything except what
> Christ has accomplished through me in leading the
> Gentiles to obey God by what I have said and done -
> by the power of signs and miracles, through the
> power of the Spirit. So from Jerusalem all the way
> around to Illyricum, I have fully proclaimed the
> gospel of Christ.
>
> (Romans 15, verses 18-19)

In Hebrews, he again links signs and wonders inextricably with the
preaching of the gospel:

> We must pay more careful attention, therefore, to
> what we have heard, so that we do not drift away...
> This salvation, which was first announced by the
> Lord, was confirmed to us by those who heard him.
> God also testified to it by signs, wonders and various
> miracles, and gifts of the Holy Spirit distributed
> according to his will.
>
> (Hebrews 2, verses 1, 3 and 4)

In fact, he also makes it clear that signs and wonders do not depend
at all on the brilliance of the preaching or the strength of a man's faith,
but simply on God's power flowing through His appointed channel:

> When I came to you, brothers, I did not come with
> eloquence or superior wisdom as I proclaimed to you
> the testimony about God. For I resolved to know
> nothing while I was with you except Jesus Christ and
> him crucified. I came to you in weakness and fear,
> and with much trembling. My message and my
> preaching were not with wise and persuasive words,
> but with a demonstration of the Spirit's power, so that
> your faith may not rest on men's wisdom, but on
> God's power.
>
> (1 Corinthians 2, verses 1-5)

It stands to reason that people will pay more attention to what you are saying if it actually works. This is different from putting on a spectacular display to try and impress people. Signs and wonders in themselves will not provide a strong foundation for a life of faith and holiness. Miracles should always **follow** the word, not be the key element in a man's ministry. Look at the evangelist Philip when he went down to Samaria. He didn't preach healing, he preached Christ. And when you preach Christ, you get healings.

> Those who had been scattered preached the word wherever they went. Philip went down to a city in Samaria and proclaimed Christ there. When the crowds heard Philip and saw the miraculous signs, they all paid close attention to what he said. With shrieks, evil spirits came out of many, and many paralytics and cripples were healed. So there was great joy in that city.
>
> (Acts 8, verses 4-8)

Notice that the crowds **heard**, then **saw**, then **paid close attention to what was said.** And the outcome of such reality and integrity in his preaching was **great joy.** So this should be the fruit of the ministry of evangelists and teachers.

Perhaps an evangelist, in particular, should think of himself as a travelling salesman (for that company I work for, Father, Son and Holy Ghost Unlimited). No self-respecting salesman would go round without free samples; he would never sell anything. And God has an unlimited supply of free samples. Freely you have received, freely give.

I recently heard about an evangelist who had great faith in God. He was in India preaching to crowds of a hundred and fifty thousand and after preaching powerfully for two hours he invited people to give their lives to Christ. No-one responded.

'Right,' he said, 'now I am going to demonstrate the Gospel to you.' He walked towards the crowd and selected three individuals who were in need of physical healing. There was a blind man, a woman born deaf and dumb and finally a woman so crippled and deformed that she could only move on the palms of her hands and the heels of her feet.

He returned to the platform with these sick people and a sense of quietness descended on the crowd. He rebuked Satan as he prayed for the blind man and instantly he could see. The evangelist then commanded Satan to loose the deaf and dumb woman, and proceeded to demonstrate her healing to the crowd by teaching her to speak in English. Finally he turned to the crowd and said, 'I have not come here to fight against your god. Let us all pray to Allah that this woman who is still badly crippled will be healed.' After a time of joint prayer he noted to the crowd that the woman was still sick and informed them that it was because their god was dead. He then shouted in a loud voice, 'Satan, loose your hold over this woman'. Immediately the power of God came over her body and she stood upright on her feet. After seeing that, the crowd erupted and many thousands decided that night to forsake their god and serve the Lord Jesus Christ.

This is true evangelism on a large scale using the gifts of the Holy Spirit, for as God's Word has stated, 'He will confirm the word with signs following' (Mark 16, verses 15-18).

The evangelist knew that because of his 'office' in the church he had access to gifts of healings for the people as he boldly proclaimed the Gospel. His faith was not in 'his faith' but in the authority God had placed within him as a holder of one of the five ministries in the Church of Jesus Christ. He knew that he represented the Kingdom of God and just as a commercial traveller would carry samples of his company the evangelist knew that he could totally rely upon God to give samples of the Kingdom.

4. Pastors

I've heard some pastors say, 'I'm just the shepherd of this church. You can't expect me to do the healing, too. I'm not that type.'

But look at what is said in Ezekiel 34:

> This is what the Sovereign Lord says,
> 'Woe to the shepherds of Israel who only take care of themselves. Should not shepherds take care of the flock? You eat the curds, clothe yourselves with the wool, and slaughter the choice animals, but you do not take care of the flock. You have not strengthened the weak or healed the sick or bound up the injured.'
>
> (Ezekiel 34, verses 2-4)

And in Zechariah 10, verse 2, we read,

> The people wander like sheep; they are afflicted for
> want of a shepherd.

A field full of grazing sheep is a scene of contentment and peace unless the sheep sense any intruders, when they will become very frightened. Sometimes the sheep can get stuck in a rut or ditch and injure themselves. At other times they find a way out of the field, lose all sense of direction and end up totally lost. All they can do at that stage is bleat and cry, hoping to be heard by the shepherd.

Jesus said that a good shepherd looks after his sheep and knows them by name. His concern for them is such that should one of his flock go missing he will leave the flock secure in the pen and go searching for the lost one until he finds it. He will carry it home if necessary, rub oil in the wounds and care for it. He is a true shepherd and he would do the same for all of his sheep. If they are sick he seeks to see that they recover. They are valuable to him, and he does not leave them to fend for themselves.

In the same way God wants and expects His shepherds or pastors to love their people, to care for and to heal the sick ones amongst their flocks. God has shepherds or pastors in a high category in His listing of offices in Ephesians 4, verse 11. Within this ministry God has placed healing gifts to release the sick under that person's care, and it is the pastors' God-given privilege and responsibility to look after the people in this way.

In God's economy then, you don't generally take sheep to a vet, that is, a professional healer, you take them to the shepherd. So pastors have healing gifts for their sheep. Not for all sheep, just their own flock. This is why church membership is not optional but essential. We need to know where we are planted so that if we get sick we can go to our pastor and ask for prayer with both of us having confidence that he has the healing gift for us.

5. Elders

> Is any one of you sick? He should call the elders of
> the church to pray over him and anoint him with oil
> in the name of the Lord. And the prayer offered in

> faith will make the sick person well; the Lord will
> raise him up.
>
> > (James 5, verses 14-16)

You are lying sick in your bed feeling awful and you feel you **have** to call the elders to pray for you. But looking up at their helpless faces, you feel a whole lot worse, and listening to their conversation gives you complete confidence their prayer won't work:

'Brother, do you feel led to pray? No, brother, you go ahead,' and so on. They are worried about **who** has the faith, who has the gift, instead of realising that, as elders, they possess **corporately** the ability to heal the sick. God has implanted in their office the anointing to pray for the people under their oversight. God is very fair and if He calls you to a position of responsibility within the body, He will give you the ability to fulfil it. The anointing goes with the calling. So if you are an elder and you consistently have no ability, then it is possible you are not an elder in the Holy Ghost - that you are man-appointed, not God-anointed. Most elders have no expectation of healing, and most people don't have faith that their elders can pray for the sick either, because they know the men and all their failings. This puts pressure on both sides. An elder should be mature enough to lay down his life for the sheep, and not say, 'What am I going to do if it doesn't work?' That's not laying down your life, that's preserving it. Laying down your life means saying, 'I don't **feel** this is going to work, but this is what God has called me to do and God doesn't make mistakes so I'm just going to believe it and accept it'.

So if you get ill, call the elders of the church. Not your favourite elder; all of them. Not the one you agree with; all of them. And they all should pray with the knowledge that in their office lies the authority to carry the gift of healing from God's hand into your body. There should be no tension, no fear, no striving. I've been prayed for once or twice when I have been ill, not in my home church, I hasten to add, and the fact that I didn't end up with a dislocated neck or a damaged spine has been purely by the grace of God because I've not simply had hands laid on me, I've had people exerting all their strength in an endeavour to bring healing. They have never thought about being gentle, but have pressed and prayed fervently, and pressed a bit harder. You start with a headache and finish with concussion. In fact, I've seen some people shake and push so much that the poor sick person has got a headache just from the rings bouncing up and down on his head. 'It's the anointing,' they say. It's not the anointing. It is the tension in the person praying. Do you think Jesus went around Galilee shaking as He prayed for people? He just spoke with authority because He knew He had the gift.

Why do you think so many people are getting slain in the Spirit? (Resting in the Spirit, some call it; or reclining worship as a dear friend of mine puts it!) It's because people are learning to relax about healing, and the Spirit of God is able to flow through the arm of the person praying, straight into the body of the sick one. Then they just relax and lie there in the love of the Lord while He sorts out their physical problem. You don't have to press on someone's head to force the gift of healing through their thick skull, for God said, 'It's not by might, nor by power, but by my Spirit'. Healing the sick isn't difficult, it's impossible, so we might as well relax in it because there is nothing we can do to make it happen. Marvellous. We must learn to let God do what we cannot do! I remember hearing a testimony by T.L. Osborne, who has a fantastic healing ministry. He started by taking a good look at his hands to see if they had any power in them. They didn't look too promising, so he said to God,

'When I lay hands on the sick tonight, Lord, You will heal them, won't You?'

'Yes, I'll heal them,' God promised.

His hands still didn't look any different.

'You really will, won't You, Lord?'

'Yes, I will.'

'But Lord, I haven't got anything in my hand.'

'That's right, and you won't. It's just a contact for my Holy Spirit to flow through.'

So let's keep our own feelings and thoughts in subjection and let God's power flow through the channel of our hand - a high voltage current through a low-resistance cable.

James goes on to say in the passage about elders praying for the sick:

> If he has sinned, he will be forgiven. Therefore confess your sins to each other, and pray for each

other so that you may be healed.

So the elders should ask, 'Have you got any confessions to make?' And sometimes the sick person replies, 'Yes, I don't believe you should be an elder, and I'm afraid I can't stand you'.

Now that situation is a non-starter. For healing to take place in this context, the sick person must respect the authority of the eldership, and the elders must be confident of the calling and anointing. Unless there is loving submission and loving authority, there will be no channel for the Holy Spirit to flow through as we have already seen the blockages caused by resentment and an unsubmissive heart. So there must be repentance and reconciliation.

> A heart at peace gives life to the body, but envy (or resentment, rebellion, criticism) rots the bones.
>
> (Proverbs 14, verse 30)

Notice that this passage says that if you are sick, **you** call the elders. The onus is on the sick person. Don't expect the elders to go round visiting with a pot of oil for anointing, and discovering by chance the people who need prayer. Get on the phone and **ask** them to come round. 'Nobody in this fellowship ever visits me,' you may say. Well, if you want to lie on a bed of self-pity, it is very comfortable - until you get really ill. But you will never get healed that way. Take the initiative, step out in faith and ask for the gift of healing which lies in the elders' responsibility. Humble yourself and believe that God will raise you up. Then, like the anointing oil that ran down Aaron's beard and skirts (Psalm 122) signifying restoration, fellowship and wholeness, you can receive and glorify God in your body.

6. House Group Leaders

Like pastors and elders, house group leaders have gifts of healing for the small flock under their care. They have assumed spiritual authority over the people in their group and should have confidence to pray for them when they get ill. Unfortunately, some people in house groups expect their leader to be of a different species, a man with tremendous faith and a hot-line to God. This puts huge pressure on him to find the faith to pray for all their problems, and it's no wonder so many leaders are exhausted and full of doubt and disillusionment. They may well have enough faith to pray for the sick on many occasions, but the strain is taken off if everyone acknowledges that the healing comes from God through the man's office, not through his faith.

I went to a church some years ago which was keen on structure and authority and had just split up into house groups. I was interested to see whether all this structure was building a house or just a piece of scaffolding, so in the meeting I picked on one poor brother and asked him how many he had in his house group.

'Ten,' he answered.

'How many are sick?'

'All ten.'

'Wonderful,' I said, 'bring them all forward.'

So they all stood up and I asked them who was the sickest among them. One chap about six foot three stood up and said, 'I've got ulcerative colitis'.

'That's fine,' I replied, 'we'll start with the worst and work down'. And turning to the house group leader, I asked, 'Have you prayed for him?'

The poor man was nearly crying. I'm sure he was wishing I had never been invited, but he stuck with it and said, 'Yes, I've prayed. I've prayed, sought God, been on a three-week fast...'

My, what love, I thought. I've never fasted for anyone's healing for three weeks.

'... but nothing happens.'

'You've prayed out of your faith,' I explained gently, 'and the trouble is you haven't any, at least, not working. Would you pray for this brother again, please?'

'But I've prayed for him three or four times,' the leader cried desperately.

'That's OK,' I said, 'just come out here, put your hand up to heaven and receive the gift of healing.'

He obviously thought I was nuts. This man was well-educated, he'd been to university, had a top-grade job, and now he was being asked to do something completely irrational.

'What on earth do you mean?' he asked, bewildered.

'Faith is the substance of something you hope for. Do you hope for this brother to be healed?'

'Oh yes, I really do,' he replied earnestly.

'It's the evidence of something not seen. Where is the evidence? In your imagination. So if he needs a new colon, just imagine receiving it from head office. God's got a warehouse in heaven with all the spare parts we need. He will send a new colon by express delivery to your hand, if you just put up your hand like a little child and receive it.'

'But how will I know I've got it?' he asked worriedly.

'Because with the eyes of your spirit you will see it.'

Looking back it was quite amusing. I have never seen such a strange expression on someone's face while praying. If he looks at God like that, I thought, God won't give him anything. But after a few minutes, this leader said, 'I can see a piece of straw, or maybe it's a piece of tubing'.

'Well, that will do,' I thought. 'I've no idea what a colon looks like anyway'.

'Now put your hand on this man's head and pray for him in the name of Jesus.'

This he did, with all the force he could muster, and then I turned to the sick man:

'Do you think you've been healed?' I asked.

'No, I haven't felt a thing,' he replied.

'I'm not surprised. There's so much tension in this man's hand, I think the gift of healing is glued to it. Let's start again.'

This poor man was very embarrassed in front of his whole house group.

'Have you got the piece of tubing?' I asked.

He nodded.

'Right. Now just relax and give it to our brother here.'

So he put his hand lightly on the tall man's head, and CRASH! Down he went, right across the coffee table, down onto the floor. I thought he would break his back, but not only was that all right but all his pain had gone.

The house group leader stood staring at his hand, saying, 'I don't believe it. I don't believe it.'

'Well, you don't need me,' I told him, 'I'm just going to have a cup of coffee and I'll be back in a few minutes.'

Fifteen minutes later, there were nine more people lying on the floor and he was still saying, 'I don't believe it, I don't believe it.'

So he certainly wasn't praying out of his faith. He was praying out of his office, his position of responsibility in the body of Christ. Interestingly, there was just one man in the group who got ill again some weeks later. And it was known that he didn't agree with the way the church was run, and found it difficult to get on with his house group leader, who he doubted had the spirituality to teach them all. So where there is not authority and submission, the gifts of healing cannot flow.

The next night we had a meeting in the town hall and over eight hundred people came. This leader was so excited by all that had happened that he said to me, 'Brother, I feel I could pray tonight'.

So I said fine, called a healing line and told him to carry on. We prayed for many people that night and two hundred or so were healed; he prayed for twenty-five and according to him, none of them were healed. Driving home together afterwards, he was crying.

'You see,' he said bitterly, 'It's just **your** faith which makes things work. When you're not there, nothing happens.'

So I asked the Lord why it didn't work, and He replied,

'They weren't his sheep. He had authority for his ten, but not over hundreds or thousands or ten thousands.'

He stepped outside his anointing.

7. Parents

It is so easy when praying for your child to let your own emotions take control:

'Oh Lord, you know how much I love little Johnny...'

And God says,

'Yes, and I love him far more than you do...'

When we try and plead with God on the basis of how much our child means to us, we get caught up with fear and tension. Pray for your children as **priests** not as parents. Stand before God, and pray for your family with authority, bringing the healing gifts for your children which God has anointed you with.

Now this will work almost 100% of the time when they are very small because they haven't learnt to doubt. But by the time they are six or seven, you may be getting problems. The children will have discovered television and will see people taking yellow pills and blue pills, and red medicine, and it's not long before they want to try these things. Then when they get to school, everyone is getting innoculated and injected, and they want it too. By this time, they will have to use their own faith. But initially they can be healed on your faith as you stand as the representative before God, and minister His life to them. Before you pray for your child, go to God and receive the gift of healing, because empty hands laid on empty heads are no good to anyone! And how do you know you have got the gift? Because you can see it. Spiritual perception, I call it, rather than simply imagination. If you can see, with the eyes of your spirit, the vague outline of a new back for someone with a slipped disc, a new nose for someone with sinus problems, then feed the revelation with prayer and praise until it becomes an assurance of a gift you can pass on to the sick person. It is not resident in you; all you have is a photograph, if you like; the real thing lies with God, and flows through you as you gently lay your hand on the person in need.

Do you realise that there are almost no prayers for healing in the New Testament? Instead, authority is taken over the disease. And God delegates kingdom authority to us. The Roman centurion whose servant was sick said to Jesus,

> Lord, don't trouble yourself, for I do not consider myself worthy to come to you. But say the word and my servant will be healed. For I myself am a man under authority, with soldiers under me. I tell this one, 'Go,' and he goes, and that one, 'Come,' and he comes. I say to my servant, 'Do this,' and he does it.
>
> (Luke 7, verses 6-8)

You too, Jesus, are a man under authority, he is saying. And Jesus conferred that same authority on those who believed and followed Him. A pastor, for example, is like a spiritual policeman. If you see a policeman standing in the middle of the road with his hand up you will do your best to stop - because he is on duty and has his uniform on. If you hit him, all the police force in the country will be after you. Now he doesn't have the physical strength in his hand to stop you and your thirty-two ton truck, but he's not standing in his own strength but in the authority of the law. One little policeman can stand up on Hyde Park

Corner and put his hand up, and total chaos will reign while everyone screeches to a halt to obey him. But if he went out there one Sunday afternoon in a pin-striped suit and said to himself, 'I think I'll have a bit of practice at traffic duty,' he wouldn't last two minutes because without his uniform on he would be mown down. When we are moving in the kingdom of God, we have a uniform, a robe of righteousness, our priestly garments, and we don't represent ourselves, we represent Jesus.

Jesus never prayed from earth to heaven. He was a citizen of heaven who prayed down to earth. He never struggled to get out from beneath problems; He looked down on them and told them to be cast into the sea.

> And God raised us up with Christ and seated us with
> him in the heavenly realms in Christ Jesus.
>
> (Ephesians 2, verse 6)

So we can see our sickness from God's perspective. And there are five steps to doing this:

1. Think God's thoughts

Don't think, 'What are we going to do with this poor person?' Think what God thinks: 'I'm going to heal him, hallelujah.' You look down on the problem and think, in the name of Jesus, that he is going to be healed.

2. Feel God's emotions when you pray

So many people pray with a tremendous burden, with great fervour and intensity - which is really a cover-up for unbelief. If you go to pray for someone in hospital and you are discouraged by the sight of how ill they are, then turn your back on them and look at Jesus. Start praying and praising the Lord and you will feel joy, because in His presence there is fullness of joy. You can declare with confidence, 'I've come to bring the kingdom of God to you, hallelujah!'

3. Understand God's plan

Know that you are not praying simply because the person is sick; you are praying to extend the reign of Christ's righteousness because of

His government there shall be no end. Seek first the kingdom of God, and all these things shall be added to you. When you pray, ask for God's will to be done on earth as it is in heaven. Is there sickness in heaven? No. Is there cancer in heaven? No. So Christ's reign on earth means health and wholeness. You shouldn't need a rhema word to tell you that; a basic knowledge of God's character should be enough. Once we are praying from a kingdom viewpoint we are not concerned for our image; we don't have to depend on our ministry, for I don't believe Jesus carried a banner around saying, 'God's anointed servant for this hour'. He was only interested in doing those things that pleased His Father. Our motivation should be a desire to please our Father with all our heart and to do His will, not a wish to build up a ministry of praying for the sick. If this were our desire I believe many of us would get a double portion, because God could trust us, since we would have died to ourselves. God's plan is to show the devil he is defeated, so we should be bringing into effect His victory in every situation.

4. Pray what God tells you to pray

There is much confusion and argument in the church about whether a Christian can have a demon, or a demon have a Christian. Personally, I do not believe that a Christian can be possessed by an evil spirit. But I do think that a great deal of sickness, perhaps 60%, is initiated by an evil spirit, and as Christians we can be oppressed, bound, vexed and depressed by them.

If you trip and fall headlong down a flight of stairs, you are unlikely (unless you are my wife) to bounce down them saying, 'Praise the Lord, Hallelujah, thank you, Jesus, Amen'. Most of us shout, 'Aaahhhhh...' And when we react in panic and fear, we are in the devil's realm. In that moment of terror, it is possible for him to slip a spirit of infirmity into our spinal column, which may prevent our back from getting better after treatment and causes the whole area to be weak afterwards. Now, if we simply pray for the physical damage to be healed, this is what may happen: as the healing power of God floods into our body, the spirit of infirmity goes further down and hides, because it doesn't like the sudden influx of the Holy Spirit. But after three or four days, it comes up again and when it expresses itself it will be painful, often worse than before.

I prayed for an elder once and the situation might have been amusing if it hadn't been so distressing to him. He had terrible sinus trouble, so I said to him, 'That's no problem. I will get the pastor of your church to come and pray for you and you will be healed.'

So the pastor laid hands on him and commanded him to be healed in the name of Jesus. At once he could breathe properly through his nose and everything was marvellous - until three days later when I received a phone call from him:

'Brother, don't talk to me about healing,' he groaned.

'What on earth is wrong with you?' I asked.

'Well, three days ago, I just had sinus trouble,' he replied, 'now I have bronchial asthma.'

I'm afraid I almost laughed. But at least it had shown me that his sinus trouble had been caused by a spirit which had taken cover when we prayed and was now reacting with a vengeance. So again I said, 'No problem. Let's pray.'

I took authority over his asthma, and cast it out. And he was never troubled by it from that day. Now I knew I was addressing a spiritual force or being, but I didn't say, 'Come out, you spirit of asthma,' because that would probably only have caused him more fear and confusion. However, a spirit **was** cast out, And without any violent reactions. And I believe that if you are moving in the authority, there needn't necessarily be dramatic manifestations of evil. Let us briefly look at how Jesus dealt with the problem:

> When evening came, many who were demon-possessed were brought to him, and he drove out the spirits with a word and healed the sick. This was to fulfil what was spoken through the prophet Isaiah, 'He took up our infirmities and carried our diseases.'
>
> (Matthew 8, verses 16-17)

When Jesus cast out spirits, **healing** took place: the devil was not allowed to get attention. And He cast them out **with a word**, not with repeated shouting or rebuking. If I come against a spirit of infirmity in someone's back, I look for a manifestation of freedom; they should scream with joy, not fear, as the disc slips back into place. Sometimes unpleasant manifestations can't be helped, but generally I don't think they are edifying.

If a person has to go into hospital for a general anaesthetic, it is wise to surround them in prayer, because I have seen people go into hospital for operations relatively healthy, and come out with something called post-operative depression. On occasions, I have come against a spirit of fear and the person has returned to normal.

Many people who experience traumatic road accidents and go through the windscreen of their car, landing on their head in the road, suffer epileptic fits afterwards. Now some epilepsy, I am convinced, is a sickness, caused by certain forms of illness such as meningitis. But in other cases, it is caused by trauma, and when we pray for someone with this condition, we should ask how this sickness originated.

I prayed for a girl some years ago who had epilepsy and she came forward in some distress saying,

'I've been prayed for before and had demons cast out of me, but it hasn't done any good and I just get all churned up'.

'Wait a minute,' I said, 'how did you get it?'

'It started with a childhood illness,' she answered.

'Well, can I pray for you?'

Immediately she looked nervous and uncertain.

'I'm not sure about demons.'

'I'm not sure, either. In fact, I think in your case, it hasn't got anything to do with demons. Let's just pray for your healing.'

So we did, and when she went back to her doctors, they found her completely healed.

Two places behind her in the healing line stood a man who also suffered from epilepsy, and he said,

'I've been prayed for that my epilepsy should be healed and I've thrown away my medication but I still have fits and I just don't know what to do, I'm in such a terrible state.'

'How did you get it?'

'Well, it started after I was thrown out of a boat and almost drowned.'

So I came against a spirit of epilepsy and he was healed.

We have to understand, then, that just because we have the gift of healing for someone, they won't necessarily be healed instantaneously by a quick laying-on of hands. We need wisdom to know how to deal with each problem. Jesus prayed for one man who was deaf by casting out a spirit. On another occasion, He touched a man's ear and healed him. If someone has gone deaf suddenly it may have been caused by a spirit; if they have gone deaf gradually, it is more likely to be an illness which needs a prayer of healing. Ask God how to pray - but don't expect a loud voice saying, 'It's an evil spirit'. You will find you have more peace praying in one way than the other, provided you are open to praying in either.

A woman came to me some years ago with a terrible pain. She didn't know what it was so I asked the Lord what was causing it. A fear of cancer, He told me. And when I questioned her, I found that Uncle George had died of cancer, Aunt Sally had died of cancer, it was in her family and eventually it would get her. As soon as she had the slightest pain, she imagined it was cancer, and the tension and fear aggravated the pain. A spirit had got into her body, lying to her, wearing her down, so that her life was dominated by this fear. When the root of fear was dealt with, the physical problem was healed.

5. Trust God with the Supernatural

When you have done what you can do, you must fall back on the faithfulness of God to do what only He can do. He promises **He** will confirm the word with signs following. Striving and fretting will only block the flow of His power.

On a practical level, when ministering to a person individually make certain that they give you their full attention. If they have understood your explanation of the Bible verses about healing, (and question them to ascertain whether or not this is so) tell them what you are going to do next - that you are commanding the pain to leave them in Jesus' name, or that you are about to lay hands upon them - and ask for the presence of the Holy Spirit to come over them. If you, as the minister, sense an outpouring of love or joy or deep peace, communicate this as well, as all these steps help release faith and enable the person being prayed over to receive from God. Pray from heavenly places down into their need or bring God's will in heaven into their piece of earth.

There must be a co-operation between the person praying and the one who is trying to receive from God and if this is achieved the Holy Spirit has a channel through which He can operate. When casting out a spirit of grief trust God to bring the release of joy, or if it is depression look for the peace of God to flood into the person. We cannot produce these emotions or psyche them up, but we can and must stand in a position of faith until we can see that God has done it. We must remember that we are not dealing with natural problems, but fighting a war against spiritual problems with outward manifestations. We have authority over the evil forces belonging to the devil.

Many people in the Bible were healed 'the same hour' or as they went upon their way, **acting upon the words of Jesus.** Unfortunately, some people today expect to feel better the same minute, and when I ask them, reply, 'I don't think that I'm any better, ' immediately after receiving prayer. They do not exercise any faith at all themselves, and are often very passive people by nature, unable to receive from God due to the presence of fears, unbelief or rejection.

One possible way to break through this deadlock is for the minister to pray the prayer of faith and hold the answer in his or her faith until the person can receive for himself. We know whether or not the prayer of faith has been prayed successfully because, if it has, we will feel joy welling up inside of us.

> Until now you have not asked for anything in my name. Ask and you will receive, and your joy will be complete.
>
> (John 16, verse 24)

So we must stand in the gap between man and God and **He** will do the miraculous.

Chapter Twelve

How to Organise a Healing Service

We begin this chapter by looking at an incident which follows the feeding of the five thousand. This passage gives an insight into the work of Jesus, and also into the attitudes of those who have seen Him at work in a miraculous way.

> Jesus answered, 'I tell you the truth, you are looking for me not because you saw miraculous signs but because you ate the loaves and had your fill. Do not work for food that spoils but for food that endures to eternal life, which the Son of Man will give you. On him God the Father has placed his seal of approval.'
>
> Then they asked him, 'What must we do to do the works God requires?' Jesus answered, 'The work of God is this: to believe in the one he has sent.'
>
> So they asked him, 'What miraculous sign then will you give that we may see it and believe you? What will you do? Our forefathers ate the manna in the desert; as it is written: "He gave them bread from heaven to eat".'
>
> Jesus said to them, 'I tell you the truth, it is not Moses who has given you the bread from heaven, but it is my Father who gives you the true bread from heaven. For the bread of God is he who comes down from heaven and gives life to the world.'
>
> 'Sir,' they said, 'from now on give us this bread.'
>
> (John 6, verses 26-34)

'What must we do to do the works God requires?' the people ask. What an opportunity! And in this passage we see Jesus taking full advantage of it to get straight to the hearts of those thronging around Him. Here we see Jesus the Evangelist, full of wisdom, rebuke and concern, cutting across people's religious ideas of pleasing God and showing that the real way to do so is to worship His Son.

Having just enjoyed a miraculous feast of fish and bread, the Jewish people and their leaders wanted to have the same power that Jesus had and to produce the same results. Maybe by working a few miracles they could deal with the problem of poverty; perhaps it would make them popular and give them a sense of power. In any event they would certainly be held in great awe. There were many other people using supernatural powers at that time, as there are today, and the same temptations were around then. Power which is misused only corrupts and never brings real blessing.

We are called to exercise discernment, as we read in 1 John 4, verse 1:

> Dear friends, do not believe every spirit, but test the spirits to see whether they are from God, because many false prophets have gone out into the world.
>
> (1 John 4, verse 1)

Signs and wonders do not tell us anything about a man's character, but the spirit in which he speaks, lives and performs them does. We should always have an open attitude towards any ministry, but if we sense, or the Holy Spirit shows us, that something is wrong, then we must believe that witness and we do not have to receive anything from the person concerned. We minister spirit to spirit, and that is why we must transmit what we have in God to one another. Jesus imparted **life** to all who would receive Him: He wanted no power for Himself but was eager to point people to the Father.

You may be asking the question, 'What must I do to work miracles?'

Jesus' response here gives us the key:

> The work of God is this: to believe in the one he has sent.
>
> (John 6, verse 29)

Before we can do the works, we have to have a revelation of who Jesus really is. He is looking for worshippers; for those who will follow Him and as a result, out of obedience, will preach Jesus and expect Him to confirm His word with signs and miracles following.

Seeing and experiencing healing for themselves may help lead people to God in devotion and service. Jesus goes on to say on this occasion:

> I am the bread of life. He who comes to me will never go hungry, and he who believes in me will never be thirsty. But as I told you, you have seen me and still you do not believe. All that the Father gives me will come to me, and whoever comes to me, I will never drive away.

> (verses 35-37)

There are bound to be those who want power for themselves, and those who follow ministries but fail to see who Jesus really is, and even reject Him. But God is still longing for people to know Him and have His abundant life, so we must have a positive attitude towards people, praying that the Holy Spirit will move on their hearts and lives.

We can learn a lot from Jesus' example. If we are eager to follow Him in a healing ministry we shall enjoy the same blessings, but we shall also face the same trials. Later in this chapter, we read a verse as sad as it is sobering:

> From this time many of his disciples turned back and no longer followed him.

> (verse 66)

Not only the crowds but His own disciples rejected Him. They turned their backs on the One with the words of eternal life.

This should warn us then that there are several hard facts which anyone feeling called to a healing ministry or wanting to hold a healing service will have to face:

i. People won't always, or even often, be led to Christ by a demonstration of the miraculous. Therefore, don't preach healing, preach Christ.

ii. Even more depressing, people often desire pleasure and power more than they value health. Crowds may flock to a healing service, but they may just be curious to see the supernatural, a show, and not really want to be healed or to make a commitment.

iii. People's hearts are hardened, their eyes are blind and their ears are deaf. Very often you will think you are making it perfectly clear that healing comes through faith in Christ, but they won't understand a word you are talking about. Pray for the spiritual blindness to be removed first.

iv. The work of God is to bring about faith; the supernatural or the miraculous is a fruit of faith.

v. If you preach the whole gospel, people will find it a 'hard saying'. You will be rejected.

We will look in more detail at the personal price to be paid for those called to a healing ministry in the next chapter. But for the moment, let us note some points to bear in mind when we are involved in a healing service, whether as an organiser, a leader of worship or a speaker.

BEFORE YOU BEGIN

1. Be completely dependent on God

We must cultivate total helplessness in praying for those who are ill, realising from the outset that no matter how much knowledge we have, no matter how much experience, no matter how many times we have prayed for the sick, we cannot use the Holy Spirit. He refuses to be used; He uses us. So if you think, 'I can do it,' God says, 'You can't'. We must put our faith in the God who heals, and be totally convinced that it is His will to deliver people from sickness.

2. Be led by the Spirit not pressed by personalities

It is important in a ministry not to feel under pressure to visit a certain group just because you are free and you feel that you cannot refuse the invitation. This problem is particularly common when starting out and you may be tempted to go where God has not gone before you. This has happened many times in our lives. A need does not constitute a calling and it is important to establish what both you and the group require before you accept an invitation. Ask questions. See that you really are the ministry that they need at that time. Is your ministry going to fit in with their overall strategy? What is the reason for holding the meeting? Where are the people in their walk with God? How many people do they expect to attend? Would it be better to teach faith first in an afternoon session and then hold an evening outreach service? What about financial commitment? It is better to be open and talk things through before plunging blindly into a situation and you will end up appreciating each other far more.

MAKING YOUR PLANS

1. Choose the right building
Much depends on the size of a fellowship and their maturity as to the size of hall that should be hired. Healing meetings depend on atmosphere a little and it is a big mistake to get over-enthusiastic and rent an enormous hall only to have it one quarter full with people.

If the sponsoring group is only small in numbers it is out or proportion to expect a thousand people to attend the meeting. So why go to all the trouble of setting out all the chairs 'in faith'? It is far better to have a hall half the size and fill it. There is far more sense of excitement and anticipation when it is difficult to find a seat. When Kathryn Kuhlman had her meetings in Pittsburg, the large Church building seemed always too small. She liked it that way, so that people exercised faith to attend the services. Many travelled hundreds of miles to attend and arrived hours early just to be certain of getting a seat in the meeting. It was not uncommon to hear of people being healed on the journey to the meeting or as they stood in line for hours waiting for the auditorium to open.

If it is possible to hire the building for six hours so much the better. The Holy Spirit will not be rushed and time is needed for Him to move and to build up faith to a point where the deeper needs of people can be met. There are realms and depths of the Holy Spirit that we do not generally touch due to lack of time allocated to an evening service. The time will shortly come when it will be necessary to hold meetings lasting four or five hours for healing and salvation, where the crowds can come and get their needs met and experience the power of God.

The first impressions people make are often lasting ones and therefore the choice of hall is important. A cold, dingy, scruffy hall is not very welcoming. Think about the old ladies and people with arthritis; they do not want to be thinking of their hard seats all evening and wondering when the meeting will end. Warmth is very important so that people can relax and a warm atmosphere, a few flowers and a brightly lit platform positively add to people's comfort and rest. A friendly welcome at the door and a song sheet on each seat helps to open up hearts. Be hospitable not nervous and have your congregation mix with the visitors. People need friends, and they may want to come to your church and know the Word as a result of the love you have shown them.

2. Think about lighting

Good lighting is very important. We have had some strange experiences that took place in local cinemas. On one occasion we discovered that the spotlights were red, green and blue and that they shone directly onto the platform; reading the Bible was impossible and goodness knows what colour we looked! We tried to turn these off and we were left with just one blinding spotlight. As we peered in the general direction of a nervous looking congregation, all we could see were spots in front of our eyes. Eye contact with the audience is essential, especially when giving out words of knowledge and looking for responses. Some people are very shy and it makes it doubly difficult when you cannot see who has raised their hand. On another occasion we really did have to walk by faith and not by sight as the two stage lights both failed at the same time, plunging us into darkness. In spite of these difficulties though there were some lovely healings. God is always GOOD. We always laugh at these incidents in hindsight, but we can learn from them as well.

3. Avoid the world's methods of publicity

I don't believe healing ministries should be advertised like a travelling circus. First of all, if you put up posters saying, 'Come and hear Ian Andrews,' you probably won't get anybody to the meeting because nobody has heard of him, and secondly, if you do find a few showing up they will probably be there out of curiosity, just to spectate. Ideally, people should be brought to healing meetings by friends as then they can be followed up afterwards. It is also more likely that their healing will be accompanied or followed by their salvation, as there will be a fellowship to provide guidance and support. And as an aside I would say that every sheep should bring forth a lamb each year anyway. If we do not lead at least one soul to Christ each year, there is something very barren about our relationship with God. We only have to ask God to lead us to someone we can talk to about the Lord.

4. Use wisdom in stewarding

If you plan on holding a healing meeting it is essential that you realise that you will attract people from all backgrounds and that they will be attending with various motivations. Some will genuinely love the Lord and be there to support the whole meeting. Others will be present because other Christians have invited them or because they saw the advertisement in the newspaper. Some will be in faith, others in fear, scepticism or tension. It is important, therefore, to have stewards welcoming the congregation, showing them to their seats and making quite certain that any people who are acting strangely are prevented from sitting in any prominent position near to the front. It is also recommended that any really serious cases are placed to one side away from the general congregation's attention.

5. Do not isolate the speaker

Ideally the platform should have sufficient room to accommodate all the supporting local team and worship group. Faith can be created for the speaker to launch off if there is a sense of teamwork on the platform. The speaker is not a floating arm unattached to the body. He needs to be identified with the local vision and flow with the leadership of the meeting. A further recommendation would be that a robust lectern or stand be provided, with sufficient light for the minister to read the Bible.

BEFORE THE SERVICE

1. Enter into spiritual warfare

If you do this, you will have the blueprint for the meeting in your pocket before you start. On several occasions I have spent time binding and loosing. If I ask the Lord what spiritual powers are influencing the meetings, He might show me a spirit of rebellion, and I would bind that and loose the spirit of salvation. In other words, I bind the enemy and loose the opposite work of the Holy Spirit. If I bind sickness, I loose healing; if I bind unbelief, I loose faith; if I bind doubt, I lose certainty. Some time ago the Lord led me to do this in a church in Chicago. The elders and I got together before the meeting, and as is the way in many American churches, it was all very organised and businesslike. A woman sat in the corner taking shorthand while the rest of us prayed, binding and loosing as the Lord directed us, binding arthritis, taking authority over slipped discs, loosing the Lord's life and healing. That evening, over 90% of what had been prayed for earlier was healed without the slightest effort. It was as if all the power of unbelief and rebellion had been broken down, and the whole meeting was surrounded in God's glory.

But it doesn't always work out that well. Three years ago I went to another church in the States and we spent three days binding and loosing before the first meeting. On the first night everybody was so excited with the anticipation of miracles, and the whole fellowship wanted to help me along a little. So I prayed and then asked, 'Who is being healed?' Dozens of hands shot up with cries of, 'It's me, it's me, it's me'.

'Great,' I said. 'Come forward and give a testimony,' - thinking that blind eyes had been opened, deaf ears unstopped, wheelchairs emptied. And all these dear people from the church came forward and said,

'I had a cold and it seems to be getting better.'

'I fell over this morning and grazed my knee and I can't feel the pain.'

'I had a headache but it's gone now.'

By the time they had finished testifying, the place was full of unbelief.

So I lost the first battle, but that just got me angry. If you have a bad meeting, don't give up. You've only lost one battle. Fight another one, and don't give into fear, discouragement and dismay. On the second night, there was a tremendous move of God's Spirit, and many people were healed of very serious conditions. These were the same people in the meeting as on the night before, but this time the devil had to admit defeat to all the binding and loosing, and God's healing power broke through.

One very sad incident sticks in my mind. I did some healing services in one city for several years and some really remarkable miracles took place in those meetings. But the spiritual onslaught on the fellowship afterwards was so bad that they agreed not to hold any more healing meetings. For if the devil doesn't attack you before, he may well have a go afterwards. And from those to whom much is given, much is expected, so if you receive wonderful healing miracles from the Lord, the depth of your faith in God Himself may be tested. Many people in the local church got sick after these meetings, and decided the Lord must be saying they should disband them. It was tragic. If you get sick after a healing service don't wonder what God is saying, because He doesn't use sickness to speak to us; the devil does, to tell us to give up. Don't accept the attack. Stand your ground. Fight the next battle and press on in the health God has already demonstrated that He has provided in Jesus Christ.

On the same theme, during a meeting, you could think of asking the Lord how many people you have faith to see saved in one meeting. When Paul preached in Lystra, everybody got saved in the city who was meant to get saved. This is the victory which overcomes the world - our faith in God. And that faith is a creative force. If God says seven people are going to make a commitment that evening, stand up at the end and say so. As soon as you commit yourself to that, something is released through your spirit and the people believe it. Seven hands will go up - and then you are left thinking, 'Why didn't I reach out for more?' But this has got to be real, an inspiration of the Holy Spirit not wishful thinking. I went to a meeting a while ago and one young girl told me the Lord had said that twenty should be saved in her church that night.

'How many have you got in the fellowship?' I asked.

'Twenty five.'

'Well, I don't know,' I said uncertainly, 'but let's see.'

Nobody got saved. It was one of the hardest meetings I have ever taken.

LEADING THE MEETING

1. Enter into His gates with thanksgiving and His courts with praise.

We need to be very sensitively led by the Spirit in this area of praise and worship when we hold healing meetings. For praise is the runway by which we ascend into the heavens and worship, and it is in this position of openness to God that people are most frequently and easily healed. For this reason, some Celebration Nights or All Saints' Nights can be a disaster as far as healings are concerned. So often the fellowship leading the meeting will only think of singing their particular brand of chorus, and all the dear people from the Anglican church and from the Catholic church, the Baptists and the Brethren, sit there thinking, 'We don't know any of these songs; don't they sing about Jesus any more in this church? It's all about relationships and covenant and commitment.' So a quarter of the congregation is getting wonderfully blessed and everyone else is sitting there stone cold, wondering what it's all about. The only way the aircraft can take off is by going down the runway of praise first. So however much we might enjoy singing, *He is Lord, He is Lord,* we don't start there. We need to draw everyone into the praise by recognising that we haven't come to the meeting just to get blessed ourselves, we have come to serve the rest of the Body. We may have spent time before the meeting praising God and so be all ready to go as soon as the meeting starts, but the people who have come rushing from their houses, after a nightmare time of giving the children their tea and putting them to bed, might be sitting there exhausted and stone cold at the start.

So I stay in the realm of praise until I begin to see smiling faces out there. It's no good thinking, 'We'll have the harrier jet today - straight up to God,' when the spiritual aircraft you have in the meeting is the old prop-shaft thing which has to trundle down an endless runway and staggers off the ground just missing the trees, then climbs laboriously up, having used half its fuel. But, if necessary, we have to go that slowly because a healing service is where God wants to manifest His love and glory to people. If we are patient, people will be saved and a demonstration of the kingdom will be brought before them. It is marvellous to sing beautiful fellowship-type choruses in meetings where everyone is a Christian and they are all good friends. But nothing horrifies me more than taking a healing service where there are fifty Christians and one hundred unsaved people, and the Christians all want to sing, *Bind us together, Lord* and put their arms around one another, while the hundred unsaved rather respectable, rather reserved, normal human beings who haven't been exposed to charismania look on dismayed. I don't want them to get put off before I have started. Possibly the Word might put them off, but if it is the Word which does it, that's fine.

So let us be sensitive, not selfish. Praise is directional. It is going somewhere - into the courts of God. Worship is already there, around His throne. The object of a healing service is to draw attention to Jesus, not to people. If no-one else is playing a tambourine, do you have to prove to everyone else that you're free? If you are really free, you might allow it to sit under your seat! We have to consider why we are putting on this meeting. Not for ourselves, but so that others will find Jesus. So bring everyone through praise and, before you minister, lead them on into worship.

2. Keep the flow of the Spirit

When introducing the meeting it is a good idea for the leader to find out how many people are in such a meeting for the first time. If you are holding a series of meetings, it is helpful to ask how many people have been significantly healed. You can then ask some of them to come forward and testify to what God has healed them from. That will build faith in others and deal with any scepticism.

Start with praise focusing on Jesus. Choose songs that are uncomplicated remembering that many people don't have the faintest ides of 'Kingdom' terminology and haven't been to the Academy of Music, but they do understand words like' Jesus', 'Saviour', 'Lord', 'love', 'joy' and 'peace'. So please keep it simple, but bright and cheerful. Remember that many people have rushed home and probably come to the meeting feeling rather exhausted. A spirit of praise lifts the heaviness and depression that may be over people. There is plenty of tension at a healing meeting, from people hoping or 'trying' to get healed, so the idea is to turn their attention off themselves. When you put a release of joy on the people and the anointing starts to flow begin to come gradually into worship, just naturally taking off on the wind currents of the Holy Spirit. I believe it helps if people are standing. They are then actively involved rather then listening to a performance. Watch the faces and attitudes of people and sense where they are so that you can move along with them into the presence of the Lord, until the anointing is not only on you but on them also. The anointing of the

Spirit brings release and peace where He is received and softens people's hearts, soothes their minds, and generally prepares them to receive God's Word. The Holy Spirit always draws attention to the central person in the meeting - Jesus.

After the Word had been preached and ministry begins we can keep the sense of the Holy Spirit's presence by having musicians softly playing in the background some extempore worship melodies. When people start to receive their healing it is most important that the attention is not focused entirely on the healings or the ministries: by going back into worship, or by having soft music, we keep people's attitudes and minds focused on Jesus. For without the Holy Spirit's presence it is impossible to do anything and people then become very disappointed, not understanding why the Lord has stopped working. We can release the power of the Lord who is present to heal as we keep faith released towards Him.

3. Don't lose the anointing

Sadly, a lot of churches break into worship to put the soloist on, or read the notices, as if praise and worship are just a little side-show, nothing to do with the real business of the evening. Good, bad or indifferent, if there is a soloist in the church, on they go, and we are into the realm of Christian entertainment, with everyone sitting there passively, instead of responding to God. Then on comes the poor speaker and he has to try and pour the anointing back onto the congregation with praise and worship again!

4. Allow room for the Spirit to move

Just before rising to speak in a healing service I have had the following said to me: 'I trust you, brother, but don't mention demons or money; it could upset some of the people.' We may laugh but it is often true that we try to control each other with our fears. Well, God is a perfect gentleman and usually obliges, but the results are like drinking a cup of half-brewed, lukewarm tea. We must not set out deliberately to upset but neither do we have to apologise for the Gospel or what God is doing. Let us be bold and radical. Jesus was. Some loved Him, some hated Him, but there was no doubt about His message and the commitment that it demanded. His words flowed out of a heart of love and were full of power.

If the local leaders have faith in their hearts to make room for the Holy Spirit to move as He desires and they release the speaker to share what he has on his heart, they will have God's best for the meeting. In our experience, this ensures the greatest freedom in ministry. It is so easy to try to please people and unwittingly put yourself under someone's control. Submission is different, in that I choose to agree for the best interests of everyone. Timidity on the part of the speaker, or a spirit of control through fear, will not bless anyone.

Recently I was asked to speak at one of the large summer camp meetings. The group of brothers hosting the event said to me, 'Look Ian, we just want you to know that if nothing much happens in this meeting, our relationship has not changed. We still love and respect you.' That is commitment. What a relief! Often one is accepted upon performance. It's too bad if it wasn't your night and not many healings took place. That is why good relationships are so important for they create a confident secure atmosphere which enables God to work.

5. Get the offering and the announcements out of the way before the speaker gets up.

If you leave the offering until the end, for example, half the people will have left and the rest will be so blessed, they won't be financially-minded! And once the Holy Spirit has started to move, it's terrible to interrupt Him to let everyone know there will be a coffee morning next Saturday. Tell the congregation that the King of Kings is present and if they don't have to go, would they kindly stay. Sometimes there is a real lack of reverence for God at these meetings; people walk in and out, chat and laugh, and seem completely oblivious to the fact that Almighty God has graced the meeting.

Once when we were taking a meeting in a cinema, those who organised the meeting felt they shouldn't mention money for fear of offending anyone, so they put a bowl at the back in case anyone would like to give. This is underestimating human nature. Most people are quite happy to pass the opportunity by! During the worship, as we were looking out on the sea of faces (which looked rather blank) God spoke to us and said that it was quite wrong not to allow and encourage people to give. Although grace is free, there is a commitment of the person in giving. Many healing meetings can be purely selfish, with the 'what-can-I-get-from-God?' attitude. Although God was longing to heal that night He also wanted people to express their love to Him, for even those who don't know God can honour Him with their substance. We can't pay for our healing but God has shown us that the principle of giving as an act of worship and thanksgiving is very important for all those involved - for those who have organised the meeting, for the preacher and for the congregation.

God blesses the cheerful giver. If the person ministering lives by the Gospel, where the giving is an offering to the Lord the preacher is received, honoured and blessed, and God seems to be received as well. It is important then that those taking the offering are neither embarrassed and apologetic, nor pressurising the people to give. It is sensible to give a little constructive teaching prior to the offering so that it is a **faith** offering and God is glorified. We don't deserve a thing, but because of God's goodness He has provided for us and wants us to come into His financial system - the law of divine supply.

We heard of a story of a lady who travelled a long way to a healing meeting, taking her very sick child with her. She had no husband and the fare and hotel bill were all she could afford, with a little money left over.

The meetings were over a period of six days and each night as the offerings were taken she delved into her pocket to give to God. The money she needed for her fare home and her hotel bill was going down quickly. Each day she brought her son (who was very deformed with twenty six major incurable problems) to the meetings in the hope that the preacher would have a word for her. She didn't miss a meeting and she didn't give up. The last meeting came and nothing had happened - she could have become angry and bitter, but when the offering came round she gave her last dollar bill to God, like the widow in the Bible who put in all she had. Her dependence and security were given, along with herself, to God. As the service began, the Holy Spirit began to speak to the preacher, giving him a vision of a woman with a very sick child. He described the boy's condition perfectly, and invited the person with that boy to come forward. This little lady had been expecting and hoping, and God had loved her faithful attitude. She rushed forward carrying the boy. The preacher then took this hopelessly deformed child in his arms and just sighed, 'Oh God, Oh God.' The love and power of God came down and the bones that had been deformed began to go into place, the crippled, stunted arms were restored and the boy began to speak for the first time. He was made 100% whole by the power of God. After the meeting people were so happy for this lady that they began pressing money into her hand. When she looked, she had enough and more to pay the hotel bill and her fare home. Her faith in God made her and her son whole!

PREACHING THE MESSAGE

1. Pray before you start speaking

I mean, pray aloud, for by this you can draw everybody in so that they feel part of what is going on, and lose some of their fear and tension about being in a 'healing service'. For the same reason, to employ some humour when you are speaking is a good idea because a lot of people are very tense when they come to these meetings. They have been dragged there by friends, and they didn't think it was a bad idea - until they arrived and suddenly felt all the pressure of, 'I've got to get healed because if I'm not, I'll let my friends down'. Help people relax so that they stop trying to **get** healed, and just respond to Jesus.

2. Be sensitive to the moving of the Holy Spirit

There have been many times over the years when I have messed it up because the message I preached last week had been really anointed, so I determined to preach it again today. Then about three quarters of the way through this message the Holy Spirit has started to move in power with this marvellous sense of the presence of the Lord, but I have been determined to get my punch line in. By the time I've finished speaking, the Holy Spirit's presence has lifted. It is better to start a message and let God finish it. 'But,' I thought for years, 'I have to give all the people all the facts, all the time', - and all they get is facts, not healing. But if we start by saying, 'Look unto Jesus,' and the Holy Ghost comes down with everyone looking to Jesus, then we don't really need to say any more. We can't organise a healing meeting to be decent and in order all the time, for when the Holy Spirit moves He will move, if not in a disorderly way, at least in a manner which doesn't conform to our typewritten order of service. So we need to get used to flowing with the Holy Spirit rather than trying to use Him by the force of our personality, because He won't be used. I have heard a lot of people stand at the beginning of a meeting and say, 'I believe God is here, and we're going to have a wonderful time tonight because God is going to do some great and mighty things…'

And when He doesn't do them everybody goes home rather empty and disillusioned - or accepts that it was just another ordinary meeting. Better to feel our way sensitively and ask the Holy Spirit to lead us in stimulating faith, rather than spout meaningless phrases which have no substance in them.

THE TIME OF HEALING

1. If you yourself are extremely ill, don't be the first person to rush forward in the healing line

This may sound hard, but the reason is that the poor preacher is trying to serve everyone and his faith is a tender plant. If he starts by praying successfully for small things, the faith of everyone will grow, and you will have more chance of receiving your healing. But don't wait until the end either! If you discern the Lord, you will go forward when you feel there is real faith in the meeting. So many people come to me after the service when everyone is relaxing and talking, and say,

'Brother Andrews, will you pray for me? I have muscular dystrophy.'

And I may well say, 'I'm very sorry, but no I won't'.

'Don't you love me?' they ask, dismayed.

And I reply, 'Yes, I love you far too much to have you disillusioned. Don't you discern the presence of the Lord at all? The Holy Spirit has lifted.'

'Oh,' they say, 'but God is always with us.'

'Well, the Bible says the power of the Lord was present to heal on some occasions, so there must be times when it isn't present to heal. It might be present if you have faith for your healing, but at this moment you haven't got any and neither have I.'

So many people want to wait until after the meeting for a sort of private consultation, and then wonder why they don't get healed. But we cannot use the Holy Spirit like that.

If you are the one doing the praying, and someone comes forward saying, 'I'm blind in one eye, I can't hear, I've only got one kidney, I have angina, varicose veins and a hammer toe. Please pray for me,' don't try and pray for everything at once or you will be worse than double-minded. Concentrate on the last thing they said and work through each problem systematically. But if you have a whole line of sick people in front of you, listen to the Holy Spirit and see who He is showing you to pray for, or which one you have faith for. If you have faith for somebody with sinus trouble three or four people back, pray for them first. You don't have to take the first one.

2. Be aware that some people come forward for prayer rather than healing

I've spent a lot of time in Lutheran circles, and one dear old lady came forward in a healing meeting in Denmark. After I had prayed for her, she said,

'Oh, Brother Andrews, thank you so much. That prayer was wonderful.'

'I'm not interested in the prayer,' I replied, 'are you healed?'

'Oh no,' she said, 'but that prayer... I shall always remember it.'

'And you will always have arthritis,' I warned her.

'What do you mean?'

'Look,' I said, 'I will pray for you again, and this time, would you just listen and receive.'

Some people are terrible at this. The moment you start to pray for them, they begin jabbering away in tongues and saying, 'Thank You, Jesus, thank You, Jesus,' until I have to say,

'Look, would you mind shutting up?'

'But I'm reaching out to God,' they protest.

'Well, would you mind not doing that? I'm the one reaching out to God. Would you just receive?'

'Yes brother, I will.'

And as soon as they close their eyes, they're off again. It's become a habit. And I have to tell them to stop again. Eventually, I have to say,

'If you have that much faith, don't come to me for prayer, just pray in tongues and get healed.' So many people don't realise it is their religious attitudes that prevent faith working. A person has to relax in order to receive.

3. Realise that you will need patience

In the middle of a healing service you may find someone standing up and saying, 'Please would you pray for Sister so-and-so?'

'Where is she?' I ask.

'Well, she's not here, she's in hospital.'

'What's the matter with her?'

'She has terminal cancer.'

'Is she expecting to get healed?'

'No,' they answer.

Or on another occasion, you may have a word of knowledge for someone with angina, and a person gets up and says, 'I was just thinking of my great aunt in Scotland. Do you think it could be her?'

These situations will need all the grace you can muster. What does the Lord think of people like this? It's bad enough using the word of knowledge with fifty sceptical, unsaved people, but when we who are Christians stand up and wreck it because of our lack of spiritual sense, we don't need the enemy in the camp; a few brothers and sisters will do the job perfectly well!

4. Be prepared for a host of different reactions after people have been prayed for

If someone gets over-emotional, sometimes it is best just to leave them as attention is what they may be seeking; they will become quiet very quickly. If another person gets slain in the Spirit, and as God ministers to them they are weeping and weeping, don't feel you have to be a mother in Israel and drape a big arm round them saying, 'There, there, it's all right'. If they are in the operating theatre of God, leave them there: they couldn't be in safer hands. Yet inevitably, someone comes along who says he has a ministry of comfort. Our human reactions so often break the power of the move of God's Spirit.

If people fall to the ground under the anointing of God, they won't hurt themselves; but if they fall over backwards because they think it's the thing they should do, they can't expect not to hurt themselves. I saw a man go face down onto concrete under the power of God without putting has hands forward - bang! I was dreading seeing the mess this poor brother's face would be in, but when he got up, he was just bathed in the glory of God. The supernatural doesn't have to be spectacular. Yet still, to my sadness (and exasperation), I get people who are almost 'professionally" sick. They have been prayed for hundreds of times by just about every ministry there is, and they have brought it down to a fine art, coming forward with every need and problem in the world, begging me to pray for them. Then, when I lay hands on them, they fall over five minutes before the Holy Spirit has even begun to touch them. This is not only foolish but very dangerous. I understand that in Finland recently, someone fell over backwards and killed himself. Well that's not very glorifying to the Lord, is it? So make sure you have responsible people standing by to catch those being prayed for, especially if there is a heavy presence of God in the meeting.

5. Don't give up

In some meetings we have to face the fact that there seems to be no anointing and no move of the Holy Spirit. But we don't have to close in prayer and go home calling it a failure. Ask if there is someone with a physical problem that your own faith feels it can tackle, perhaps a sinus problem or kidney trouble, then say, 'Come forward and I will pray for you and God will heal you'. That will stimulate faith. If you say, 'Come forward and I'll pray for you and we will see what God can do,' you will have unbelief everywhere. But if you say God will heal them, you are committing yourself to a level of your communion, or personal faith, and God will honour it for He said, 'All things are possible for him who believes'.

Then if you get a handful of people healed of smaller problems, bending over and touching their toes and generally manifesting joy and health, you will find faith in the meeting, and a growing and tangible sense of the presence of God.

But it is no good producing a word of knowledge if there is no resting place for it. Noah sent out two birds from the Ark. The first, the raven, flew to and fro across the earth unable to find any dry land and was never seen again. When the dove went out, she too found no place to set her foot the first time, but on the second occasion she brought back a freshly plucked olive leaf - there was somewhere to receive her; the third time she flew off and found a home. Noah waited seven days before sending the dove out the second time. If we get no response with a word of knowledge, it might be best to wait until the waters of unbelief have subsided a little.

TWO THINGS LEADERS NEED TO DO

1. Discern people's ministries

I believe that we must do this much more than we do at present. A sick person may have more chance of getting healed through one person than another, and we should recognise the boundaries of our own anointing and refer people to another ministry if we can see they will not receive much from us. For example, I normally pass the really serious ones over to my wife, Rosemary! Actually, there is some truth in this because she has tremendous faith in God in areas where I have very little. That's why God has put us together. If I have been anointed in a meeting with a **gift** of faith, I can believe for any condition to be healed. But in the cold light of day, if a person wants prayer counselling, they will generally receive more if they go along to Rosemary. The trouble is that I know some people feel they are being palmed off. They have got their attention focused on my ministry rather than on the Lord, and when she tries to pray for them she can see they have got one eye on me at the other end of the church and they are not really listening to a word she's saying.

Generally though, most people are submissive and needy enough to go and do it, but we had a desperately sad situation with a woman a couple of years ago who came to me with terminal cancer. She was very ill indeed, and looking at her I knew I didn't have faith to pray for her. I knew Rosemary, on the other hand, wouldn't be discouraged by her condition, so I told the lady to go for prayer with her. She refused angrily, even when I insisted that her healing lay through my wife's ministry. In the end, I said quietly, 'I'm afraid you will die then'. And she walked away to die.

We should not feel threatened or have a sense of failure if we admit we don't feel able to pray for someone. We are all members of the Body of Christ, and it is His life not our own which we are ministering. And the glory is His too. At the end of everything, we are still unworthy servants. We must simply employ our talents wisely. It doesn't matter if we have three or five to start with; they are all given by the Lord. But He will be looking for fruit in appropriate measure through our faithfulness and wisdom. Some people have very particular ministries as if they are 'specialists' in the Body of Christ. I know of someone who has faith for teeth! He asks people to hold their mouth open while the tooth is being fixed. Can you imagine looking inside someone's mouth and seeing the gold being poured into the tooth? He prayed for a friend of mine who happened to be a dentist and my friend managed to scrape some off and analyse it. The results were amazing. It was gold but not gold, wonderful gold but not gold as we know it, of a quality we could never afford to use, a perfect consistency so that it would adjust and never fall out. Make of this what you will, it is certainly a fact that some people have particular success in praying for specific ailments - for backs, for cancer, for blindness and so on. Jesus healed **all manner** of diseases, and I suppose, as individual members, we fulfil different functions and so, corporately, perform the work of the kingdom.

2. Recognise the importance of discernment and the word of knowledge.

There are two gifts particularly related to the healing ministry that I would like to comment on briefly as we end this chapter. Basically, there are three gifts we control - prophecy, tongues and interpretation of tongues - and six which are in the control of the Holy Spirit - the word of knowledge, the word of wisdom, the gifts of healing, the working of miracles, the discerning of spirits and gifts of faith. I do not have a faculty of discernment, a telepathic ability within myself. I cannot look at people and read their thoughts, or know everything about them. If I can I have the wrong gift from the wrong source, or at best, I am critical - I must look for Christ in my brothers and sisters and if God wants to reveal something He will. But He won't reveal it to give me knowledge so that I have power over people; He will reveal it in order for me to minister life to them. I stayed with a pastor once for five days, and all through that time he looked at me very strangely. Then at about three o'clock in the morning, just before I was going to leave, I was woken by this man shaking my shoulder.

'What is it?' I asked, struggling to wake up.

'I want to talk to you,' he said urgently.

'What a time to pick, three o'clock in the morning,' I protested.

But he ignored me and insisted, 'You know something about me, don't you?'

I looked blank. 'No.'

'Yes, you do. The way you've been looking at me, you know something about me.'

I was just about to tell him not to be so ridiculous and to go back to bed, when I realised he was speaking the truth. In an instant, the Lord had told me he was a homosexual. I had been in his house for five days, but nothing I had seen with my eyes had told me that. The Holy Spirit within me had discerned the spirit within him, but it didn't come out of my own sixth sense. I prayed for that pastor and he was gloriously set free.

The discerning of spirits often goes hand in hand with the word of knowledge to enable us to get to the root of problems. Jesus said we should lay an axe to the root of the tree, not merely chop off a branch, because if we take out the root, the whole tree will die. So if someone comes to me saying, 'I can't stop drinking because I'm depressed,' I am asking the Lord, 'What is it?' And He gives one word - loneliness.

'Are you lonely?' I ask the man.

'Oh no, I go to all the conferences.'

'Yes, but do you have a compulsion to go to all the conferences?'

'Oh yes, I want to get really spiritual.'

'You can't bear to be alone, can you?'

And that touches the hurt. Thirteen years of alcoholism then gets broken by one prayer because the Holy Spirit has revealed what the root is.

Sometimes God reveals the root, and sometimes He doesn't. So we can't hope to get a wonderful counselling ministry just through words of knowledge because we can't switch on this power to order. The Lord knows every thought in a person's heart, and although someone may appear in desperate need, only God knows if they have come to an end of themselves. Because, generally, God doesn't set people free to be free. He sets them free to follow Him. He breaks the yoke to bind them to Jesus.

Many of us probably aren't aware if the Lord is giving us a word of knowledge or not. Prophecies are usually fairly insistent - definite words or phrases repeated two or three times - but the word of knowledge flows at a tenth of a decibel rate and often it comes only once. It is then usually followed by a doubt because the devil doesn't want us to believe the truth. Sometimes it comes as a very faint thought - there is somebody here with diabetes - and then it's gone. Sometimes it will come as a mental picture: there you are, praising the Lord, and suddenly you see in a vision a hearing aid. Now I'm not talking about three dimensional technicolour trances that take ten minutes to go into and ten more to come out of. It is just a swift visual impression, again, usually followed by a doubt. On other occasions, we will have a sensation or pain in our bodies. Jesus is touched with the feeling of our infirmities, so if we have His life flowing through us, we too will be touched by other people's sicknesses. We may not feel a terrible pain in our back or something, but a certain pressure will simply draw attention to some part of our body. If you have been preaching and the power of the Holy Spirit descends, it is possible somehow to follow Him as He moves round the room. You may have a knowledge that two rows from the back, someone is getting healed, and a few seconds later you will be aware that He has moved to the left-hand side, and someone there is being touched. Once you get in a flow of the Holy Spirit you may find yourself saying things that are by-passing your mind, or pointing to someone quite naturally in the congregation to say they are being healed. This is the place in the Lord where it feels most comfortable and God leads your thinking and feelings under His anointing. It is a combination of the openness and faith of the people trusting God working through you, the support of those around you leading the meeting, and your own trust in God's ability in your weakness.

This is a sensitive issue because in the Bible we find no teaching on how the power gifts work and so they are open to abuse, or attempts at abuse. But they are supposed to flow out of a life of worship and consecration to God, so it is not a game; it means dedicating ourselves to God's service. He can use us if we are yielded to the Holy Spirit, relaxed and waiting for Him to move. The trouble is that every time we step out in the gifts of the Spirit, a great trench of fear opens up in front of us and we may start striving, trying to produce the miraculous. But as we worship God, our earthen vessels become filled with the treasures of God.

Chapter Thirteen

The Healing Ministry - A Price to Pay

God has been leading us more and more to teach others how to pray for the sick and it is for this reason that we have been holding training seminars throughout the world for some time now.

Judging by the response, it seems people are really keen to get involved. So many people have benefited already and we have had very encouraging reports from those who have stepped out into a healing ministry and started to pray for the sick.

In view of this enthusiasm, I feel it is very important to point out that there is considerable cost involved and it is an area where we can be very vulnerable. Having been engaged full-time in this ministry myself for nearly twenty years I have had my fair share of experiences - some of which I would not like to repeat - but I can at least pass on to you what the Lord has shown me through them. It is easy to look back and laugh when the actual experience is way behind you, but at the time it can be extremely painful. You suffer, you make your nearest and dearest suffer with you, and someone else often has to pick up the pieces.

Many people are obviously attracted by the thought of being able to perform miracles. But if that is our motivation, whether unconsciously or altruistically ('I will be able to help so many people'), then we probably won't see any. For more than any other ministry - because in reality no-one can produce the miraculous through his own ability or strength - healing requires a complete surrender of our own life. A person can appear to be an inspired preacher but in face he is simply an eloquent speaker and it would be possible for him to deliver a brilliant sermon (intellectually) without needing the Spirit at all; someone else may seem to prophesy powerfully, but often there is more of Joe

Bloggs than of God in it. No-one can make a crippled person walk or a person with terminal cancer live, on the other hand, unless the Holy Spirit within them touches the person who is sick. So it is from a position of complete weakness and surrender that God leads us into a ministry of healing. We are thoroughly dependent on His Spirit.

It takes a long time to realise the truth of Jesus' words,

> Except a corn of wheat fall onto the ground and die,
> it abides alone, but if it dies it brings forth much
> fruit.

We know that Jesus has already died in our place but we have to identify ourselves with that and so bring forth fruit out of that death. Paul exhorts the believers in Rome,

> Therefore, I urge you, brothers, in view of God's
> mercy, to offer your bodies **as living sacrifices**, holy
> and pleasing to God - which is your spiritual
> worship.
>
> > (Romans 12, verse 1)

Because of God's goodness to us, which means that we have received what we don't deserve - His redemption with all its benefits through His sacrifice for us - we should give our whole lives over to Him. This is a once and for all experience when we accept His salvation and Lordship of our lives, but it is also an ongoing commitment, which gets tested at various points in our lives as we move forward in faith. We may be like Peter who was very extrovert and raring to go, or we may be like Moses who was afraid to speak, but in both instances their lives were refired and their commitment tested as they responded to God's call in their lives. It wasn't an easy life for them, and it won't necessarily be one of ease for us, but in all the trials of faith and seemingly depressing circumstances, Jesus is there to encourage us to rise up and walk on.

James is able to view his own difficulties and trials for being a follower of Christ in a remarkable light:

> **Consider it pure joy,** my brothers, whenever you

> face trials of many kinds, because you know that the
> testing of your faith develops perseverance.
> Perseverance mush finish its work so that you may
> be mature and complete, not lacking anything.
>
> (James 1, verses 2-3)

James obviously shared Jesus' vision of their joy which lay on the other side of the Cross. But I know 'pure joy' isn't usually our reaction when problems arise, and the going gets tough. Especially when we haven't been this way before and every step is one of faith. It's easy to become discouraged or cynical, blaming our own failings, or God's people, or even God Himself. But God loves us too much for us to stay the way we are, and as we embark on ministry, He does a little pruning and character building here and there. As God said to a friend of ours once, 'I am **FOR** you, not against you!'

Jesus wants us to know this, and by encouragement and love beckons us to walk on, to go deeper into the waters of His Spirit and swim in them (Ezekiel Chapter 47). (In my own experience I wanted to test the temperature of the water first - to put in my big toe and then, as my feet found their hold, go a bit further amidst the stones and swift current.) As we step out, we gradually find that our footing becomes less fearful and unsteady; once we have got used to being knee deep, we dare to let go and plunge in until the water supports us completely. Entering the healing ministry is rather like going through the waters of baptism - it involves a kind of death as we allow our lives to be hidden in Christ.

I once went to a very large church in Canada and as I got off the aeroplane, I spotted a newspaper which had a huge advertisement in it:

BRING THE LAME AND BLIND AND SEE THEM HEALED!

MINISTER FROM ENGLAND, IAN ANDREWS, PRAYS FOR THE SICK.

My heart sank and I said, 'Lord!'

And His reply was, 'Don't try and heal the sick this week because I'm not going to'.

'But you've got to, Lord,' I spluttered, panic-stricken. 'It's in the papers.'

'Don't tell me what I've got to do,' He answered sternly. 'I'm not healing the sick this week.'

'You wouldn't do this to me, Lord…'

But He would, because He knew that dear men of God had invited me to preach to help draw in money for their massive building programme. Every week they invited a different healing ministry to attract the crowds so that they could get the millions of dollars to build their church in the centre of the city. Somehow I don't think God was too pleased with this, because at the start of the week we had a thousand in the first meeting, and by Friday night we got down to three hundred, just those people who really wanted to hear from God - and then God started to heal the sick. He wanted to be gracious!

So God dealt with my fears and the pride and motives of the leadership in that church but it was painful for all concerned. If we are bothered about our reputation we shouldn't consider the healing ministry, because there is nothing we can do to save our own name or impress people.

> For the kingdom of God is not a matter of talk, but of
> power.
>
> (1 Corinthians 4, verse 20)

And ironically, we will find that even if we are seeing miracles happen when we pray for the sick, even this will make people criticise and reject us. 'You can't do it that way,' they say; 'That's not scriptural,' says another group; 'It's all fixed,' say the sceptics. Jesus said:

> The blind receive sight, the lame walk, those who
> have leprosy are cured, the deaf hear, the dead are
> raised, and the good news is preached to the poor.
> Blessed is the man who does not fall away on
> account of me.
>
> (Luke 7, verse 23)

The RSV says, 'Blessed is he who takes no offence at me'. Even healing miracles won't win you a fan club. Quite the opposite. People will often take offence and you will find you are being ostracised just when you thought you were getting established. You will be tempted to give up not only your ministry but your whole faith. But through all this, cling to the Lord. He rewards faithfulness not success, and He promises to give the Spirit without measure to those who make Him Lord.

Is it all worth it? You are probably wondering why anyone would seek a healing ministry. First of all, of course, we don't pray for the sick for what we get out of it, not even to appease the tremendous compassion we might feel. We pray for the sick because of the terrible suffering Jesus went through to heal them; we pray for the sick because it is part of the gospel; we pray for the sick because God is love. Secondly, though, God is no man's debtor. If we give, He will give to us good measure, pressed down shaken together and running over. What will He give? He gives like for like, so if we surrender our lives as a burnt offering, He will give us the life of Jesus which has been through the fire of Calvary. There is limitless potential then in what we can receive back if we only have faith and commitment. For Jesus says,

> No-one who has left home or brothers or sisters or
> mother or father or children or fields for me and the
> gospel will fail to receive a hundred times as much in
> this present age (homes, brothers, sisters, mothers,
> children and fields - and with them, persecutions)
> and in the age to come, eternal life.
>
> (Mark 10, verses 29 and 30)

We need to be dedicated in the face of failure - and in the face of success. One person who had that tenacity, that vision, that boldness was Elisha.

First of all, look at Elijah in 1 Kings 19. One moment he was performing incredible miracles through the gift of faith on Mount Carmel, and the next he was sitting under a broom tree in the desert wishing he could die. Jezebel was out to murder him and he felt as if he had not a friend left in the world.

'I've had enough, Lord,' he groaned, and exhausted with disillusionment and despair, he fell asleep. Be warned, this is a common situation after an intense outpouring of spiritual power. It happened to me once in Sweden. The day started unpromisingly. While I was praying before the afternoon service, I had a vision of an empty wheelchair. I was terrified. It was in the early days when I had absolutely no confidence anyone could be healed through my prayer, and I was sure I was going to be way out of my depth that evening. I tried desperately to think of how I could get out of going to the meeting, which didn't impress Rosemary and we had an argument. At four o'clock in the afternoon, I walked into the little church and there under the pulpit was this wretched wheelchair - occupied. And the devil said, 'If husband and wife aren't right, your prayers are hindered'.

And I replied quickly, 'Don't worry, I've no intention of praying for that, I have absolute faith she will hurt herself if she tries to get out of that chair.'

I was feeling useless so I tried to preach faith, and the more I preached faith, the further into unbelief I got. Eventually, I thought I'd better try and pray for the sick by the word of knowledge.

'Somebody here has got a headache.'

(That was about my level at that moment...) Someone responded and immediately the pain went.

'Somebody is suffering with sinus problems. You are now healed.'

And a woman exclaimed, 'Yes, it's me. It's wonderful!'

After three or four successful words of knowledge, I suddenly felt a pressure across my chest and I said, 'There's someone here who has difficulty in breathing.'

And the dear old lady in the wheelchair squeaked, 'It's me!'

For a moment I felt I could have given her difficulty in breathing, but I rejected the thought quickly and went over to her.

'What's going to happen when I pray for you?' I asked.

'I'm going to stand up and walk,' she replied without hesitation.

I was staggered. 'You are?'

'Yes, God has told me I'm going to be healed tonight.'

There was no way out.

I put my hand on her head and prayed, 'Father, in the name of Jesus, heal her.'

Slump. She sank back into her wheelchair for a moment, but a second later she asked me to help her up. I was so frightened. I knew she wasn't healed and I was sure she would do herself terrible damage by trying to walk. But she insisted I helped her out of the wheelchair, and she staggered three or four steps before I saw an empty seat and thankfully guided her to it. Good, I thought, you can sit there safely and afterwards you can just go quietly home. But suddenly I sensed the presence of the Holy Spirit, and for the first time in my life I experienced the gift of faith. The anointing of God rained down upon me and I felt about six foot wide and nine foot tall. I didn't have a doubt in my being. Then I heard the little old woman's voice saying, 'I have pain in my ankle'.

It had never occurred to me that she was sitting in the wheelchair because of her ankle. I had thought she was there because she couldn't breath properly. But looking down, I could see her ankle was grotesquely swollen and as I took it in my hands, it felt just as if oil was flowing down through my hands and over her ankle. Instantly the swelling shrivelled before our eyes, and before I could stop her she had jumped up and went running around the church. When she came back I asked her what had been the matter with her leg and she explained that she had been sitting in the wheelchair for nineteen years, had received many operations on her foot and now had a steel bar going from the base of her foot up through her leg which meant she would never walk again.

I turned around and there was a man almost bent double leaning heavily on crutches.

'Pray for me,' he pleaded.

I hardly knew what I was doing. I just stood under the anointing and said, 'Be healed!'

Suddenly my hand flew upwards as he straightened up like a soldier standing to attention, and the cancer of the hip disappeared as God put in a new hip-bone.

Next a huge goitre stood in front of me. It was hard to see the woman it was afflicting for it dominated her whole aspect. Her story was tragic because she said she was an opera singer but could no longer sing a note, so restricted was her throat by this hideous lump. Again, I could hardly believe the words which came out of my mouth, but I told her that I was going to touch the goitre and then she should start singing, 'Our Father, who art in Heaven'. I placed my hand on the swelling and in a moment the church was filled with the most beautiful heavenly singing as she worshipped the Lord. The goitre vanished.

For the next ten days not a soul got healed, not one, not even me with a cold. And I came back from Sweden thinking, 'Did that happen or didn't it? Am I saved or aren't I?' The intensity of that anointing had been so great, the feeling of confidence, energy, strength and power so overwhelming, that when it lifted it was like being plunged into the depths of despair. I hardly knew who or where I was. At times like that, it is a great help to have someone in the family who is in the faith, like your wife, who doesn't go down with you, but can encourage you. And it is also a great help if you have a strong and caring fellowship to support you.

Which is what poor Elijah didn't have, of course. But in the absence of all human help, God sustained him and sent an angel to feed him and strengthen him so that he could carry on until he reached the place where God had planned to meet with him. And in the loneliness of the cave, God invited him to pour out how he was really feeling. Out came all his hurt, his rejection, his indignation and his sense of isolation. Yet he didn't curse God or put the blame on Him, though it would have been easy for him to feel full of anger and self-pity. He was still able to discern the voice of the Lord, a gentle whisper after all the drama and spectacle of the wind, the earthquake and the fire, as if he knew that after all the excitement of the miraculous events on Mount Carmel what was more important was his relationship with God and his ability to recognise the real presence of the Lord. He didn't hide from God with a sense of failure, guilt and resentment but stood right before the Lord with total openness and honesty, and repeated his despair. He acknowledged that he had come to an end of himself. He didn't beg or shout at God to do something; he simply gave himself and his problem over into the Lord's hands. And God didn't let him down. He didn't agree it was all a bit of a foolish waste of time, or a big mistake (as the world tells us), but He told Elijah to **go back the way he came,** retrace all those painful, disillusioned steps, and just do two or three small jobs - anoint two kings and pick his prophetic successor. How Elijah found the strength and courage to obey God is almost beyond me - except that I know he must have had an extraordinary confidence in God's love and faithfulness that must have stemmed from an understanding of covenant commitment. And as Elijah responded to God's commands, the Lord played His trump card:

'Oh, and by the way, I have reserved seven thousand Israelites who haven't given Me up and worshipped Baal...'

Out of the darkest of situations and the helplessness of human despair, God brought a glorious hope and a future. Elijah returned with a deeper trust in God, but also a knowledge that the ministry he had been given required a total self-sacrifice, for Elijah had laid down his head to die and from that time he had lived by God's Spirit. So he walked on until he found Elisha ploughing with twelve oxen. Now Elisha wasn't sitting under a tree twiddling his thumbs until Elijah came along, he had been getting on with ordinary life, and evidently with some dedication and ability. Yet as soon as Elijah threw his mantle over him, Elisha knew what he had come for, as if God had already prepared him for this moment. But there was a time gap between the promise and the fulfilment. So it is worth noting that if we receive a prophecy that we are to have a healing ministry, it doesn't necessarily mean it will happen immediately. The prophecy doesn't produce the ministry; the anointing and our obedience to God do. There may be an intermediate period of testing and discipline when God often reveals what is hidden in our hearts.

But Elisha knew his time had come at last. Running after Elijah, he asked only to go and kiss his parents goodbye. And Elijah replied, 'Go back. What have I done to you?'

How's that for encouragement?! But maybe Elijah was testing Elisha to see how serious he was about coming along. The way was going to be so tough, it would be no good if Elisha got cold feet halfway through. Also, Elijah was making sure that Elisha wasn't hero-worshipping him.

That is easy for us all to do without realising it. I was at a prayer meeting one evening and God spoke to me:

'You worship idols.'

'I beg your pardon, Lord. I do not.'

'You worship idols - Cerullo, Kuhlman, Branham…'

'But Lord,' I protested, 'I just see You in them.'

'You don't need to,' He responded, 'You can see **ME.** You don't need to look at a reflection when you can see the real thing.'

Elisha did go back home - but only to prove that he was completely dedicated to following Elijah. He kissed his mother and father goodbye and:

> He took his yoke of oxen and slaughtered them. He
> burned the ploughing equipment to cook the meat

and gave it to the people and they ate. Then he set
out to follow Elijah and became his attendant.

(1 Kings 19, verse 21)

He made a public statement that there was to be no safety net in
case it didn't work, no regrets. He was determined to have what Elijah
had, no matter what it cost.

In 2 Kings 2, the Lord is about to take Elijah up to heaven in a
whirlwind, and Elisha knows it. Imagine how he felt when Elijah
turned to him and said, 'Stay here, the Lord has sent me to Bethel'.

After all they have been through, is Elijah rejecting him? Elisha
could have taken it like that, but instead he saw it as a test of his
dedication and faith. He swears not to leave his master. Then the whole
of the company of prophets come out and ask, 'Do you know that the
Lord is going to take your master from you today?'

And Elisha replies curtly, 'Yes I know, but do not speak of it.'

'Hold your peace; I don't want your discouragement, I don't want
your information, I don't want to get side-tracked. My eyes aren't on
what's going to happen, they're on Elijah, and I'm going wherever he
goes.'

Now Bethel is the first place inside the Promised Land. Elijah is
offering Elisha a soft option, if you like: stay here. It's a place of
dedication, a place of rest, comfortable and sociable. And the
temptation to us is to sit securely in our little charismatic nest, just
speaking in tongues and prophesying, and having a happy time. But if
we want to go on with God, we have to push past all the
discouragement and 'good advice'.

So Elijah and Elisha went on to Jericho, the place of faith. It wasn't
just a miracle place. It was a place of faith. For six days, two million
people walked round the walls once a day without murmuring. That
was a miracle in itself. Can you imagine what it did to the enemy?
They were all on the walls looking down, wondering what on earth
these people were doing walking round without a sound. And on the
seventh day, when they all gave a huge shout, the shock was so great,
the walls fell down. It was a victory of faith and obedience. Elisha was
determined to go on into a deeper realm with God. Again he received
more discouragement for he got the same treatment from the prophets
at Jericho. And once more, he gave them the same short answer.

Finally, Elijah declared he was going on to the Jordan, the place of death, and he urged Elisha to stay at Jericho. (Stay in a place of faith and the supernatural, but don't go on to the place where you may lose your life completely!) But having come this far, Elisha was not going to miss what he had set his heart upon, no matter what it cost, so the two of them went on to the banks of the Jordan. Then Elijah took off his coat, rolled it up and struck the water with it, and the water divided so that they were able to cross over on dry ground. And when they had crossed, Elijah said to Elisha, 'Tell me, what can I do for you before I am taken from you?'

And Elisha replied quick as a flash, 'Let me inherit a double portion of your spirit'.

This was the vision, the goal, which had fuelled his dedication all along. Elijah said, 'You have asked a difficult thing'.

I am a great believer in setting goals, but there is no point in setting goals so low that we can't possibly miss them. Set a goal perhaps just outside your faith capability and pray for **God's ability** to bring it to pass.

'Yet if you see me when I am taken from you,' continues Elijah, 'it will be yours - otherwise not.'

This is the crux of the matter in the healing ministry. Where will we fix our eyes; what will our attention be on? Will we be looking at the supernatural events and desire to perform them? Will we look at the hopelessness and need of so many sick people and be daunted in our faith? Or will we concentrate on the God with whom nothing is impossible? I found in the early years of my healing ministry that I could pray for anything I couldn't see. If people looked healthy, that was fine, but if they looked as if they were dying on their feet, I found it very difficult to pray with any confidence. At first it was OK because I tried not to notice people who looked really sick, but then God began to bring all sorts of strange looking people to my meetings - the crippled, the maimed, the deformed, the handicapped - and I cried out to the Lord, 'I can't cope with this'.

And He said simply, 'Seek Me'.

That didn't seem like a solution at all so I thought of going to the Morris Cerrullo annual convention.

'Seek Me,' He said again.

…Or maybe I could go and see Kathryn Kuhlman. Somebody

offered to pay my fare to America so that I could attend one of her meetings and I was full of joy. All I needed was a visa. So I went along to the American Embassy and was told basically, 'You haven't got a job, you reckon to live by faith (crazy), we don't like your face, we don't like your type, and we don't want you in America'. Three times I went back to the Embassy and kept getting the same wretched man:

'Can I have a visa (in the name of Jesus, in the name of Jesus…)

'NO!'

I was so depressed. I had my ticket paid for, and spiritual progress was just across the Atlantic, and the **devil** was blocking it!

I was staying in the house of friends at the time and on the day before I was meant to fly, the lady of the house came over to me and said,

'I believe I have a word from the Lord for you:

"Your appointment is not with a man, not with a woman, but with me," saith the Lord. Goodnight!'

I knew I couldn't go to bed until I got through this, so I stayed up far into the night praying and asking God what was going on. Then at about three in the morning a light appeared in the room and suddenly Jesus stood before me. In an instant I hit the ground at His feet, and the Spirit of God was surging through me in such a mighty tidal wave that it was impossible even to pray in tongues. I was just groaning, yet without any sound, and the only word which escaped was, 'Lord, Lord…'

Then Jesus spoke to me and said, 'In that day you will know that I am in you and you are in Me'.

That day I did know it. That day I knew that Jesus Christ was alive and **alive in me.** I didn't know it because the Scriptures said so, or because it was church doctrine, but because I had actually seen Him.

The next morning, I went round to the Embassy, saw the same man, and was granted a visa without any trouble! I discovered at the same time that all the previous day's planes had been grounded by fog for twenty four hours, so I was able to use the same Apex ticket I had got for the day before. I went straight to the huge Cerullo convention in California and there was a great sense of the anointing of God. In fact, he said, there were people in the convention who prayed for the sick, and if they would come forward they would receive a special anointing from the Lord. Everyone went running down, and he took one look at me and exclaimed, 'Brother, I can't pray for you, you've already got it!'

The next thing I knew we had all collapsed on the ground under the power of God. So I never did receive it from a man.

From there, I went to the Kathryn Kuhlman service and I sat there minding my own business - just praying desperately that she would get a word of knowledge like,

'There is someone here from England who stammers...'

When suddenly she pointed her finger in our direction and said,

'There are some people here from England. Stand up.'

My two friends and I immediately looked round to see if anybody else acknowledged this, but fortunately they didn't. Hardly able to believe it, we stood up. Then she said to us,

'Come up on to the stage.'

We went up in a kind of daze.

'Tell me,' she said to me, 'What do YOU do?'

I could hardly speak for a moment. My mind was reeling.

'I've got a hhhhhh-healing ministry,' I spluttered.

'W-o-n-d-e-r-f-u-l!' she replied.

She went on to explain that the Lord had told her He was going to send people from all over the world because He wanted the healing ministry to expand everywhere. Then came the crunch:

'Do you want more of God or would you like to be healed?'

Now what can you say in front of thousands of people? God had set me up magnificently! If I had been like Elisha, I would have said, 'Both,' but I didn't have the nerve. I said, 'More of God,' of course, (but inside I was thinking, 'I will come back in six months' time and get the healing!')

My ministry was enlarged from that day. When I got back to England, I found I was praying for seriously ill and crippled people. I could actually feel deformed limbs and bodies straightening out as I closed my eyes and reached out to the Lord, and when I looked, they were completely restored to wholeness; healed and good as new. I was amazed! It had to be the anointing!

So back to Elijah and Elisha. 'You can have it if you see me go up.'

This was to be the final test of Elisha's single-mindedness and commitment. Would he be distracted by the spectacular events God could produce, or would he keep his eyes on the representative of the Holy Spirit?

As they were walking along and talking together,
suddenly a chariot of fire and horses of fire appeared
and separated the two of them, and Elijah went up to
heaven in a whirlwind.

If I had seen horses of fire, a whirlwind and chariots of fire zooming
through the sky like a divine sledge, I'm quite sure I would have taken
a look at it. Particularly as these heavenly messengers actually drove
between them and parted them just as they were enjoying a quiet
conversation together. There was nothing to prepare Elisha for the fact
that this was the moment. Suddenly he was on his own. But he kept his
eyes on Elijah:

'My father! My father! The chariots and horsemen of
Israel!'
And Elisha saw him no more.

When my wife and I went to another Kathryn Kuhlman meeting I
thought at the start that I was going to miss out on all the blessings,
because I found myself stuck behind a huge concrete pillar in the
auditorium. When Kathryn Kuhlman walked on to the stage, I couldn't
even see her. I was getting very frustrated as I tried to lean first one
way and then the other to catch a glimpse of what was going on:

'Lord,' I cried out, 'I can't see a thing.'

Don't worry, I put you there,' He replied.

'Why? Don't you love me?'

Just as I asked that, Kathryn Kuhlman's voice rang out,

'Second row in the balcony, there's a person there who is being
healed of a brain tumour.'

And it was the woman next to me. Just the other side, somebody
else got healed of epilepsy. She went down the whole row and missed
me out because I was hidden behind this wretched pillar. I was wild
with impatience. Peeping out from behind the pillar, I looked down
resentfully at everyone below, and thought, I bet all those Christians in
the front row come from Pittsburg and they come for this every week.
I've come almost five thousand miles and I can't even get a decent seat.

I'm glad God has gifts for the rebellious.

He said to me, 'Don't panic. I've got you here for a purpose.'

'But I can't see anything,' I almost shouted.

'No, that's what I mean.'

Then a few seconds later an extraordinary thing happened. I could almost physically see the person of the Holy Spirit. Somehow I could see Him moving right across on the far side of the church and a moment later Kathryn Kuhlman said,

'God is moving over there now, and somebody is being healed.'

And I knew what they were being healed of. So I asked the Lord what He was showing me. And He said,

'Me. Do you see the miracles, or do you see the God who does them? For only those who see the God who does them can actually move in this realm themselves.'

That is double portion stuff, looking away from the signs and wonders and keeping your eyes firmly on the God who works miracles. Elisha saw Elijah go up. He hung on to the end. He needed no further word or commission. The contract had been fulfilled on both sides. Now he had only to receive. So he picked up Elijah's cloak, went back to the Jordan and struck the water, fully expecting it to part. Hundreds of years before Christ, Elisha illustrated the reality of the miraculous ministry which is available to us if we steadfastly look to Jesus, allowing our own lives to be used so that we can pick up the mantle of His anointing. For Jesus said,

> Believe me when I say that I am in the Father and the Father is in me; or at least believe on the evidence of the miracles themselves. I tell you the truth, anyone who has faith in me will do what I have been doing. **He will do even greater works than these because I am going to the Father.** And I will do whatever you ask in my name, so that the Son may bring glory to the Father. You may ask for anything in my name and I will do it.
>
> (John 14, verses 11-14)

It sounds wonderful, doesn't it? Who doesn't want to do greater works than Jesus? Let's all be where the action is. But it was Kathryn Kuhlman who once said,

'There is nothing God has given me that He won't give to you, if you are prepared to pay the price.'

When God called me, I thought I had given Him everything except my car, my 1959 Volkswagon with 135,000 miles on it. Somehow that was mine, a symbol of **my** identity, **my** independence, **my** security and **my** achievement. And I wasn't going to let God get His hands on it.

'That's my car,' I told Him.

'No, it isn't,' He replied. 'Sell it and pay your bills!'

I couldn't do it, but a few weeks later I lost my job and the car had to go. I went from £3,500 a year to £387 and 2 shillings, which was all I received from living by faith, (mostly cleaning the church floor in those first twelve months!) so I didn't tithe that year; God just took 90%.

I worried while my wife prayed and God answered her prayers. That's how we survived our initial training experiences of living by faith. The problem was that God had the blueprint for our lives and I wanted to be one step ahead to prevent any calamities from taking place. I wanted to be in charge as I had been at the office in the past. It was like playing a game of chess with God, and no matter how hard I fought and dreamt up strategy, He always won. I was the clay and He was the Potter. My fears were numerous and were always being brought to the surface by His tactics. In the end I had to trust in God for our finances and in everyday problems, as well as in our ministry.

Had I envisaged what being a disciple would entail I might never have signed on in the first place. However this is what discipleship is about - doing what we don't want to do, going where we don't want to go - in order to do the work of the Master. 'Go and get a donkey.' I'm sure the disciples didn't think that was a very glorious or exciting job. But we don't experience the power and joy of Pentecost unless we are faithful first in the small things. And even if we are faithful in the mundane tasks, and in the greater ones too, we are still just unworthy servants. We may find though, to our humiliation, that we don't succeed even at the small things. Don't worry, this is a necessary part of the training too. We have to be prepared to make mistakes: better to be making mistakes than to be making nothing at all; better to pray for ten people and for only one to be healed, than to pray for no-one. If we are not willing to be a fool for Christ's sake, then we are too big to be used. After all, just because something doesn't work out, it doesn't mean we are failures. We are simply people who have had a failure.

Peter had more failures than any of the other disciples: he tried to walk on the water - and nearly sank; he fell asleep at the transfiguration; he fell asleep in Gethsemane; he cut off the ear of the high priest's servant; he even denied Christ. I think most of us would have given up if we had made a mess of things that often. But Peter accepted the death of his pride, and so God was able to exalt him. Through all his mistakes, Peter's heart was right. He wanted to serve Christ no matter what it cost, and significantly it was to him and not to, say, John the contemplative, the apostle of love, that God gave the revelation of the nature of Jesus. And in response to Peter's declaration of faith, Jesus promised him:

> 'Blessed are you, Simon (meaning a reed), son of Jonah, for this was not revealed to you by man, but by my Father in heaven. And I tell you that you are Peter, (a rock), and on this rock I will build my church, and the gates of Hades will not overcome it. I will give you the keys of the kingdom of heaven, and whatever you bind on earth will be bound in heaven, and whatever you loose on earth will be loosed in heaven.'
>
> (Matthew 16, verses 17-19)

Then on the day of Pentecost, we see Peter entering into the fullness of his ministry, preaching to thousands, healing the sick, establishing the church. But God made him go the first mile. He paid the price - and he paid it all through his life, with persecution and suffering, and eventually a terrible martyrdom, but he kept his faith, just as Jesus had promised him.

> 'Simon, Simon, Satan has asked to sift you as wheat. But I have prayed for you, Simon, that your faith may not fail.'
>
> (Luke 22, verses 31 and 32)

Just as He changed the water into wine, Jesus can transform the weak water of our natural lives into the rich, full wine of His supernatural life. And just as the master of the banquet tasted the wine, so God samples the quality of the life within us, to see whether the bouquet carries the fragrance of Jesus, looking for the fullness and strength of the life of Christ. It may be that the wine of our lives needs more time to mature. The cloudiness and impurities of our inner selves must be refined until the glory of Jesus alone shines through us. For,

> We, who with unveiled faces all reflect the Lord's glory, are being transformed into his likeness with ever-increasing glory, which comes from the Lord, who is the Spirit.
>
> (2 Corinthians 3, verse 18)

And the glory **is** the Lord's. We must be so careful never to claim it for ourselves. If the power of God heals people through us, it has nothing to do with our ability or spirituality. It is simply that we have decreased so that He might increase; it is that we have died so that His life might come through us. If we commit ourselves to that double portion and pay the price, God's grace will draw us into an ever-deeper experience of His power and love, so that we, too, can say to the Lord:

> Everyone brings out the choice wine first, and then the cheaper wine after the guests have had too much to drink; but you have saved the best till now.
>
> (John 2, verse 10)